Daily Fresh

Jory Post

copyright © 2021 by Jory Post

All rights reserved.

No part of this book may be reproduced or transmitted in any form or by any means, electronic or mechanical, except for the purpose of review and/or reference, without explicit permission in writing from the publisher.

Cover artwork copyright © 2021 by Janet Fine

Author photograph by Karen Wallace

Published by Unruly Voices
unrulyvoices.com

An imprint of Paper Angel Press
paperangelpress.com

ISBN 978-1-953469-44-1 (Trade Paperback)

10 9 8 7 6 5 4 3 2 1

FIRST EDITION

*In memory of my mother,
Jeannine Post,
who made my life so wonderful!*

Foreword

Make It Fresh
by Dan White

IN THE SUMMER OF 2020, at the height of the Covid pandemic, Jory Post enrolled in a memoir and personal-essay class that I was teaching. Perhaps the act of signing up for the class—the swooshing sound of the email he sent to me, expressing interest—was a catalyst. Maybe that email was a trip wire. Jory must have been waiting for a prompt, a signal, a loud report from a starter pistol. Somehow, his statement of intent—"I'd like to sign up for your writing class"—was the pistol shot. And then he was off in a sprint. He wrote—one entry per day, without fail. Day after day, week after week. It was as if he'd put on a pair of bewitched red shoes and could not for the life of him stop dancing.

In these pages, Jory—or should I say, the Speaker, the Narrator, the Designated Muse-Representative of Jory—roams the world. We move forward and backward in time, from the wilds of Norfolk Island to the football fields of Watsonville High School. It's all here—sex and romance, the peculiar decor and rituals of doctors' offices, the lonely ghosts of extinct birds, and the delicious agony of a redwood-deck project that Jory describes as a labor worthy of Hercules. In one marvelous chapter, the Speaker, while lying down for a nap, breaks free of his body and skates across the surface of a cloud like a wheeling seabird. In a burst of freedom, the "unprompted" writer, with no goal in mind, soars low to the sea, "watching for whales and dolphins, clusters of kelp, not hunting, not seeking, simply observing what is there for my eyes to bring in":

> I've never flown like this before, never had my hands on the wheel with the ability to control my flight pattern, but I gladly take the reins, appreciate this newfound joy in flying low with no concerns of crashing or landing, just a glide, an airless, breathless floating above the waves, the coastline, the places where I have spent nearly sixty years of my life, bodysurfing and mat surfing at the Cove, 26th Avenue, parties on the beach, parties in high school at the Lincolns' house on 16th Avenue, and in this plane ride, I can let my hands off the wheel, think about where I want to go, what I want to see, and the gentle swerve takes me there.

I've read that passage many times, and it still gives me a feeling of buoyancy. Jory, a protégé of the beloved poet and poetry teacher Danusha Laméris, is a master of light and shadow. In this book, you will find moments that will rend you, and others that will patch you together again. And what is the beat that pulses through the book? The beat is the long hand of a ticking clock. In late 2018, Jory was diagnosed with pancreatic cancer. He had been writing for years, but the detection of a devastating disease and his intensive treatment unloosed something inside him. Imagine a pressure cooker left on for too long, the pressure going up above two atmospheres, causing a rupture.

The result was an astounding period of creativity: prose poems, short stories, meticulously crafted dream boxes inspired by Joseph Cornell, and a novel, *Pious Rebel*. All this alongside the forays that make up *Daily Fresh*.

It would be one thing if Jory's daily musings were just blurting, getting random thoughts on the page. But that's not what's going on here. *Daily Fresh* isn't purgative. These pages are roomy and inclusive, inviting you to dwell inside them. If you spend time with this book, walking its corridors, exploring its attics, basements, and mudrooms, I can guarantee one thing. It will make you take stock. You will look back on the loves and friendships of your life. You will reframe your relationship to illness. In Jory's pages, illness is more than a diminishing, more than a deadline, and more than a form of subtraction. It is also a magnifying glass, a mortal enemy, a muse, a dream box, a dwelling place, a flashlight, and a wall to kick off from.

There is refreshment here, and renewal. In one lovely chapter, Jory casts himself forward as a benevolent spirit, giving comfort to his grieving widow, Karen. The piece left me breathless because of its empathy and propulsion. There he was, sitting down to write, while contemplating life going on without him. A similar impulse led him to write a mordant, funny poem in his wonderful book of prose poetry, *The Extra Year*, in which he thinks about the music he wants mourners to play at his funeral, including John Prine's "Please Don't Bury Me" and "Another One Bites the Dust," by Queen.

In a sense, *Daily Fresh* is also a mixtape. The sequencing is masterful. Just when he gets you in a somber mode, he'll upend the mood with mischief, hilarity, and wild invention. Consider the chapter that delves into Jory's career as an educator. He and his elementary-school students turned their classroom into a small city, using its own currency, holding elections, and selling real baked goods from its Lilliputian bakeries. In another uproarious passage, Jory talks about celebrating the artistry of a deck installer by crafting a miniature version of the deck and presenting it as a gift to the hardworking artisan. In a sense, this book, like that mini-deck and shrunken city, and like the dream boxes that Jory crafted with Karen, right up to the final months of his life, is a container. My advice is to open it and take a stroll through Jory's recollections. Make yourself comfortable. You could read it all the way through if you're so inclined, or "finger-dip" your way into passages at random. There is wisdom in these pages, and the best sort of recklessness.

Jory was a big-hearted, lyrical writer, and he was an insubordinate student in the best sense. He would not be penned. He would not accept the rabbit-hutch confinement of genre restrictions.

I hesitate to call this a book of pure nonfiction. Some chapters, including one in which he turns himself into someone else and changes his name, flirt with fictive realms. What, then, should I call it? It's not a memoir. Labeling it a journal feels like a cold, clammy cop-out. Journals are expulsive, while this book invites you in. And this book is much too unruly to slap it with the boring label of personal-essay collection. And I wouldn't dare call it a self-help book—Lord, no!—though this book helped me. I defy you to read these pages without feeling a sharp kick. *Get on with it,* the pages say. *What do you think you are doing, saving up your best ideas? For when? Spend them all. Spend them now. Don't wait for some undetermined later.*

Still, I must call this book *something*, so I will place it in the category of "fictography," Jory's wildly inventive version of autofiction. In it, he comments on other pieces he was working on and tests out ideas for future works. He holds his dread at bay by staying busy, considering the nature of the subconscious, and letting the currents of his thoughts carry him. But make no mistake. *Daily Fresh* is not just the staging ground for future art but a work of art in its own right.

And speaking of definitions, what was Jory getting at when he talked about this concept of "Daily Fresh"? Here, I'll let the author speak for himself. Daily Freshness is all about the mystery of creativity:

> About how the words come to me, what vehicles they have crammed themselves into to be delivered to my pen, my keyboard, my brain, to mine them from the rabbit holes as if they were solid gold, or platinum, or maybe even the explosiveness of uranium.
>
> I'm ready. I'm poised. I'm borrowing the nurses' haloes and using them as receptors for waves sent from distant planets and brought to earth by extraterrestrials eager to share, eager to teach us what they already know about travel and distance and time and the relative importance of ideas and transmission of knowledge and information. The freshness.

Santa Cruz, California
September 2021

Contents

It Was in a Dream 1
Agendas 3
Sometimes I'm Unexplainably Calm 8
I Know It's a Good Day 12
A True Daily Fresh 17
Just Any Word 19
One Day at a Time 21
Cheryl Morris-Vieira-Dixon-Brothers 24
A Nap 28
Contrivance 30
Karen, My Karen! 33
What I Avoid 37
Detritus 40
Poison Darts 42
A Thematic Infusion-Inclusion-Intrusion 45
Loose Threads 47
The Every-Other-Wednesday Way 50
Taking Care of Business 64
"V" Is for Verve 67
Adrift 70
The Value of Statues 73
Every Day Is Tuesday 76
Atasky 79
Cliché Watch 81
Slippage 84
I Lie Better Than I Examine 87

Dear Sandra—8-1-20	90
Pressure	97
The Lists	104
A Crumbling Cracker of Communion	111
Ms. Bossy Pants— Otherwise Known as CHETKO	115
Side by Side	119
Style-ish	123
The Urge to Submerge	127
Extracting the Fossil	132
Mel Ott vs. Willie Mays	136
Another Good Week	142
My Summer Fog	146
A Deep Clean	148
The Moan of Lisa	153
A Shift in Focus	159
The Defiance of Reliance	163
One Step Beyond	169
The Failure of Immune Systems	201
What's Next?	206
"They Got the Fire Down Below"	211
A Matter of Principal	215
Evacuees—What Is Left Behind	218
Magical, Mysterious, Magnificent Art Workshop	223
December 7, 1932—Santa Catalina	228
Reset	235
Apologizing for Priorities	241
The Compound	246
Perspective	251
A Little Bit of It in Everyone	255

Every Hug Is a Small, Soft Jail	257
Quietude	261
Night Walk	266
The Next to Last Supper	272
The History of Fried-Egg Sandwiches	278
The Golf Fade	282
The Gamester	287
World Series of Poker, Lake Tahoe—5-4-2005	292
The Art of Deflection	300
Carryover	304
The Sleep of Goddesses	308
Widow's Lament	311
The Students	315
Great Scott! 50 Reasons Why Scott Is My Friend	318
When the Music's Over	328

It Was in a Dream

IT WAS IN A DREAM EARLY THIS MORNING, during that time where it doesn't feel like a dream, but more as if I'm sitting there with these two guys in this office where it feels like I'm supposed to help with ideas, with completing copy for a newspaper, writing stories, thinking about story lines, writing notes in a very old notebook that seems rare and antique, and I don't understand why we're using it to write on now, and eventually one of the guys says, "Why are you writing on this?" to which I say, "Yeah. It looks pretty valuable." And he proceeds to thumb through the pages, showing us a series of very detailed characters for cartoon images, images I fall in love with quickly. This sequence was connected to a number of other pieces which aren't bubbling up to the surface right now, but it seems like there was some mayhem in the streets, maybe fire, maybe Molotov cocktails and police wearing armor, and we had to get into this office and get to work because the work was important to get out to the people to change the mood, to redirect their anger and disgust in a way that provided solutions, looked at ways out of what appeared to be a dead end.

Agendas

MY BRAIN HAS BEEN FUNCTIONING BY AGENDAS for quite some time. For years I have started my morning journal entries with To Do lists, which are agendas of sorts. Sometimes the agenda is short, just a line or two of a poem I'd like to write. The lines come early in the morning, usually before I move from my horizontal pose. Other times lists of things appear and I try to find places to stick them, create a memory palace, attach the revision of the *Smith* novel to my foot, so that when I put the first foot on the floor, I know to head to the computer and modify; connect the *Zoom Forward!* tasks of the day to the tingling in my fingertips, knowing touching the keyboard will remind me to address needed issues; take my first drink of morning water to unplug my throat and remember to continue to build my streak of Daily Fresh, now at two days.

But these days, before I even open my eyes, before the crack of light appears in the eastern sky just above the mountains across the valley, I am building a daily list which I have zero control over. It's the deck project. The massive deck that courses across our backyard and hovers above the canyon is thirty years old. Was thirty years old, built by Stephen Burt and crew in 1989. The majority of the nails used to attach the boards to joists were sticking above the boards by a quarter inch. It was dangerous, not only to the humans who occasionally walk out there but also to the wildlife that visit.

On one hand, we can't really afford the exorbitant cost of a deck at this point in our lives, and on the other, I guess we really can, given that we won't be taking any vacations anytime soon given the combination of Covid in the world and my pancreatic cancer in my world. With that in mind, I priced out the cost of a new deck, using three different possible decking materials: Trex, regular redwood, con-heart redwood. Because our brother-in-law Chuck, who managed Big Creek Watsonville forever before he retired, could get us his discount, we went with the con-heart option, nearly 2,300 board feet at $2.95 a foot, that ended up costing nearly $8,000 with all the accoutrements. Next was a conversation about costs with our handyman Terry—well, to put it accurately, our good friend Lisa McKenzie's good friend Terry, who successfully completed two earlier projects for us and who charges less than the going rate, partly because he's most likely not bonded and doesn't have a contractor's license, and because he works with an engineer's mind, and because he's sixty-eight years old (which translates to being slow, but accurate). His initial estimate for removing nails and boards, laying down new boards, power washing the railings, flipping the top boards of the railings, sanding the deck, and staining the deck came in at 140 hours, or $3,500.

As of this morning, as of the writing of this Daily Fresh, we are at approximately 129 hours of Terry's time, and he has two major sections of decking left to lay, including removing of nails and boards for one section, and most likely having to rebuild substructure of the final section, as he has had to do for every section. Therein lies the rub. The occasional rotten substructure boards needed redesigning, engineering, recreating, and using a method called sistering, where he uses old boards to pair with the existing rotting boards, which takes, how do I say it nicely, well I guess I don't, forever!

So before my feet hit the floor, before my eyes opened, before I knew I wasn't dreaming, the agenda of the deck formulated on that incessant screen inside my head that tracks untrackable things, beginning with a helicopter view over the deck, me perched in the passenger seat, hanging my head out the window, surveying the current status of the job. The first item I add to the agenda is the three huge dumps of nails pulled from old boards that were piled into a plastic tub, then dumped into our wheelbarrow. They need to be moved, emptied, dealt with, so we can have the use of our wheelbarrow returned. The next item on the list is the large pile of lumber scraps and sawdust amassing under the chop saw, which is Terry's primary tool on the job. Next are the piles of old boards, some as long as twenty-four feet, stacked in various spots around the property, which need to find their way to the front yard for Dave Culver to haul away for kindling when he visits on Wednesday, which is tomorrow, which is chemo day, which means that when Stuart, Lisa's son, gets here today to work, that will be one of his first tasks, at least on my agenda, if not Terry's.

More surveying of the job from my view from above takes a look at the con-heart boards spread around the backyard, at least now moved into the backyard so inspectors can't see them, unless they have a helicopter of their own, ready to be moved, cut, set in place like a puzzle, screwed to the sister joists using the special Camo tool we bought. But most of this view is the preliminary look at the work, like when Terry says, "I won't charge you for my thinking time," and he does so with a slight grin, moving from the saw to the current deck section where he is placing a piece of his reconstruction puzzle.

Now comes the true agenda, me thinking in terms of half days—$100—or full days—$200—and I'm hoping the current section he is working on will only take a half day of substructure reconstruction, and in fact it takes a whole day, with no boards being screwed down, and I'm wondering if we will get all the boards in that section screwed down today, or if it is going to take two or three days—$400 or $600—and while Terry is doing an excellent job, the deck so far looks great, and it will probably be sturdier than the sheer panels in the walls of our house added after the 1989 earthquake, we are heading for the land of over-budget.

By the end of day today, we will be very close to the 140-hour estimate, which is where my head travels to the next section of the agenda, the lower deck where the hot tub used to sit, where none of the nails have been removed yet, which I imagine is going to take another $200 day to complete, maybe more. And once those nails are removed and dropped in our garbage can for Waste Management to haul away, we will discover the truths of the next item on the agenda: the status of the substructure in this final section of deck. Most likely there will be two or three more days of sistering, two or three more days of screwing boards down, and now we are liable to be almost doubled in terms of real versus estimated hours. Which is when I round out the agenda, add the remaining phases of the project, the cleaning up of the yard, getting rid of detritus, and as Terry said in his original estimate, power washing the railings, flipping the top boards of the railings, sanding the deck, and staining the deck.

Holy shit! What have we gotten ourselves into? Let me restate: the deck is gorgeous, sturdy, is where we should go for safety if there is another earthquake, but holy shit! But, like I said, we most likely won't be taking any more vacations, so we will stay-cate in our backyard, on our gorgeous new deck, with a view over Rodeo Gulch Road, invite our friends over for a socially distant gathering. The first such gathering will be Lisa, Steve, Stuart, Terry, and Deborah, to show off Terry's work, to have people jump up and down on the deck so they can feel the hidden substructure of Terry's engineering genius doing its work. I figure this project will end up costing us $13,000, but hey, a new car would have cost three times that much, and we couldn't afford that. Maybe we could hire Terry to retrofit our 2010 Prius, work on the substructure, give us an estimate, see how things go. Within two weeks, our bank account will be drained, and the deck agenda will be gone, replaced with something new, finishing the extinct-bird project, finalizing *Capture and Release*, working on *Lonnie and Art*, more, so much more!

Sometimes I'm Unexplainably Calm

SOMETIMES I'M UNEXPLAINABLY CALM, and other times I'm impatient. Not unexplainably impatient, because I'm certain I can come up with an excuse every time. I become impatient with redundancy, when I hear people say the same thing two or three times in a row even though they tried to use different words each time, as if they were trying to trick you into hearing what they had to say in three different ways. Maybe it's not impatience. Maybe it just pisses me off.

As I wrote yesterday, I have an impatience with the progress on the deck-building in our backyard. I won't go into a redundant rant on that process. I'm impatient about my body. But when I say that, when I think that, I ask myself, "What is it that I'm waiting for, what am I antsy about?" Yesterday after orgasmic sex with Karen I experienced immediate excruciating pain in my upper back/neck area. I've had similar feelings maybe a half-dozen times in the past, but not the depth and duration of yesterday's event, and I think I'm correct in calling it an event, because it was different, because I didn't know if it was going to subside or if Karen was going to have to call 911 or if I was just going to roll over and die. It's this impatience with my body that haunts me. Am I waiting for that final unknown episode to whisk me away? I don't think so. Not waiting for it, but knowing that it's most likely out there and that I have no idea how or when it will occur. Thus the impatience.

To counterbalance the impatience, I try to keep busy. No, it's not even a trying, there is no concerted effort that *trying* suggests. I just keep busy because I have a long list of projects to complete. I am driven. I have my priority list and I know where I'm headed, know that *Pious Rebel* is off and running and looking for a home. Know that *Smith: An Unauthorized Fictography* is in Kathy's hands for a copyedit. Know that I'm taking *Capture and Release* with me to the chemo chair today, hopefully for a sustained six-hour look at reviewers' comments and whether or not to continue on the pathway of having Louise deal with pancreatic cancer or let her be, go back to the original draft and clean it up as is. The question about Louise is not a simple one. Well, the question is simple, but not the answer.

Within a few weeks of completing the first draft was when I received my diagnosis, in October. That diagnosis made me think that my book, mainly about death and dying, had no character like me, with the worst possible cancer available, and made me think about giving it to Louise, because I had been told in comments that she was a one-dimensional, flat character. But, as I learned more about my cancer, as I joined Danusha's poetry workshop, I was able to think and talk about the cancer through over 300 poems written during the next twenty-one months. Thus, Louise disappeared, headed to Canada for a long train trip from British Columbia to Nova Scotia I jokingly say, meaning I didn't need her to tell the cancer story anymore, meaning I now need to think about whether *Capture and Release* really needs that story line, and if I'm willing to go through the work to sustain that thread throughout the book, which means changing her relationship with everyone she knows. One day I'm leaning toward leaving Louise cancer-free, and the next I'm leaning toward continuing the thread, because I like the two chapters I wrote about her when she first hears about the cancer and undergoes the first treatment.

So much of that is behind me that I'm not sure I want to dig in and regurgitate it again. Will I make that decision today, while sitting in the chair, while receiving my IV doses of Zofran and Emend and Oxaliplatin and Atropine and Irinotecan? Will I watch the nurses doing their crazy-fuck jobs of keeping themselves up and happy for the purpose of keeping their patients up and happy? Will I watch them fill IV bags across the fourteen chairs and stations scattered around the infusion room? Will I listen to them tell their jokes, laugh loudly, watch them sidle up to a colleague, lower their voice and share a secret, something they watched on TV last night, something they ordered out from a local restaurant, a walk they took with their husband through Arana Gulch, a conversation they had with a child who shared that he was sick to death of sheltering in place? Will these angels continue to lift me on their wings, wear their haloes proud, guide me as I make this important decision about Louise, about myself, about how my writing life proceeds?

Yes, they will, and *Capture and Release* will move its way to the finish line. One month is all I'm giving myself on this one, which means by August 8, I will have another draft to be copyedited, maybe by Scott, or maybe it's time to hire a professional so I can take the burden off Kathy and Scott. And at some point, this Daily Fresh column will venture out into something more than a personal journal entry, grow into something that is truly FRESH and allows me to find and occupy a rabbit hole with windows to the universe that teach me new ways of thinking and living and writing and sharing unlike anything I've ever known before. It will be about how the words come to me, what vehicles they have crammed themselves into to be delivered to my pen, my keyboard, my brain, to mine them from the rabbit holes as if they were solid gold, or platinum, or maybe even the explosiveness of uranium.

I'm ready. I'm poised. I'm borrowing the nurses' haloes and using them as receptors for waves sent from distant planets and brought to earth by extraterrestrials eager to share, eager to teach us what they already know about travel and distance and time and the relative importance of ideas and transmission of knowledge and information. The freshness. What comes out new and unrecognizable because of a new dress, a new pair of shoes, a different way of looking at oneself and the world, of oneself in the world, of the eventuality of oneself out of the world. This is what is fresh. It's *Lonnie and Art* fresh. It's that first sentence on the page which is not new but is still fresh: "Lonnie lives on the streets. Art is her friend." That's what I mean. The two living side by side, intertwined, the polishing of the one while birthing the other. The polishing of the many while the birthing of many more. As if time were not an issue. As if time were the most important issue of all.

I Know It's a Good Day

I KNOW IT'S A GOOD DAY WHEN I WAKE UP ... Maybe I should just stop there, knowing it's a good day because I *did* wake up, but no, that's not my point, my point being that I know it's a good day when I wake up and don't care about the chemo pump hanging round my neck, when I see the fog floating over the con-heart redwood forming our rebuilt deck, and instead of focusing on nausea, the first thing that comes to mind is making Terry, who is rebuilding our deck, an awesome cup of hot chocolate with miniature marshmallows floating on top to help him fight off the chill.

My day made already, before nine o'clock, and with this starter to another Daily Fresh. And while I'm at it, at this thing about thinking about how to make others happy, or to help them solve a problem, I remember that Mom and Shelly have questions about summing a column of figures in an Excel spreadsheet, so I add it to my To Do list, one that I'll tackle as soon as I finish this piece. This piece, whatever it is, whatever it may become, the flip side of yesterday's theme of impatience, even though waking up on the same side of the bed, doing so with a different brain, one ready to take on the world anew, dare I say fresh, dare I say both hands on the wheel, driving foot to the floorboard, careful to hug the road, endure the curves, avoid the cliffs. I'm not sure if my arrival justifies the speed at which I traveled, or if the speed negates the need for an arrival.

Either way, I'm here, feet back on the ground, maintaining my wider stance to keep myself from tipping over, using a wall as needed, ready to cut some bird maps, to put a *Done!* tag on the sarcophagus for the Norfolk Island Kaka. By the end of day to have one of thirty done, to take its picture, share it with a few friends who are interested in the progress, who may actually have been more interested in the lack of progress, who care about the successes that help keep me alive, help all of us stay alive and looking for and finding the positive aspects of a planet spinning out of control.

One purpose for this Daily Freshness can be the development of characters. Lonnie and Art have been in my mind, fingers, and stories for a number of years. They reappeared in the final line to *Pious Rebel*. As with all my characters, I've written about them for years, but I tend to slip into their minds, their situations, their everyday living, and forget to provide my audience, whomever that might be, with details that help to paint an initial view of who they are, that allow the reader to immediately invoke an image whenever they see or hear the name mentioned.

It's Lonnie I'm interested in as the protagonist of a new story, or as an expansion of an old story. There's some backstory about her that needs to be clarified. Most of her life she sold real estate. Beach properties and hillside estates that generated nice commission fees. She bought a nice house overlooking the San Lorenzo River, across from the Boardwalk, where she and her husband lived happily and a little too high on the hog, an extremely well-stocked liquor cabinet, throwing weekly weekend parties on their deck, inviting friends, neighbors, clients, sometimes all three embodied in one person.

That was when the husband, who will remain unnamed because we don't care about him, may never hear him mentioned in the story, that was when he started the first affair Lonnie knew of, with the neighbor next door whose husband was always out of town on business, the one who sunbathed in the nude on her own deck, the one who drank all of the fine scotch at the weekend parties. Until then, Lonnie had been a moderate drinker, a glass of red wine, an occasional silver gin fizz at brunch, but now that the husband had brought something new into their marriage, now that he expanded the circle of love, of sex, Lonnie drank more. Vodka tonics, *mai tai*s, shots of tequila. Her real estate work suffered. She quit making cold and warm calls and expected people to find her if they wanted. She fell out of the million-dollar circle, and was soon digging into her meager savings to pay for her booze. Food was of no importance. She'd eat nuts and chips at the bars, would go home with strangers and have unsafe sex just because she wanted to, wanted some temporary relief from her cascading life.

It didn't take long for the first STD to appear. She took out second and third mortgages on the house. Eventually the banks foreclosed and she lost the house, moved into the back seat of her BMW, took most of her belongings to Goodwill, except for the grungy stuff that she walked over to the neighbor's yard and dumped in a big pile in front of her garage door. She started parking at Twin Lakes Beach at night, until the same cop kept driving up behind her, turning on the flashing lights, telling her to move on. She ended up in the driveway of a real estate friend, until the car was repossessed, and the friend let her stay in a spare room inside for a couple of weeks. That dried up quickly when the friend found Lonnie passed out in the bathtub, drink in hand, nose and chin nearly under water. That's when she ended up on the streets, under trees by the highway, nestled in wherever she could up and down the stretch of River Street, always gave her address to folks who asked for it as 101 River Street.

Was Lonnie a bad person? A few clients toward the end whose deals she messed up may still think so. But the husband who started the avalanche, once he finally left the neighbor, didn't think Lonnie was a bad person. He thought he was the bad person, that he was the cause of all Lonnie's problems. Which of course was not completely true. When Lonnie was at her peak, she had weekly sessions with her stylist at the salon, who streaked her hair with blond splashes, made her look young, attractive. Her skin was moisturized with all the right creams. Her body was tan. Her teeth were perfect. It was more about the liver and her mind as time went on. More blood tests. More visits to the doctor to talk about cirrhosis. Fewer visits to the hair stylist. More visits to the discount liquor store where she could get hard booze by the half gallon. No more blond streaks in her hair. The grey edged out, took over, frizzy edges, split ends. She quit brushing her teeth and flossing, instead rinsing her mouth out with a shot of Patrón before falling into bed, or the back seat, or under a bush at Pogonip. She had sold most of her clothes at yard sales before she lost the house. Kept a few things in a suitcase that she stored at a homeless locker.

In the beginning of her life on the streets, she would use the laundry once a week. Not anymore. It didn't matter what she wore. It didn't matter how she smelled. Two long dresses were her favorite, so she didn't have to unzip pants to go to the bathroom, just squat and drop. Her arms were tan from all the time pushing carts up and down River Street into town. But the rest of her looked ashen, bland, a lump of flesh unkempt and abandoned. Her fingernails were either too long or broken, chewed off back to the skin. Her daily life consisted of finding something in a trash can to eat for breakfast, gathering bottles and cans to sell at the recycle place, picking up a burrito from Taco Bell for lunch, walking, a lot, her calf muscles being the healthiest part of her whole body. Huddling with acquaintances along the river.

Which is how she met Art. On the levee. She hadn't encountered too many sweet men on the streets, not that she ever expected to, was leery of all of them, until she met Art. Seeing him every day made her want to brush her hair, wipe the dirt out of the expanding wrinkles in her forehead.

So there's a little bit of Daily Fresh about Lonnie and her friend Art. Just 1,000+ words of backstory that may help launch into something brand new, something that *Pious Rebel* characters Alice and her daughter Lisa Hardrock considered throughout their lives.

A True Daily Fresh

A TRUE DAILY FRESH TODAY. I watched Terry working away on the deck, figuring he's at least another week out. I've been trying to think of something to make him in the workshop, kind of an Oscar or Emmy for woodworking. While I haven't been happy with his speed, I am happy with the quality of his work. I started thinking of how I could use the laser cutter to create a miniature replica of the deck that I would glue together and give to him when it's completed. We'll have a deck party with Lisa, Steve, Stuart, Terry, and Deborah, and present it to him then.

I created a design in Illustrator that roughly matches the dimensions Terry drew of the proposed deck replacement. I created a template with replicas of sixteen-foot 2x6s, and the laser cut it out perfectly. Tomorrow I'll cut some sides so I can piece it together. Railings will come later. The only piece that is a little off is that the top of the boards have the wood burn from the laser,

Daily Fresh

so it looks brown instead of red. After I glue the pieces down, I might be able to sand it, but I doubt it. I'll create a plaque on the laser cutter that says: *Refurbished by Terry Miller from June 15 through July 17, 2020.* That's about as fresh as it gets today.

Just Any Word

JUST ANY WORD. Like *round*. What is roundness? This is where my good friend Don Rothman would come in handy, would shine, would light up like a well-traveled neighborhood at Christmas. Wordsmith, indeed! He might talk about the roundness of a pregnant mother's belly, having seen it directly at least twice. He could talk about the roundness of a well-formed, well-shaved head. Together we'd envision circles and orbs and rings and globes and planets. We'd play with basketballs and hockey pucks and Frisbees and golf balls and softballs and hardballs and throwing the discus at a track meet.

We'd debate the value of wedding rings, of tradition and being told what to do by overbearing forefathers and mothers. We'd sit 'round campfires, we'd round up cattle into their pens, we'd round up old friends for a reunion. We'd round out a discussion, round up to the nearest whole number. To end the

Daily Fresh

day, we'd spin our Hula-Hoops, think about our spheres of influence, head downtown to the Poet and Patriot and buy a round of drinks for everyone there.

One Day at a Time

WILL I TALK MYSELF OUT OF continuing to write these Daily Fresh pieces by beginning to think they are simply another form of navel-gazing? I hope not, because even though they are initially prompt-less, eventually a prompt appears that guides me forward into a near-stream-of-consciousness pathway that occasionally produces something of interest.

So onward I go, watching a very large blue jay outside my slider filling itself with seed, guarding its domain, pushing would-be collaborators away from the tray, this ever-present pecking order that birds are governed by, not unlike humans, who also enjoy getting a leg over, especially poets on the rise, spreading preciously couched words from one coast to the next. The birds must know I'm thinking about them, writing about them, as they've temporarily disappeared, left me alone to invent my own prompts, find my own way through without their assistance. But it's too late. They are in my blood. They inhabit my workshop, make nests tucked just under my cerebellum, are with me through every dream, through every waking morning moment, whether extinct or living. And as soon as I recognize their disappearance, they return, in my face, reminding me that I have no power to predict the future, to track their movements and patterns, not because those movements and patterns don't exist, but rather because I don't have the scientific genes to study and research with a voracious appetite until I have picked them down to their tiny little bones.

They know I drift, they have studied me well enough to know my patterns, to know that when I drift I may forget about them for a while, as I see the deck below them in progress, them knowing I'm waiting for its completion, for another backyard phase, with socially distanced masked parties and antique glass-top tables, a pretense of normalcy in a world that has spun so far away from normal that the definition has been removed from most dictionaries, except for the one currently used in urban dictionaries, the one that says "a word made up by this corrupt society so they could single out and attack those who are different."

Now *normal* jumps to the front as prompt, and the idea that every person has his or her own definition of normalcy to explain away their differences, to look at so many others as abnormal because they don't live up to either a social or personal set of standards scaffolding a fragile existence. Every one of us takes our unique place on that ever-present spectrum that gets bandied about so much these days. My grandson, clearly on the spectrum, at ten years old doesn't speak, doesn't understand most of the normal world. He lives his normal existence that the rest of us don't understand because we can't find the right code to unlock his mind, his way of knowing that we will never know.

My sense of what is normal is so different than what it was twenty-one months ago. It was once normal to attend two or three movies a week, to think and write about them. It was once normal to go to the Spa Fitness Center and lift weights and ride the exercycle. It was once normal to assume that I would always be overweight given the diet I grew up on that included Grandma Esther's cookies from Sunshine Biscuits, the Mounds bars and almond clusters she traded for, the cases of soda pop my dad traded for drug samples with the guy who lived next door, the Michelob on tap in a red refrigerator in the garage next to the pool table. With one CT scan that sense of normalcy disappeared. It became clear that normal was a mindset that could shift as quickly as a 7:15 a.m. call from a doctor. That what was going on inside of one's skin changed the nature of normalcy of what was going on outside one's skin. It's now a day-by-day, minute-by-minute occurrence.

There are a few things I can predict based on my chemo and other schedules, but mostly I leave predictions behind me now. I'll make To Do lists so I can be as productive as possible, but I understand that the predictions may be a waste of time, because the notion of what is normal, a key ingredient of successful predictions, is no longer a reliable resource. Like the writing of this Daily Fresh piece—no idea where it would begin, where it might end.

And here I am, birds gone once again, my cerebellum feeling the itch of their nests, knowing that there is no one in the world that matches my current definition of normal, knowing that it will change as the day moves forward, as I make my way through extinct bird maps, laser cutting miniature 2x6s for a replica deck, talking with my friend Kathy for two-plus hours today on Zoom, just getting a text from my granddaughter Georgia who is coming over this afternoon to look at the studio, another way to look differently at the world, the house we live in, the people we live with, the people we love.

Onward! One day at a time.

Cheryl Morris-Vieira-Dixon-Brothers

I MET CHERYL MORRIS-VIEIRA-DIXON-BROTHERS IN 1980, when we hired her to become the principal-superintendent of Happy Valley School on Branciforte Drive, where I was a fifth-sixth grade teacher. I was quiet, introverted, had been so my whole life. Cheryl was the opposite: bubbly, effusive, always up, at least on the surface, hiding it well when she wasn't. I was in my fourth year of teaching, not flailing but not shining either. I was recently divorced, and was making up for lost time. Partying. Dancing almost nightly. Drinking. Smoking pot. A little bit of cocaine introduced to me by Happy Valley parents.

At age thirty, I had no idea what I wanted the rest of my life to look like. Not sure teaching was the right fit. And although we had our awkward moments—like when my car's battery was dead and Cheryl tried to help me out and switched the cables in the wrong direction and the battery exploded and acid splattered over my shirt, eating holes into the cloth, leaving me looking like Swiss cheese, luckily not reaching skin—our relationship and long-lasting friendship falls in the 99.9% range.

Cheryl was a go-getter, nothing out of her reach. She knew how to think, plan, act, and make things happen. Like convincing me that I was a natural-born teacher, like talking me into applying for the Master's in Educational Administration program at USF. Which I did. By 1985, I had completed my master's, had quit using drugs and mostly given up alcohol, became closer with Cheryl as both mentor and friend. Cheryl was never afraid of ideas. And she wasn't the type who thought only her ideas were good. She listened to everybody, nodded her head, looked for ways to make things happen, make people happy. Cheryl believed, as did most of our staff, in an eclectic approach to teaching and learning. The key to her philosophy, and therefore ours, was the love of learning. That was our number-one job. To make kids thrilled to be coming to school every day, to be learning something new, to be working together with others, collaborating on group projects like Dig and Caravans, taking science trips to Camp Hammer and Camp Koinonia, creating arts-based mini-courses on Friday afternoons, helping to organize fundraisers for sick students.

There were very few dull moments during the twenty years I was lucky enough to spend with Cheryl. There was the year she turned sixty and I rented a limousine and we tootled Cheryl all over town. There was the year Jonathan was born, and I was there, video camera in hand, ready to capture the whole event on film, though a last-minute caesarian altered our plans, me waiting in the lobby until Jon appeared.

One thing we shared were common enemies. Well, really just one. He was the loudest-mouthed, reddest-necked man living in Happy Valley. I leave his name out of it, as he's now passed, so no need to malign him. He came after Cheryl because she lived her life the way a strong woman should live it, independent and according to her own code. I came to her defense. The same person came after me as he finagled his way onto the school board and tried to get me fired because he had seen me take a hit off a joint at a community party—a joint that he personally handed to me. He was a sick, unhappy man, and Cheryl and I stood arm-in-arm against him and prevailed.

The biggest effect Cheryl had on me was the drastic change of consciousness I underwent by being in her presence. Life was good. Regardless of all the little things that could throw you off course, life was good, and was always getting better. I met Karen, well, re-met Karen, whom I went to high school with, in 1988 at our twenty-year high school reunion. Cheryl was/is a huge fan of Karen's and let me know quickly that she approved and that I would be an idiot to let her get away. As always, she was right, and I took her advice, held on tightly to Karen in my life as my wife, and held on tightly in my life to Cheryl as one of my longest and best friends.

When I was diagnosed with pancreatic cancer in October 2018, Cheryl was one of the first people I told. She was devastated. I could tell that my poor health was affecting her health. But it didn't keep her away. She brought flowers, and squash, and strawberries, and anything she could think of that would make my life easier. When my first book of poetry was published, she supplied all the flowers, vases, and arrangements for the tables at the Food Lounge where we had 130 folks show up. She has always been there for me. And I have tried to always be there for her. Cheryl was the first person I gave a copy of the Italo Calvino box, the crown of my artistic creation so far. Gary found a perfect glass enclosure for it, and it sits on a table in their house. In our front yard, we have thriving angel trumpets that Cheryl gave us ages ago. They remind me of her every time I walk outside and smell the fragrance, hear the bees buzzing.

When I think of superlatives to describe Cheryl, the first that comes to mind is bubbly. Then there's effervescent. Enthusiastic. Avid. Passionate. Warm. Willing. Zealous. Devoted. And spirited.

There is no other single person in my life who has had such a drastic and positive influence on my life, who turned me around and taught me to open my eyes and pay attention to the world and people around me.

Thank you, Cheryl. For the love, the friendship, for the forever kind of thing that we have always had and will continue to have.

A Nap

A NAP! AN HOUR'S WORTH OF SLEEP in the early afternoon can make all the difference. And today it did. Refreshed me. Ready to take on another chunk of the world. Maybe a small chunk—finish gluing the railings to the miniature deck I'm building Terry. Maybe working on cutting and gluing maps for the next extinct-bird sarcophagus. And definitely getting this ninth day of Daily Fresh logged before we head to the Crow's Nest to pick up family dinner for four. Probably the roast chicken, with mashed potatoes, gravy, mixed vegetables, and eight of their awesome brown rolls.

I should let Karen convince me of the value of the nap more often. To close my eyes and not think of nausea is a gift. To wake up to the ringing of an obnoxious telemarketing call and discover that I'm rested and can leave my anger about the call aside and smile at my good fortune.

I'm not prompted yet today, flying my plane low to the sea, watching for whales and dolphins, clusters of kelp, not hunting, not seeking, simply observing what is there for my eyes to bring in.

I've never flown like this before, never had my hands on the wheel with the ability to control my flight pattern, but I gladly take the reins, appreciate this newfound joy in flying low with no concerns of crashing or landing, just a glide, an airless, breathless floating above the waves, the coastline, the places where I have spent nearly sixty years of my life, body surfing and mat surfing at the Cove, 26th Avenue, parties on the beach, parties in high school at the Lincolns' house on 16th Avenue, and in this plane ride, I can let my hands off the wheel, think about where I want to go, what I want to see, and the gentle swerve takes me there, to Buena Vista Road in Watsonville where I picked olallieberries, to Watsonville High School where I played in football games against the Wildcats, up the coast to Davenport and beyond, where I took my parents' Camaro for a very fast ride through Four Lanes, near the dump.

It's a soft flight, like resting in a large marshmallow, sitting afloat a huge mug full of high-end hot chocolate which soothes my stomach, my life, prepares me for the soft landing on the second-story deck of my house, where the birds are waiting for me, asking me where I've been, where I'll go next, and I tell them I've been to see their ancestors, been to Mauritius and New Zealand and Iceland and Tasmania and Hawai'i to visit the lands where their relatives became extinct, where humans viewed the planet as a place for their taking, a place where no other species need be considered as they crafted the world to meet their every desire.

Contrivance

CONTRIVANCE. There's a word worthy of study. "The use of skill to bring something about or create something." And "a device, especially in literary or artistic compositions, which gives a sense of artificiality." Or "a thing which is created skillfully and inventively to serve a particular purpose." I'm not sure I like the use of "artificiality" to describe the creation that occurs when one sets out to contrive intentionally. Like what I'm doing now.

I woke up to an email that made me unhappy. No, first it made me angry. Then I tempered it down to unhappiness, so I could have a conversation with the person who sent the email. I had the conversation, and now I'm attending to the tenth Daily Fresh in ten days. To loosen the grip of unhappiness, I contrive, I build this or these paragraphs to vault me into something worthy of consideration, to occupy my brain with the creation of sentences which may find some future value or use. So I have contrived this prompt for today, this contrivance thing which may explain everything I've ever written, every thought I've ever had, every relationship I've ever had or may have in the future.

From the Middle English "to invent" and Old French "to find." I like both of those explanations better than "artificiality." But somehow it all comes back to "fictography". Everything always does. The beginning and the end. I'm inventing the pathway of this Daily Fresh entry with each pluck of a key, with each completion of a word, with each compilation of a sentence that stacks together with others to form a paragraph. And as the Old French suggests, I am finding my way as I go, like my character Lisa Hardrock, who wields a sharpened machete and hacks through underbrush. A difference is that she has a destination in mind: a Land of Medicine Buddha she knows will eventually be there when she cuts through. Mine is to some degree unknown, lies at the end of a 500- or 1000-word invention that helps me to find the end point. Like Kathy Runyan in our improv group, who would always finish with a Nadia Comaneci landing for her final sentence of a piece. That's what I hope for. That's where I'm headed. Even though I have no map, no blueprint to guide me along, no James Patterson framework and team of writers to point me to the end. Mine flow. Fall out, sometimes like rainwater down a drain spout, furious and unleashed with gravity in control. Other times more like molasses inching its way out of a bottle at the same pace as banana slugs working their way across a driveway.

A key assistant to this contrived presence is patience. Waiting. Not forcing out words that make no sense, words that, when combined with other words, are built into sentences solely to increase a word count. Sometimes in NaNoWriMo that was the goal, the intent, to reach x number of words per day—say

2,000—so the thirty-day goal of reaching 50,000 words could be seen as something achievable, something reachable with room to spare. Thus there is a clear contrivance at work in today's session. Putting my brain to work on this partial-page piece that keeps me far from anger, takes me in a positive direction away from thoughts that can pull me under, in a time when pulling oneself under can be detrimental to productivity and the dozens of tasks that await my time, my energy, my focus. And thus, the landing point, at 10:52 a.m., one final phrase, sentence, as I prepare for my Zoom meeting with Scott at 11:00 that I so enjoy. One of the key thought partners of my life.

Karen, My Karen!

I TELL PIECES OF THIS STORY MULTIPLE TIMES in various forms. It appears in poetry, it oozes out in journal entries, and of course it influences the traits of numerous characters in novels and short stories. And now, it's time for the straight-on personal essay that spills it out in all of its glorious splendor. While I use those superlatives—*glorious* and *splendor*—lovingly, there are no better words to quickly capture the essence of the primary person in my life for the last thirty-three years.

Karen Lynn Wallace has been my partner, my wife, my love, since that first dance we shared at the Cocoanut Grove on the Santa Cruz Boardwalk on August 1, 1988. It was our twenty-year high school reunion. We had been given hints by a mutual friend that we were both single, and possibly available, so we sought each other out early in the evening, found each other and secured a table with others, went through the buffet line, and then danced, all night long, until she needed to head home to get some rest for an upcoming race the next day.

A few weeks later she called and we scheduled a date on her thirty-eighth birthday on September 11. She was living in a house she bought on Paul Minnie Avenue, occupied by her oldest daughter, Jeannie, and occasionally her younger daughter, Ali, and, perhaps most notably, a ghost who kept them company. I don't remember now if the ghost had a name, but it was often talked about.

At the time, I was dating two other folks. Three was too many. Two was too many, but I was not clearheaded in those days. I ended one relationship which had always been difficult. But the other had been present in my life for a number of years. I was honest with Karen from day one, said, "If this person leaves her husband, I would definitely be with her." This had to be a ridiculously difficult thing for her to hear, and live with, but I felt it was more important to be honest about it up front and not spring something on her later.

As it turns out, I probably should have said nothing, because nothing came of it, and because my growing love of Karen negated any long-term feelings I might have had for someone else. When I say I should have said nothing, it's because even thirty-three years later, Karen carries some heavy jealousy and anger when it comes to that other person in my life. It would be better if that wasn't an issue that pops up sometimes, especially since I was diagnosed with pancreatic cancer and have a shortened timeline of years, months, days left to live. Enough of that worn-out topic.

Onward to more superlatives that describe the love of my life. She is an excellent mother, who is always concerned for the health and well-being of her daughters. And even a better grandmother to Hannah, Georgia, and Owen, doing anything and everything to make their lives better. I was lucky to find myself in a relationship with built-in family, knowing I would never have children of my own.

It's not easy to explain the symbiosis that we have achieved as a couple, as partners, as lifelong friends. I think about the majority of relationships that I've witnessed, or lived in, and I imagine those wooden toys with a hammer where we pounded round pegs into round holes, and so often in those relationships folks struggled for lifetimes pounding square pegs into round holes. It has never been like that for us. We have always fit together perfectly, and it never took any pounding. Instead we glided together as if our bodies and minds had been forged side by side and felt as if we were the thousandth piece of a thousand-piece puzzle that fit in place and ended the search.

My search ended thirty-some years ago. Since then, more superlatives have fallen into place. *Bliss* is one. *Blessed* is another. I'm sure I could come up with another dozen "b" words, but these first two explain a lot. Bliss and blessed have a lot to do with luck. My luck began at Soquel High School when we were sixteen years old. We had a couple of classes together, chemistry with Mr. Dick and Spanish with Mr. Denton. We were friendly, liked each other, but ran in different circles, and I was shy, didn't put myself out there on the dating scene. But getting to know each other in a friendly way as teenagers was a staging that I think was predicated on luck.

Twenty years later, it wasn't so much about luck but more about serendipity, that we had both been married to people who weren't our life mates, that we both removed ourselves from those relationships, that on a hot summer night in August 1988 we parlayed the luck, the serendipity of the moment, took advantage of the situation, and managed to get our heated, dancing bodies as close together as possible with clothes still on.

That first date that culminated at my townhouse on Dover Drive clarified how well we fit together. Part of it, of course, was need, the need to be with someone who was loving and caring, and to be honest, the need for a good physical fit, a mutual sexuality that has never waned. Yes, we were both lucky and we learned how to use that luck, turn it into something solid, made of platinum and gold.

She taught me how to love her daughters, which grew into love for our grandchildren. I shared with her my love of theater, of writing, of movies. In addition to loving each other more every day, month, year, we learned to love the things that each other loved.

Usually when one speaks or thinks of thirty-three-year relationships, one talks about the ups and downs. For the most part, I only remember the ups with Karen. The downs were always minimal and forgettable. The ups, however, fill photo albums, fill our memories, fill a house full of gifts. My time with Karen has always been up. There are too many ups to count, but let me try to list a few: sitting in a hot tub on a new deck in 1989; traveling to Tahoe to gamble and relax; spending loving hours with grandkids; taking a book-arts trip up the West Coast; creating a marvelous workshop together; working on art projects together; working Open Studios together; doing everything together.

And now we get to learn how to do this final thing together. To live strong, focused, impassioned lives while staring in the face of a shortened timeline. We cry when we need to. We joke whenever we can find a way to do so. Karen acts as my legs, my arms, my chef, my friend, my everything. I try to act "normal" when I can, not dwell on what's in front of us, or actually, yes, dwell on what's right in front of us, the day to day, the minute to minute, the love that only strengthens over time.

What did I ever do to deserve Karen in my life? I'm not sure. But, oh, what a perfect life it has been. I love you!

What I Avoid

ANOTHER ONE OF THOSE WORDS. *Avoidance.* If used well and appropriately, it can sink one so far below reality that one can struggle to get back to the surface for the better part of a lifetime. But therein lies the dilemma. The original intent of the acts of avoidance was to bury one so far away from truth and knowledge and understanding of the real world that one could exist in fantasy for as long as possible. So in many cases, there is no struggle to return. The initial struggle was to figure out how to successfully avoid those things that might make life unbearable, or at least too difficult to handle for any length of time.

Today is Friday, July 17, 2020. What I choose to avoid today is different than what I chose to avoid, say, two years ago, or in February, or in three months from now, or even yesterday. Let's look at yesterday, for example. Every day for a month I've been waking up and falling asleep thinking about the large deck rebuilding we got ourselves into. Okay, thinking is probably not the best verb to use. Stewing, worrying, consternating, all work better and more accurately describe the state of my brain. But yesterday I told Karen I couldn't take any more of the daily strife and that we needed to make a decision together about whether or not we would take the deck project to its fruition, to the point where it looks good and complete, even though it would cost us twice as much as Terry's initial bid of $3,500. We made the decision, figured out how we would move money around to pay for it, and at that point, I decided to avoid thinking about it any further. It was now in Terry's hands to do a good job, make sure we have the supplies to finish the job, and get on with it. This avoidance was helpful to me, is helpful to me. It allows my thoughts to focus on what it is I want to get accomplished with the daily hours in front of me. Working on these Daily Fresh essays. Working on the seventeen projects I've prioritized for completion. Eventually getting out to the workshop and gluing maps for the extinct-bird project. Dealing with *Zoom Forward!* tasks as needed. That this avoidance is a form of productive procrastination is clear.

What are the other areas of avoidance that I've mastered over the last twenty-one months? The largest area is spending too much time worrying about when and how the cancer will take me out, or if the chemo will beat the cancer to it. It's impossible to completely avoid it because it is such a large part of my life. The biweekly infusion and pump treatments, the ten days of side effects that accompany it, that it repeats every two weeks. Impossible to ignore, but avoiding always thinking or worrying about it is not so impossible. I do a fairly good job of getting on with the daily business of living and hacking away at my To Do lists. It's an avoidance well worth the effort, that pays its dividends immediately.

Probably the largest avoidance I have undertaken since March 2020 is ignoring the massive amount of information generated almost hourly on TV, Amazon Echo, and every other source of communication and thrown in our faces these days about Covid-19. It is clearly a killer that has most folks in the world concerned about their futures and those of their friends and loved ones. For the most part, I don't want the daily inundation and reports. I know it's bad. I know millions will die, and I know the U.S. leadership is either in complete denial or, worse, is involved in a conspiracy to eliminate those whose age makes them susceptible to the disease, the same group that also taps into Social Security and Medicare.

I wear my mask everywhere. I practice extreme social distancing when friends do come over. I am angry about the cavalier behavior of youth and others who think it's a hoax or that they're invincible or "Let the old folks die." But I refuse to watch minute-to-minute reports that increase angst and cause a lapse in focus. I avoid it. I keep it out of my day-to-day existence as much as possible. Because I have work to do. And if I choose the correct things to avoid, my work can flourish. And if I'm not successful at those choices, my work will suffer. At this point in my life, it's about the work. The work of these Daily Fresh essays, where I talk about the love of my wife. The love of my friends. The work of continuing to be productive, which helps me to avoid staring into the daily face of mortality. I know it's there, but I also know that avoiding the worry of it will help me survive longer in ways that keep my focus attuned to accomplishments rather than disappointments.

Detritus

I'VE ALWAYS LOVED THE WORD *DETRITUS*. The way it sounds, the way it forms in the mouth, pushes itself off the tongue like the balls of feet pressing against a diving board to thrust a body forward. I have no idea where I first heard it, what author plugged it into a sentence to intentionally showcase the process of decomposition at work, or the result of that decomposition. My use of and thinking about the word has often been erroneous, I discovered, as I sit here with split screen, Word document on the left side, Wikipedia on the right. What I didn't know about detritus is that it is primarily "dead particulate material, as distinguished from dissolved organic materials." It turns out that detritus appears to be a mix of dead bodies and fecal material, and it "hosts communities of microorganisms that colonize and decompose it." Who knew?

I'll never think of detritus the same way again. Instead of imagining inert material blowing into a pile against a fence or under a deck or piling up in the corner of a closet, now when I use the term in a sentence or to make a point, I'll be conjuring up colonies of microscopic bugs working away at decomposing feces and other materials. In my short Internet search of things detritus-like, I discovered a book on Amazon called *Debris & Detritus: The Lesser Greek Gods Running Amok,* written by Patricia Burroughs. I love the title and hope that it holds true and that Burroughs has invented two Greek gods who go by Debris and Detritus. I delve further into the description.

It turns out that Burroughs is the editor of this anthology of stories written by over a dozen authors. Yes, as it turns out, these lesser gods, Debris and Detritus, are written in as characters in every story, wreaking havoc as they go about their work and play. In the foreword to the book Rhonda Eudaly says, "It's a collection of mostly women writers, which I find amazing—but as I've heard Ice-T say of *Law and Order: SVU* writers, 'Women writers write the sickest stuff.'" Makes me curious, but I'm not sure it would be my next purchase.

Poison Darts

THERE ARE MORNINGS WHEN I WAKE with poison darts dangling from my skin. Not so many that it feels like I've been trapped in a net and shot through with them, one after another, so the tiny feathers overlap, leaving very little skin to view. No. Just a few. Today maybe three or four. These are the self-inflicted darts that push themselves from inside out, originating in my brain after a viral thought has worked its way under my skin, kept me awake, like knowing that I have been remiss in sending an agenda on Saturday to prep for my Sunday meeting. It's tiny, doesn't cause much disturbance, but it's there with me on the pillow when my eyes first open to see the digital clock is still flirting with 5:00, teetering on 4:56, about to move forward to 4:57. The sting is minor, as if I'd brushed up against a nettle plant. I feel the tingle, wonder why I didn't get to the list yesterday, wonder what will make it onto the list today. As I said, it's small, I'll figure it out, send it off before 8:00.

What will be more difficult is trying to ignore the few other darts that remain attached, or trying to remove them. The one about Terry and the deck and his change of plans yesterday and lack of communication about it is the hard one to let go, as if the minute amounts of poison leaking into my system are taking it over, spreading cell by cell throughout my body. That's the one that feels like it affects my nausea, makes me wonder if my large cup of hot chocolate with miniature marshmallows melting on top will do its job again of calming me down. I'm certain it will. Which is how I disentangle the darts from my body, by focusing on what is good in my life, that I still have a life, which is a minor miracle of its own.

That today is Sunday; that I have my 10:00 standing meeting to look forward to; that the new deck will be completed by the end of this week; that I got to play some online poker last night with eight folks whose faces I loved seeing in their *Hollywood Squares* Zoom windows; that we completed another successful *Zoom Forward!* event Friday night; that I am sheltered in place with the best possible person on the planet; that my sister seems happy moving to my mom's; that my granddaughter Georgia seems happy to be moving into the apartment; that Hannah seems to be enjoying her role in *Zoom Forward!* and *phren-z* literary magazine; that Karen is out on the streets for her daily walk; that her sciatica seems to be improving; that Dave Culver will be back on Tuesday to carry away some more used lumber and sit and talk at a safe, masked distance; that I just received an email from Terry apologizing for his scheduling confusion; that I have completed *Pious Rebel*; that I have completed *Smith: An Unauthorized Fictography*; that I am back into *Capture and Release*; that I am thinking ahead to next projects like the short-story collection, the Zoom play night, *A Matter of Principal*; and that as of today I will have completed fourteen Daily Freshes in a row.

Daily Fresh

See how easy it is to remove the darts, cover oneself in flower petals and incense, and know that I have lived a charmed life that **continues to stretch itself out much longer than I expected?**

A Thematic Infusion-Inclusion-Intrusion

I HAVE THEMES THAT RUN THROUGH MY LIFE, my head, that appear in my thoughts and writing whether I invite them or not. I'm okay with that. It's okay with me that the falls at Big Creek appear in multiple pieces of my work. It's okay with me that the foods in my life reappear in everything, those foods that led to my diabetes and most likely the pancreatic cancer. *Zen and the Art of Motorcycle Maintenance* has raised its head a few times, and one of these times I'll do it right, reread from cover to cover in one sitting and reevaluate my age-old fascination with it.

My writing tends to focus on women, women on the verge of something, though I can't steal "women on the verge of a nervous breakdown," not only because it's been taken, but because my women are on the verge of a breakthrough rather than breakdown; having suffered through a lifetime of abuse and being under the thumbs of others, mostly men, they are ready to celebrate their independence, to showcase their strength, to move forward into the world with confidence and verve. I think I write women better than men. Maybe because I recognize my own foibles in the male characters I write, maybe because I believe it is time for feminine guidance and rule. The falls and hike to Big Creek appears everywhere, can't keep it from flowing through my head, my fingers, my work. The cleansing effect. The freshness. The erosion. And then there are the events that never seem to fade. The maggots on the meat in the plastic barrels in the back of Country Boys' Market that made their home on the top of floating pieces of rotten meat intended to be put back in the meat case to be sold as corned beef.

Loose Threads

Usually on socks, sometimes on a pair of pants or a t-shirt. The proper solution is to find my way to a pair of scissors and snip it clean back to the cloth. But the immediate response is to grab the thread between fingers and twist and pull until it either breaks away from the fabric or uncovers an even longer thread that just makes it worse. The same loose threads that appear in writing and thinking are ones that I enjoy, that I take advantage of by spending time looking at their construction, if they are frayed, if I think they can be extracted or not, if there are improvements I can make, rabbit holes that might be fun to bury myself in for a while.

Like this one. Came from nowhere I can think of. Just jumped to the top as a title and gave me an inkling of an idea of how to proceed. Sometimes I like to think of my mom, nimbly playing with embroidery threads to weave a project of beauty. I wonder how her brain operates. How she decides to pursue a project. If it is always pattern-driven or if she ever just starts from scratch, lets herself go wherever the moment and fingers and threads take her. I know that's not her usual style. But I do have one quilt hanging on the wall, of branches with white leaves, and one of the leaves has fallen to the bottom, outside the frame, and I love it, because it is so different than everything else she's done. What I don't know is if the pattern called for the fallen leaf, or if it was innovation. Not that it matters, but my curiosity grabs it and runs with it, and I crawl inside her brain and try to discover how the idea moved through her head. I'll jump on a blood cell, ride it like a bronco, discover whether or not I'll get tossed off simply because I tried to discover the answer, or because I shouldn't be jumping into people's circulatory systems trying to discover secrets available only to scientists and surgeons.

  A loose thread that appears today has to do with all those that dangle from the whiteboard in the foot-of-the-bed writing studio, all of the unfinished projects that are beginning to breathe, that show me their hearts flexing, wanting to surge to life, wanting my attention, each of them dangling with threads to be pulled, clipped, frayed, tied to other threads, shortened, lengthened, ignored, incorporated, isolated, split into smaller pieces, wound around fingers and slipped between moist lips. They beckon, some louder than others, those that have gained personality over the years, those that have remained dormant and not complained, knowing that I would eventually return, find my way back to the core thread that made me begin thinking and writing about an idea in the first place. With some of them I want to grow them, twist them, make a head full of dreadlocks that I love looking at even though to think and write about it could be construed by some as cultural appropriation because I will never have dreadlocks, have no friends with dreadlocks, have never held a dreadlock in my hand, have only observed them from distances, usually through a TV screen of someone who might live 5,000 or 10,000 miles away. And the threads of dreads are anything but loose. They are twisted tightly, organized, orderly; merged with colors and metals, they reflect off the teeth of those who wear them, they attract others, they want more for themselves and the person who grew them and that person's children and grandchildren. They want to grow old and watch the grey slowly infiltrate and evolve into another level of beauty.

That the world is comprised of billions of threads that are unrecognizable to many, or are ignored by most, makes them that much more enticing to me. Undiscovered worlds, words, stories, and characters that link together in a body of work whose origins began as loose threads and move forward into a more cohesive existence where they are no longer loose but eventually grow connected, to the soil, to the trees, to the axons and dendrites in my head and others' heads, that they grow into something unimaginable, something they or I never knew could be possible and achievable.

Give me more. Loosen me up. Strengthen me.

The Every-Other-Wednesday Way

AT THIS POINT IN THE CYCLE, it was less about decision making than it was about memory. Always some of each, but after twenty-one months, rote behavior demands its place.

"Last name and date of birth?"

"11-30-50. West," Mark answered. He attempted a quick calculation of the number of times he'd provided this information since his diagnosis in October 2018. But it wasn't quick, so he gave up, but knew it was well over a hundred. His nurse's aide today, Elena, slipped the identification badge over his wrist.

It had begun the night before, the Tuesday before the Wednesday, the day reserved for eating and drinking things cold for the last time in two weeks, the day scheduled for a sex date, the day to pack the bag in preparation for the six-hour sit in the infusion chair. The small plastic bag containing two Imodium and two Tylenol, just in case, just in case the chemo drugs blast through his skull and cause a throb. Just in case they disrupt his digestive system and he needs some help with blockage. The sketchbook in case he felt the urge to pull out a pen and draw the scene, which he had never done. Pens and highlighters placed in their designated slots in the bag. Printouts he might choose to use for his projects. The masks. One that his wife made for him with a literary theme. The other a basic powder blue sold by the boatload throughout the world. He preferred the one with "Emily Dickinson" stitched across the front, but had once been denied entrance into the facility because it was "floppy," according to the nurse.

Getting in the passenger seat with bag in hand, masks in pocket, wife behind the wheel, ready to drop him off, activating the memory. Had he forgotten anything this time? Yes!

"Wait!" he yelled a little too loudly. "The cell phone."

His wife went back to the house to retrieve it from its charging spot upstairs. It was a key ingredient in the day's events, as he never knew when they would reach the end, release him, and he'd need to text her with the estimated pick-up time. Had to have the phone.

At the corner of Thurber Lane, they turned right onto Soquel Drive. So many medical facilities in this two-mile stretch of pavement. So many memories. His father died at Dominican Hospital situated on the right side of the road. And Mark's infusion center was just across the street on the left side of the road. Today was different. Thinking about it brought immediate tears, so he kept his mind busy on other things.

He was hungry, had chosen not to eat breakfast. That's when the decision-making process overtook the memory process. Or actually paired with it. He remembered how sometimes while sitting in the chair he had to move quickly to the bathroom or suffer the public humiliation of an accident.

The recollection of those events caused the decision to skip the fried-egg sandwich, the bowl of steel-cut oats with banana, and the Eggo waffles drenched in syrup.

Being hungry was much better than having to go through the gyrations associated with an accident. He'd gotten better at it. At home, he put an extra pad and pair of scissors in the drawer next to the downstairs toilet so he could cut his way out of the sharted pad rather than go through the full process of undressing, taking off shoes, socks, pants.

While there were a few decisions that had to be made, every-other Wednesdays were mostly about letting the rote behavior have its way and guide him through the six-hour ordeal without any significant modifications. Ordeal. That was a word left over from the early days. He had viewed it as an ordeal then, but that felt too much like self-pity, which he was trying to eliminate from his life. Now it was just a biweekly event to put on the calendar. Like attending a class. A class on survival. Showing up, taking notes, highlighting phrases and sentences that could be useful in saving his life, or if not saving it, extending it, giving him time to complete unfinished projects.

The "chemo holiday" he had enjoyed from August 2019 to February 2020 ended with the results of the Stanford CT scan. It had metastasized to the liver. Two lesions.

"How long?" Mark had asked the oncologist.

"A matter of months."

The following week his oncologist chose not to rest on the Stanford results, quickly moved back into another twenty-four-week cycle of chemotherapy.

As his wife turned into the parking lot at the infusion center, he remembered this was week twenty-two, cycle eleven of twelve. What a long haul. He was amazed that one of the three "C"s hadn't killed him yet. The cancer was mixed. The tumor had never grown since its initial sighting. The latest CT scan showed that one of the liver lesions had grown by two millimeters, and the other had disappeared, or at least was not visible. The chemo was not pleasant, but his side effects had been much less intrusive than he expected. The nausea and diarrhea were always at play, but no vomiting or pain. But then the third "C" appeared on the planet. With a depleted immune system, trying to avoid Covid was the latest event that changed the nature of his life, of everybody's lives.

They didn't kiss goodbye, as they avoided kissing these days, out of a habit and frame of mind to not swap fluids. Mark strapped his bag over his shoulder, slid his literary mask up over his nose, and stood on the blue-tape line at the entrance to the facility. It was 7:30 a.m. He was always first. No other cars in the lot. No sick people in line. Just one nurse.

"Good morning," Leo said.

"Good morning, Leo. How's your day?"

"Very good," he said. "Have you experienced a fever, cough?" Mark no longer verbally responded to the same list of questions he heard a dozen times a month. He shook his head No as the questions continued. "Have you been tested for Covid? Have you been around anyone who has been tested for Covid? Have you traveled out of the country?"

Mark lowered his mask, waited for Leo to slip the thermometer into its thin condom and slide it under his tongue.

"98.4." Leo completed the pink slip of paper that was his entry ticket, allowing him into the facility as long as he was under 99 degrees. Only twice had he failed the entry exam. The first time he had been cold and cuddled back into bed under the electric blanket before he jumped in the car and made the short trek down Soquel Drive.

"99.4," the nurse had said.

She had Mark sit down on the bench outside for a few minutes so the temperature could decrease, which it did.

The second time was more recent. His wife had found a new powder for making hot chocolate called Sillycow Farms Chocolate Truffle. He had quickly become hopelessly addicted. Two heaping teaspoons, almond milk heated for three minutes in the microwave, miniature marshmallows floating on top. He had forgotten about how the heat in his mouth affected the thermometer. Again, a one-minute sit on the bench allowed the number to decrease appropriately.

Carrying his pink slip, Mark walked past the clerk's counter, said hello to Crystal and Laura.

"You're all checked in, Mark!"

He nodded, took a seat, and within a minute Elena arrived in the lobby.

"Ready, Mark?"

"As ever," he said.

First stop, the scale. 175.3. A little lighter than last time, maybe a pound, but with all the blowouts he had suffered over the past four days, he wasn't surprised. Plus no breakfast.

"Jo will be your nurse today."

"Very good," he said. Jo hadn't been his nurse since his second week here. She was good, friendly, knowledgeable, a real pro.

He was the first patient in, as always, and because he was first, he was always offered his choice of stations. The fourteen chairs were situated on two walls. Twelve of them were out in the open. Two were more private, like cubicles, with two walls and a curtain. He preferred being in the center facing the nurses' work area, where he could watch them all, see everything that went on, every new patient who came in, which nurses were assigned to them, watch the nurses sidle up to the pharmacy window to get the next course for their patients.

So his day in the facility began with another one of those decisions guided in part by memory. A few times he had come in with a rough stomach and needed to be closer to the bathroom. Today he was hoping the Imodium would keep his bowels secured for six hours, so he decided on the middle chair where he had the best view of everything.

Orientation. Going through the rote activities that would make him most comfortable for the day. Unzipping the Patagonia jacket so he could accept the blood pressure monitor more easily. 145 over 75. The more important reason for unzipping the jacket was exposure to his chest, unbuttoning his surf-themed short-sleeve shirt with the Giants' logo. He didn't like logos on shirts, but it had been a gift from his stepdaughters. He did like the Giants, although they had stunk over recent years. The unbuttoning gave access to his right-side port. It was always the first question asked by the assigned nurse of the day. Today, Jo, who said, "Left or right?"

Mark pointed to the right-side port and Jo proceeded to remove the plastic that Mark had placed over the Emla that numbed the skin surrounding the port. That had been rote. No decision needed. He knew by now to numb the skin an hour in advance before they stuck the Huber needle into him, reducing potential pain. She cleaned the surface of the port, gave him a three-count, and on one he exhaled deeply as the sharpened tip pierced the skin and port.

He liked that there were no decisions required of him once he sat in the chair. He gave himself over to the nurses. Not unlike letting a masseuse have her way with him. A relaxation of the brain. Letting down the side rails on a hospital bed, something that his nurse-wife hated to see on medical shows. But he felt safe with these nurses, almost every one of them. The only things close to decisions were if he wanted a pillow, if he wanted water, when he was ready to head to the bathroom. But really, the biggest decision was what to work on today, how to take advantage of this block of time where he was a captive audience and couldn't be interrupted by phone calls, knocks on the door, text messages, or a kitchen and refrigerator loaded with food and drink.

But this decision had been made the night before during his Tuesday-night prep session. In bed he had begun building the frame for today's work. He had been working on his short Daily Fresh essays for sixteen straight days, and today would be number seventeen. Most days he had no prompts, no conscious beginning points, just let his fingers rest on the keyboard and find their way forward. Today would be different. He wanted to capture this every-other-Wednesday experience from A to Z.

Jo was across the room at the pharmacy. But he wanted to slow down, felt he had jumped forward a bit, needed to back up and take a snapshot of the room, the infusion center, his home away for so long now. His chair had the best view. He took out his cell phone and took three photos that provided a panoramic view. On the left side of the room were eight other chairs, mostly identical to his. All blue. All with little metal ledges that pulled out from the bottom where patients could rest their feet. Every chair had a remote that allowed patients to tilt back, almost lay flat if they wanted. Mark had never used it. Needed to sit straight up and have access to the computer that he would remove from his pack and set on his lap. There was a bathroom on the far left near the entrance, just across from the large brass gong hanging on the wall, the gong that chemo graduates got to bang on their way out. Straight across from Mark's chair was the nurses' station. A thirty-foot, four-foot-high wall with a counter on top. Desks on the other side of the counter with a bank of computers where the nurses do their research, their charting, their After Visit Summaries as soon as a patient walks out the door. Mark remembered how he'd sometimes leave, and as he entered the car driven by his wife, he'd get a ping on his cell phone with a link to the After Visit Summary. The station was large, deep, probably thirty feet by twenty-five feet, with nearly a dozen computers scattered throughout. Against the back wall were three rooms. One where blood draws were taken by a phlebotomist. A middle door Mark had wondered about but hadn't known what was behind until today. He asked Jo.

"It's a storage room related to the pharmacy."

Now it was time to talk about the pharmacy. There was a large glass window that went all the way to the ceiling. At the bottom of the window was an opening with sliding doors where the pharmacists slid out the next course of poison for nurses to take to patients. He never had a full view of the room, but what he could see looked spooky, technical, full of metal stacks and pharmacists in blue gowns. Even before Covid they all wore masks. Poisons. All day long. What a life! Mark remembered a friend telling him how much it cost every time he sat in the chair. Fifty thousand dollars! When Mark first heard that, followed by his oncologist saying he wasn't sure that Medicare would cover a non-stage-four diagnosis, he told his wife and close friends to not be surprised if they received a phone call saying he had stuck a hose in his tailpipe in the Happy Valley School parking lot and ended his life rather than depleting his wife's resources to pay for a bunch of poisons that might kill him anyway.

On the far-right wall hung a couple of photos with sunset views of the ocean. Beneath the photos were seven containers of gloves, apparently to accommodate the seven sizes of nurses' hands. In the far-right corner of the room was the other bathroom, the one Mark preferred to use because it was closer. On either side of Mark were chairs, about eight feet away. Before Covid he had never really noticed the curtains. But now, the nurses pulled them shut to reduce the potential of exposure to the coughing or sneezing of others. Every twenty feet scattered throughout the room were the WOWs, Workstations on Wheels, that used to be called COWS, Computers on Wheels, until nurses complained about it. Everything known about patients is stored on the WOWs, so nurses can be sure to follow proper protocol and make sure the patients are receiving the appropriate drugs and doses.

When Jo finishes attaching the Huber needle, she brings the first bag of drugs from the pharmacy, the Zofran that will help to alleviate the future effect of the two-hour poison drug to come. The Zofran takes thirty minutes to infuse. Jo is fast. She doesn't waste time between courses. As soon as the Zofran beeps from the IV stand, indicating that it's complete, Jo hooks up the Emend for fifteen minutes. And then comes the first monster. Oxaliplatin. It is one of those heavy-duty drugs that requires a med check, meaning a second nurse comes over to verify that everything is correct, matches what's in the charts. Two hours' worth! Sometimes Mark will close his eyes during this phase. Get some rest. The first session back in December 2018, he meditated the whole time, recited his mantra internally—*gate, gate, para gate, para som gate, bodhi svaha*. For six hours. He thought it might have helped.

Not today. Today he needs focus. A freshness. Needs to capture this every-other-Wednesday way like he has never done before. He's mentioned it to folks. He's put pieces of it into poems. But never written the whole story. This fresh essay that is both new and stale, both from memory and based on decisions of the moment, decisions about word choice and sentence structure and how long to stay seated in the chair before giving in and getting up to use the bathroom. He cranks. Views his surroundings. Listens to the nurses talking with patients about their histories, their meds, their granddaughters who live up north, share pictures of their kids, talk about whether the husband or wife is the better cook.

The Oxaliplatin hours pass. The IV beeps. Jo returns. Time for the Atropine. A short one. Just fifteen minutes. It helps to alleviate the side effects of the upcoming monster. He's on rote now. Just keep it coming. Get him out of here as quickly as possible. The collective memory of nurses and WOWs and doctors allow him not to think about it. Until. Until Jo says, "Would you like a second course of Atropine? Given that your diarrhea has been acting up?"

Damn! Mark thinks. This is a decision point. He's never been asked directly before. It's been mentioned in passing that he usually doesn't get the second course of Atropine. But Jo is good. Thorough. Is thinking about his well-being once he walks out the door. He appreciates it. Not the needing-to-think part, the need to make a decision, but that Jo has given him the option. He doesn't know the answer yet. When the first Atropine has completed, Jo quickly grabs the Irinotecan from the pharmacy, brings it over, calls for a med check, and plugs it in. It's 11:00. Jo is so fast. Much faster than the others. An hour and a half for this one. Should be done by 12:30.

He has this time now, this ninety-minute block, to complete this project. To look back and add details. To talk about the nice garden on the other side of the window behind his head, a garden that two weeks ago he had watched a patient roll his IV stand out into and rest in the sun. He had never seen that before, didn't know it was allowable to roll out there and have your poison plied under direct sunlight. He has time to listen to the sounds other than the voices of nurses. The occasional chatter of patients, telling their stories. The fan or air-conditioning that appears to be nonstop now that he's paying attention. Footsteps on linoleum. Truck and cars passing by on Commercial Way. The rolling wheels on carts that nurses move around like castles and knights on a chess board. A sneeze. A cough. A cell phone ringing. His cell phone. Says "likely SPAM." And he gets embarrassed. At the loudness of the ring. Worried about bothering patients in the vicinity. But he doesn't turn it to Silent. Doesn't put it on Airplane Mode.

Mark looks at the countertop. There are three plants. Not the orchids that the physician's assistant Teresa used to bring from her neighbor. Three indistinct plants. But next to them he sees some fired pieces of pottery. Small pieces. There are seven of them. He has never seen them before, or at least doesn't remember ever seeing them before. It looks as if they're all turtles. The Magnificent Seven. One of them might be an owl and not a turtle. He'll need to look more closely on his way out. He'll ask Jo if they are new or if he has been turtle-blind for the past twenty-two months. Wait! Right in front of him on the counter, perched underneath the largest plant, are two more turtles. Large turtles. Four or five times bigger than the others. The curtain has been pulled between him and the patient on his left, so his view of half the counter is obstructed. He wonders now if there are more turtles. Are they everywhere? Do the nurses bring them in to share with each other? Do the patients bring them in for the nurses? Mark wants to bring them a turtle. Make them a turtle. Maybe a book in the shape of a turtle.

He spends the next fifteen minutes thinking about the book, how he would make the covers, where he would find images, if he'd steal content off the Internet, if he'd write fresh turtle poems to populate the pages of the book, if he'd draw turtles, fill them with multiple colors. Tania comes by with a cart of meds for one of her patients. He calls out to her:

"Hey, Tania. Have those turtles always been here?"

"That white one on the end is new, but the rest have always been here."

"Wow! Twenty-two months and I never noticed."

She smiles. "You've been focused on other things."

Yes. He has. Things like whether or not cavalier, narcissistic people will start wearing masks and stay off our beaches. Things like identifying other stories along Soquel Drive to inhabit the future novel-in-stories project. Things like his mom, who is across Soquel Drive in room 2244 of Dominican Hospital, the same hospital where his father died on October 31, 2005, at age 73. Things like the wedding photo of his mom and dad in front of a building in Reno, Nevada, in March 1950, him aged 18, her aged 17, theoretically not pregnant, as the math would attest to, that photo now open on the desktop of his computer as he types, as he looks up and watches the nurses work, listens to them give reports to other nurses as they prep to go on their lunch breaks, looks again at the turtles, chuckles at himself, at the other things he's been focused on instead of turtles. The neuropathy in his feet, his prioritized list of writing projects (this not being one of them, yet), the harebrained idea of establishing a literary trust, of naming a literary trustee, of establishing a team, of creating a fund, of receiving a response from the attorney who holds their living-trust documents, of his continual use of the phrase *delusions of grandeur* as he thinks and talks about the advantages and disadvantages of a literary trust. That the most ideal solution is to stay alive and active and writing as long as possible, bringing as many of the seventeen writing projects to fruition as possible.

So, of course, he hadn't seen the turtles, had looked past their ceramic faces into the lively faces of the nurses doing their work at their computers.

12:00. A half hour more of Irinotecan. What was his mom doing? Were her eyes open? Did she know what was going on?

What new drug had they stuffed into her? Had they done an MRI yet? Did they have any better idea about whether or not she had Parkinson's? Would she ever make it out of Dominican, or would she die within a hundred yards of where Dad died? Would she ever make it home?

He stared at the photo of the eighteen-year-old dad and seventeen-year-old mom. What was in their brains back then? How much of it was hormonal? How much of it was love? No way of knowing.

He wished the next steps with Mom could be rote. Driven by positive memories and photos of the past. He wished he could walk out of the infusion center at 12:45, have his wife drive him across Soquel Drive to Dominican, sneak in the back entrance, take the elevator to the second floor, slink through the hallways until he found room 2244, unhook Mom's IV, wheel her to the elevator and into the parking lot and lay her in the back of the Prius and get her back home and into her bed.

It probably wouldn't go like that. There would be clear decisions to be made. Skilled-nursing facility. Home. An urn for ashes.

12:15. Mark decides to skip the second dose of atropine. Jo brings out the pump, plugs it into his port, which gives him forty-six more hours of four poisons, a return trip to the center on Friday for a disconnect and a shot of Neulasta to help keep his white blood count regulated.

"See you next time," he says, pump hanging from his neck, pack wrapped around his shoulder.

He takes time to steady his balance, widen his stance, all actions based on memories of the previous ten times he's done this. What is new this time is the decision to turn and look into the garden. There are dozens of turtles. He looks at the section of counter he hadn't been able to see from his chair. More turtles. Everywhere.

He stops in the bathroom, knows to empty his bladder now while he still has control. No reason to wait. He walks past the gong without smashing it, not yet a graduate of this phase of the program, knows he'll be back in two weeks for the twelfth cycle. Maybe it would be the last one for a while. Forever. That was a decision the oncologist would make, not him.

He's just along for the ride, is happy to be told when it's time to hop out, take a walk, save Wednesdays for something completely different.

Taking Care of Business

WHAT IS THE BUSINESS OF THE MOMENT? It can change faces with the flip of a coin, the drop of a hat, an unexpected phone call, an irregular heartbeat. Today is Thursday, so my business is somewhat different than it was yesterday. Today I have to nurture the pump full of poison in the little black nylon bag that carries an eighth-inch plastic tube into the port in my chest. Nurture means to take care to remember that it's plugged into me, that if I forget it, the plastic tube will tug on the Huber needle stuck into the port and possibly dislodge it, spraying poisons everywhere. Wearing it around my neck like an ugly and large pendant, hauling it with me four or five times a night to the bathroom so I can empty my bladder. Listening to it whir every twenty-seven seconds throughout the night and all day long.

And any email can change the business of the moment, of that which keeps one's brain and fingers busy. Like an email from someone I've known for forty years who has never reached out to me until I include PST in a posting related to the time of a Zoom reading. Then a second email. Both of them complaining about the accuracy or inaccuracy of the use of PST. Never an email to thank me for showcasing his partner's work. Never an email to thank me for the series of *Zoom Forward!* meetings. It becomes the immediate business because it irks the shit out of me. But it's not the real business. It'll pass.

The phone rings and it's the hospitalist at Dominican Hospital with an update on my mom's situation. She has had a discussion with Mom and she was sweet and friendly, talking about her marriage and other topics. The Covid test came back negative. The physical therapist had success walking with her this morning. She does have Parkinson's. They will send her home with a prescription for Sinemet. She will have an outpatient MRI next week, and a video visit with her primary doctor. That was a business call. Short and to the point related to a half-dozen issues. We can take her home sometime today. We. Not me. I'm worthless. Shelly and/or Karen will bring her home. They will probably call the fire department at the end of Mom's street to come lift her from the car and take her up to her bed.

These are the important things that define a day, that help us keep busy at keeping busy. Writing a $5,655 check to Terry for completion of the deck project. So nice to have that business transaction behind us. Having a Zoom rehearsal with Steve Kettmann and Wallace Baine, working out the details for their Friday-night reading, who goes first, who introduces whom, what books they will promote for Bookshop, how long they get to read. The business of agendas and itineraries and protocol. The regular stuff that needs to occur weekly. Starting to think about next week's reading, trying to get a little ahead of the game. Noticing that the business of writing these Daily Fresh pieces feels more like business in the afternoon rather than the morning, because it feels like a business now having written them for seventeen straight days. I imagine Labor Day coming around and me having just completed my sixtieth essay in a row that could very well fill a 300-page book. With what theme? Is it the business of freshness? Is it the willingness to sustain an activity, a thought, to keep busy with the thinking and doing and living of this life in whatever fashion makes most sense in the moment?

Yes. I think so. Something like that.

"V" Is for Verve

THE WORD *DECLENSION* FLOATED THROUGH MY BRAIN most of the night. I don't know why, because I've never really known what it meant. Upon googling it, I prefer the second definition to the first. The first has something to do with the structure of language that I never really learned in any class I attended during my seventeen or eighteen years of schooling. But the second definition gives me something a little more to bite into: "a condition of decline or moral deterioration." Even though it's listed as archaic, it rings truer to me given the current state of the world. Because I'm vowing to avoid topics and issues that pull me into a depression that could further deteriorate my immune system, I let go of declension, and move to the other word that danced with it all night long: *verve*.

I have always loved this word. It will never pull me under, will always lift me, has always raised me above the fray, even before Verve Coffee Roasters opened their venues in Santa Cruz along with others in San Francisco, Palo Alto, and Japan. Vigor and spirit or enthusiasm. Synonyms: energy, pep, dynamism, go, elan. I find this interesting graphic tracking the mentions of *verve* over time:

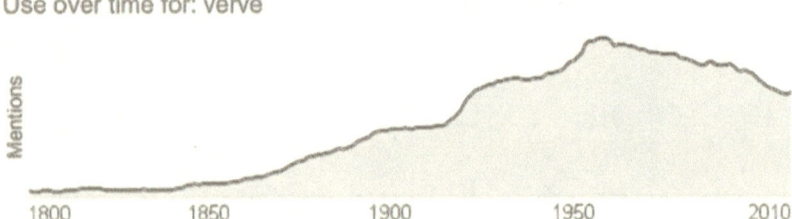

Looks like it reached its peak around 1955, when I was five years old, the year my sister was born.

When I think of the word, I drift to *swerve,* think about movements of the body in curves and arcs, a dance with oneself, an entrance into a world of magic and mysticism and unknowns just waiting to be discovered. Other "v" words come to mind—vivacity and vitality and vim—and a couple of "z" words: zing and zip.

It's a word I want to keep with me, wear it around my neck mounted inside a piece of antique amber, tattoo it to my chest in a semi-circle around my port, use it as an ankle bracelet that tracks my mood, keeps me up, keep it folded and tucked into a secret spot in my money clip, and share it with others when I open my palms, my mouth, my heart.

Its roots have to do with artistic composition and expression, especially with words, which makes sense to me, as I feel the electric waves pulsing from brain to heart to fingers, through the whole circulatory system, as I construct phrases and sentences intended to counter the antonyms, the lethargy and listlessness and sluggishness and torpidity. I leave them behind, forget what they mean, find no partners for them to wrap themselves around and cause senseless mayhem.

I move forward into the unknown with juice and bounce and moxie and sap and snap, implant *verve* just beneath the surface of my gold crowns, use it as the product that makes my hair stand up like David Lynch's, polish my fingernails with it before my fingers touch keys and begin to sing.

With *verve* as my anthem, my mantra, my mode of interaction with others, I march on, baton and wand in hand, waving away anything and everything blocking my path.

Adrift

On one hand, probably the left hand, being in the hemisphere controlled by the right side of the brain, I float adrift like an untethered helium balloon seeking a final unknown destination. I could travel so far and fast and high that the gas depletes and the sack carrying me shrivels and fizzles back to earth. Or I could be sucked into the Southern Hemisphere's polar jet stream and spend the remainder of my gas and time circling Antarctica. I'd rather find a polar jet that would wrap me around the planet until the west-east pathway eventually dropped me into the Hawaiian Islands, leaving me just enough ballast for a gentle landing in Hana, Maui, a soft approach where my feet dip into the waters of the seven sacred pools at 'Ohe'o, or find myself nestled in a flock of nene geese.

On the other hand, the right one connected to all things logical and mathematical and scientific, as soon as my toes felt the icy water, I'd be looking for the safety of land, pull out my journal, begin counting the nene, now two thousand strong after wavering on the edge of extinction. Simply watching and living among the nene for a few minutes provides enough verve to fill my sack, to lift me up and away to continue my continental drift, what feels like a reenactment of my life even though I'm still alive. In the reenactment, someone else inhabits my body, an actor who has muscles and the ability to survive physical obstacles, not a Dwane Johnson who busts out of his skin like the Hulk, but more of a Brad Pitt or Xena the Warrior Princess.

Likewise, my brain would be occupied by someone who has no fear of exploration and experimentation, not an Einstein, who would not fit easily into my brain, or Marilyn vos Savant, who has the highest recorded IQ in *The Guinness Book of Records*. No. It would be someone who loves crossword puzzles and every word game ever created. Someone who would keep my brain fresh with daily exercises to fend off what is waiting, what is knocking, what creeps into a liver, bones, dreams, and wakeful memories.

As it turns out, both hands are needed to extend this complicated flight, to keep the sack buoyant and just far enough above the earth to prevent it from being grounded, to keep from being pulled down and isolated by Covid and any other "C" words that think they can throw their weight around and have their way at will. It's not as if the two hands need to work together in a frenzied dog paddle, but more so the elegant stroke of the Australian crawl, a sideways movement and interchange of hands like a *tai chi* or *Qi gong* maneuver.

As it turns out, to thrive, I need both, the logical to create agendas and To Do lists and have rough ideas of where I might be headed, and the artistic, that allows me to open my mind to any unseen opportunities that might arise as the journey continues. And to appreciate my life so far, to show a standing ovation for this miracle of existence, I need to be able to smash the palm of the left hand into the palm of the right, offer up a loud and vibrant applause that becomes contagious.

The Value of Statues

DANA MASSIE HAS A STATUE INSIDE HIS HEAD. It's not there all the time but projected on his internal screen when he chooses to recall his father. Dana doesn't call it a statue, but I do. Dana might call it afterlife, replacing the typical definition of heaven and hell with one that he carries with him in the present, in this life that he lives now. It's about recollection, a re-collecting of images, thoughts, events, sayings, body structure, a grin squeezed out at appropriate moments.

And with the recollections comes the chipping away at a large hunk of marble that sits in the living room, the kitchen, the bathroom, the slow and steady remembrance of the man who brought him into this world, forged half of his genetic makeup, probably forged more than that of his psychological makeup. With small tools, sandpaper, steel wool, he modifies the shape of the marble, makes errors and embellishments in his father's profile, gives him a larger nose than the photographs show, like Michelangelo giving David those monstrous hands.

I call Dana's remembrance of his father a statue only because I have one as well. Mine is not marble, because my dad loved wood, so I have one in black walnut, another in basswood. When I conjure them up, I smell the sawdust, taste the years it took to grow the tree to its adult stages. I work on two statues at a time, and in time will probably add oak and cedar, have a gallery of carvings dedicated to the many facets of Teddy. They named him that—not Theodore or Ted, but Teddy. I've never heard, or at least don't remember hearing, the story of how he got that name, but I always imagine it had something to do with Teddy Roosevelt and the Rough Riders.

My dad eventually became a Ted, and he was not a rough rider. The black walnut statue shows him young and strong with a big grin on his face. He's got a baby at eighteen, a wife who's seventeen. Wears the outfit of an Otis Elevator operator. He still has hair, which looks good in dark walnut. I apply 100-grit sandpaper to dig through the layers of protection he used to build himself up during his youth where older brothers made him dog-food sandwiches they stuffed in his bag lunch. When I get beneath the surface, I'll switch to 400-grit, make my way softly into his core, look for the pathways that connect his heart to his brain, sand a vein sleek and narrow and follow its journey. I discover the bleeding ulcer buried in his stomach that the medical profession won't find for another decade until it's a bit too late. I find a love for my mom that beats hard and strong.

It's the basswood statue that uncovers more than I could ever remember or imagine. The wood is softer, easier to work with, easier to find a quicker access to what's inside, what's changed, the sarcastic smile clenched, teeth hidden, surgical scars leaving trails in the grain. I did not want this statue in my head, was not happy when I woke up one morning with the slab of wood sitting at the foot of the bed, carving tools neatly in order, fresh packs of sandpaper and steel wool awaiting, requesting me to get to work on this legacy of his, of mine. But I could not refuse, grabbed a hammer and chisel, began to give form to the rectangular hunk waiting for me to do my duty. I chipped, I pounded, I smashed, I rested, drank beer, pulled out the old photo albums and refreshed my memory. Made modifications as needed. This statue is thinner than the first. Lost over one hundred pounds, required thinner chisels to interpret baggy clothes, to uncover the red veins of pain hidden in the eyes. The leg and arm bones spindly. But I could still sand my way to the heart, the pulse, the desire to live and make others happy with his telling of jokes, his life-of-the-party demeanor.

I really do need both statues to recall my father as accurately as I can, which still falls short. I'm certain I'll wake one night at 2:00 a.m. and find a hunk of cedar sitting in the workshop, waiting. The smell alone will take me to places I'd forgotten, a cedar-planked floor in a closet on Peach Street in Oakland, a small carved elephant on a shelf in a glass cabinet. The oak will come, another side of him emerging that I had forgotten, teaching me how to throw a knuckle curveball alongside our house on Twin Hills Drive. The alcohol and cigarettes seeping out of pores.

I worry that my brain is not big enough to hold all the statues that might appear through my carvings over time. I wonder if the next piece of wood that appears, maybe a teak from Hawai'i, might be a request to carve my own statue. "Is it time?" I'll ask.

"It's always time and never time," the answer might come.

I think of Dana's father, whom I never knew but whom I can imagine by thinking of the statues in Dana's head, the similar processes we both went through to keep our museum of carvings alive, dusted, polished. How we both built images of our fathers in their afterlives, to keep them alive in our own lives.

Every Day Is Tuesday

I'M BAFFLED BY WHAT SEEMS TO BE the unraveling of the Gregorian calendar. As long as I've been alive, or at least as long as I can remember being alive, the world and my life have operated on the 365-day calendar named after Pope Gregory XIII, who introduced it in October 1582, a little before my time. It has endured, and its seven-day weeks have clearly defined my life, letting me know to go to work on Mondays, to watch *Saturday Night Live* on Saturday nights, to tune into golf tournaments on the weekends, and to remember to empty trash cans on Monday nights before the Waste Management trucks rumble down the street on Tuesday morning to empty our cans.

But in the last two years, something drastic has occurred. Most mornings I wake not having a clue what day it is. In the past it mattered, but now not much matters in the realm of time. It's more about the events that occur from sunrise to sunset. The looking at the digital numbers of the clock slowly changing, sliding by like molasses on steroids. The early-morning pee. The locating of reading glasses. Opening the computer. Emails. Spelling Bee. The crossword puzzle. The letter-boxed puzzle. A hot chocolate with mini-marshmallows on top. A fried-egg sandwich. Or three Eggos with maple syrup. And as of the past few weeks, the writing of a Daily Fresh essay. Eventually working my way into a project or two of the day. Like working on the extinct bird maps. Engraving something on the laser cutter.

The anomaly occurs early in the daily cycle. While sitting at the computer, working my way through the tasks that provide me with reason and continuity. It starts with noise. It growls from a few streets away. Sounds like the wood chipper in the movie *Fargo*. Doing its assigned job, getting things done, the things it's scheduled to do. On Tuesday mornings. The noise gets louder as it nears the corner of my street. A series of clunks and clatters. The growling more like a labored breathing, an inhale of waste and an exhale of completion. Air brakes releasing and holding, louder as it approaches our house. And finally, our cans being lifted by the mechanical arms, our trash being slammed into the metallic bin, slapped back down on the pavement, air released as it moves to the neighbor's house and cans.

None of this so far is a surprise. Expectations are met.

What is odd is that this happens every day. It's not a surprise that my habits are repetitious. I look forward to that. Keeps me moving forward. Gives me a purpose. A leaning into the future, to what's next.

But when I hear the grumble of the Waste Management truck every morning, I become disoriented, a little dizzy, have to grab walls and railings when I try to stand, find balance in the real world with what I can see and touch. Because the sounds are out of sync, make me wonder if I've missed out on six-sevenths of the

Daily Fresh

week. For some insane reason, every morning has become Tuesday. Every morning has become trash day. I try to think back about the previous six days and what I've accomplished, but it doesn't matter. This is not about accomplishments. This is a new version of *The Twilight Zone*. Of the acceleration of time.

How can we generate so much trash that it needs to be picked up every day? The deck is finished, so we don't fill cans with rusty nails and wood scraps. Shelly doesn't live with us anymore so her trash fills Mom's cans instead of ours. Maybe the neighbors are sneaking over in the middle of the night and dropping their sacks of chicken bones and coffee grounds into our cans. Maybe the neighbors continue to have unmasked birthday celebrations and need to dispose of used and exposed party supplies.

It makes no sense to me. But not much does these days. The lack of touch. The isolation. The shrinking of the real world. Relegated to the walls and rooms inside a house. Holding a palm up to a computer screen to simulate a hand squeeze, a fist bump, a skin-on-skin simulation that only goes halfway.

A mind altered by so many variables that didn't exist two years ago. Well, that didn't exist for me. Variables that cause hallucinations and forgetfulness and sleights of hand and body and noise that could easily account for Tuesdays taking over every other day to make sure the trash cans are emptied as quickly as possible.

I can live with daily Tuesdays. I've learned to adapt.

Atasky

I HAVE NO IDEA. Just woke up this morning with this non-word in my brain. At first I thought it was *Alaska* and that I had to return to *Pious Rebel* and revisit my Alaskan salmon man, Zack, and rewrite his character, make him more multilayered, have Lisa get more upset that he was heading back to Juneau to tend to his estranged wife with the nervous breakdown. But no. I had to let that one go. It made no sense. Not that anything will make sense with this one, but I'll try. *Attaché* came next. It doesn't sound like it, though. Just looks a little like it. But I don't think in my sixty-nine years on this orb that I have ever used *attaché* in a sentence. It means either "short for attaché case" or "a person or staff member of an ambassador, typically with a specialized area of responsibility."

While it's interesting to consider jumping down a rabbit hole chasing either of the attaché meanings, I think I won't. I'm still reeling today from a number of rejections yesterday, a friend reviewing a piece of my writing saying, "My guess is that overabundance of imagination is one of your great virtues and reigning issues writing fiction. It's one to be proud of as well as curse." He could be right, but I don't want to think so. I want to think that there is no such thing as overabundance of imagination, that it is in fact a value rather than a curse.

I don't have the correct state of mind to be writing this Daily Fresh today, this place where I have attempted to stay up and positive and forge new pathways. Today I have nausea, not sure if it's being generated from my anxious brain or that I haven't taken a Zofran in a while.

Onward! More than anything else *atasky* sounds like McKaskey, the family name of my cousins Dennis and Stephen and Robert, who got it from their father, my uncle George McKaskey, and which must have Irish roots given the Mc prefix. It makes me consider their family, the conservative roots that have taken them to the Mormon church.

Truthfully, I think *atasky* leaked out of an oozy hole in my brain during the night when this headache I'm experiencing now originated. I'm not sure if one letter at a time pushed its way out, found a place to sit in my "overabundant imagination" while watching each subsequent letter find its freedom. The "a" waiting for the "t" to emerge, or maybe it didn't come out fully formed as its own word. Maybe the "y" appeared first. Maybe when they all sat next to each other on that mental ledge it read *yaskat*. Maybe they played musical chairs, became *skaaty*, then *katyas*. I like *katyas*. I think about a chorus line of Eastern European dancers kicking their legs up, smiles on their faces, trying to convince the audience and the world that everything is really okay, that things are looking up. And *Katya* sounds much better than *atasky*.

Cliché Watch

WHEN MY BRAIN MELTS into a puddle of mush, regardless of whether it's accompanied by walnuts, bananas, and brown sugar, I fall into the pit of relying on overworked clichés to describe my condition. "Time heals all wounds" drifts to the top, but what wounds have I really endured? They aren't really wounds. There have been no weapons with sharp tips applied into and through my skin and body. Just words dropped into my brain that slow me down, make me want to become an icy glacier frozen to itself and the granite mountain beneath its mass.

"You should be over it by now." Who is it that is telling me what I should and shouldn't be thinking? And how fast I should be doing it? Two days ago my agenda was filled with rejections of various sorts from various people. A few of them hit deep and hard and made me question the value of anything and everything I've been doing to keep this bag-of-bones body vertical and attending to business. Words have been my "saving grace." Ah, there's one, though not of the same flavor as the others I'm tracking today. Give me maybe one more day and I might be over it.

"You have to keep busy." It's a pretty weak cliché and in this case it's ironic because the rejections have caused me to bury myself a bit and be less busy than I have for the past few months. The busyness of fingers on the keyboard does help. Reminds me that at least my brain is functioning even if the phrases and sentences aren't lyrical and poetical and earth-shattering. Even if they are only basic and provide some idea of what's rattling around my head.

"A blot on the landscape." That one's better. I can relate to this one. A blot, a black mark, something that mars or alters a perceived reality. That makes sense to me. I can see it there. And it's on my landscape. The one I've been drawing in pen and ink, going over with oils, trying to urge into some lifelike vision that represents my life. Then the blot appears. The blotch. The smear. The thing that hides what's really there, blurs what I thought I was seeing.

"Ignorance is bliss." Is it? My last two days have suggested that my blind ignorance as to the value of my work, my thinking, my writing, has been guiding me in the wrong direction, highlighting my concerns about delusions of grandeur, making them stand out even more in very tall flashing neon letters that are permanently nailed into the roof of my house. Ignorance is not blissful when pointed out by others, when it spills open the internal frailties and possible waste of time of what remains of life.

"A chain is only as strong as its weakest link." Really? What if all the links are weak? What if what you thought was the one weak link turns out to have spread like a virus to every other link in every other sentence and paragraph and story and novel? What if the chain you thought was holding everything together disintegrates into a pile of metal shavings that a gentle wind can easily blow away?

"A fish out of water." "A fly in the ointment." At the moment, I am both the fish and fly. I am the "frog in my throat." I am a "leopard changing my spots." I am the man whose "castle has crumbled." I am "experiencing the sea change." And if there were a mirror nearby, I would certainly be "a sight for sore eyes."

But for now, I'm thinking about that "wolf in sheep's clothing." This wolf made no attempt to hide itself. He came out with teeth bared, dripping with blood. Full from the recent feast, but ready for more. I appreciate his direct hunger. His letting me know that there was no kiss to precede his ripping of my flesh from bones. No. His was more of a "So what are you going to do about it? Are you going to let me finish tearing you to shreds? Are you going to wither and die?"

No. I have too much invested to make an "about-face." I am "after my own heart." I am "all dressed up with *somewhere* to go." "I've already got one paw on the chicken coop," so I might as well finish the job and raise the other paw.

I am as "busy as a bee," as "fine as frog's hair."

For the last two days I have been "asleep at the wheel."

No more. I am at "the eleventh hour" with only one to go, so I will relish all sixty minutes, all 3,600 seconds, get "back in the saddle" and quit "banging my head against someone else's wall." You can "bet your bottom dollar" that one way or another I will "blow your mind," because "I'm on a roll," and "in cahoots with" the "milk of human kindness."

Slippage

THIS IS NOT REALLY FICTION, but it will be written as if it's fiction.

Mom falls. I get angry. I feel sad. Responsible. It's nearly 2:00 in the morning. I call my brother and sister-in-law who live a mile away. She comes down and we lift. I'm not writing this. My brother is writing this. He'll try to climb into my head and pretend he knows what I'm going through. But he doesn't know shit. Well, he knows plenty of shit. His own shit. But not my shit.

We get Mom up to a chair and the Alexa Show is sitting there on the kitchen table watching us. She is trying to prompt us to ask her questions. *Ask me about the cat who caught Covid from her owner.* No. I don't want to hear it right now. *Ask me if the Giants won their major-league baseball game over the San Diego Padres.* No. I don't care. I think about the éclairs I picked up at Gayle's today. Mom loves them. They're not especially healthy, but that's not the point. The point is calories. The point is trying to keep her body in a thriving mode.

At 1:45 we were both still awake. I asked her if she'd like an éclair. She shook her head. She didn't say, "No thank you, I'm good." She didn't even say "No." She avoids words, or doesn't know how to produce them much anymore. But she shook her head. Made her point. Or so I thought as I got up and tended to one of the hundred things on my list, on my mind. I heard the thud. The one I've come to recognize, the one I've come to dread. I ran back to the table and she was gone. She was on the floor in the kitchen.

"Mom, are you okay?" She nodded. "Any new pains?" She shook her head and said, "Sorry. Éclair." Once I was sure she hadn't broken anything again, I went for the phone to make the call. Should I ring the fire department, who told us last time this is their job? They're less than a quarter mile away. I can see the red lights on the building at the end of our street. No. I should call my brother and sister-in-law. That's what they want. That's what makes sense. Less foofaraw to do it that way.

Alexa flashes a new command. *Tell me your birthday. I'll give you some fun facts.* Mom is calmer now. I look at Alexa and say, "December 4, 1932." Mom says, "My birthday." This is what confuses me about her. Her sometimes cognition. That she heard me, and that she recognizes her birthday.

Alexa says, *I know about three events that occurred in 1932. Great Depression. Chancellor Schleicher meets with Gregor Strasser and offers to appoint him vice chancellor and commissioner. Hitler will support his government. Michele Lupo is born in Italy. The birth of Roh Tae-woo, South Korean general and politician, sixth president of South Korea.*

I wonder if Michele Lupo and Roh Tae-woo are still alive. They would be 87 years old like Mom. I wonder if either of them fell on the stairs on Mother's Day and compound fractured their wrist. I wonder if their pill containers are as full as Mom's. I wonder if one of their children moved in with them full-time to help make sure they ate food, drank liquids, walked with a four-pronged cane, helped reduce the number of times they fell.

I ask Alexa if they are both still alive. They are. Alexa doesn't know anything about their children. Mom seems confused by Alexa and the events that occurred on her birthday. So am I. So is my sister-in-law. We gently lift Mom out of the chair, walk her down the hallway to her bed, get her tucked in. "Sorry," she says again. I believe her. She is not falling to gain our attention. She has way more of my attention than she would ever have imagined. She falls because she is a strong independent woman who has been on her own for fifteen years. She falls because she doesn't want to bother me when she needs to pee or hunt for the fresh éclairs.

We—me, my brother, my sister-in-law, her friends—do not want her to end up in a skilled-nursing facility like her mom, our grandma, who died alone in Pacific Coast Manor on Wharf Road. Especially since Covid would lock us out from ever seeing her again. Is that what this will come to? Dropping our parents off at the doors of facilities to die, to wave goodbye, watch the sunken expressions on their faces as we tilt our masks up over our noses and leave? We resist. I resist. Mom wants to die in her own home. She's been here for fifty-five years. We don't want her to die at all, but we want her to be comfortable.

I Lie Better Than I Examine

WHEN I RECEIVED AN EMAIL containing the thought "I lie better than I examine, it turns out," I replied to the friend who sent it that I would add the line to my journal next to one of my light bulbs, signaling it as a future prompt. He wrote back and told me he didn't consider it a prompt. I let it go.

Am I writing this piece to disprove his assertion? Or am I writing this one simply to prove that everything I see, hear, touch, imagine, or invent is fodder for a prompt, ready for placement after a light bulb to reside in my journal until I'm ready to drift back over the pages and focus on it? As it turns out, as with most questions, it's a little of each.

I've come to know and trust and love prompts, and this one feels as if it's as good as any, feels like I might be headed somewhere, to a place that makes sense of the initial line and finds a landing point worthy of the venture.

This prompt from my friend was in response to me asking him if he'd be reading fiction or nonfiction at an upcoming Zoom event. The comparison of fiction as lie to nonfiction as examination is fascinating to me. I agree that much of what we label as fiction is driven by an "overabundant imagination," as the same friend said of a recent piece of my work, which is clearly aided by a healthy sprinkling of lies and fabrication. Whether the lies are intentional, to throw the reader, the characters, and the author off track, into rabbit holes and sideways ventures, or whether they are accidental artifacts of bad memories and misinterpretation of photos in albums or the misremembering of conversations with aunts while drinking Harvey Wallbangers in the bar of what was once a monastery in the hills above our house doesn't matter. A lie is a lie regardless of intent. It colors and directs the writing, points the reader down a specific pathway.

For my friend to suggest that his fiction is better than his nonfiction is a questionable assertion. He implies that the examination necessary to write good nonfiction could be lacking. I've read his nonfiction. There is no lack of insight, forethought, examination, or research. But I guess I shouldn't argue with his own interpretation of his abilities and skills, should trust that he lived with both animals for many decades of his life, and ironically, his own examinations of each have led him to the belief that his fiction is better than his nonfiction. Or maybe it's not that it's better given a set of personal criteria he's created, but maybe it's that what he really enjoys is the weaving of tales. I listened to a Book Passage Zoom discussion between James McBride and Susan Orleans where McBride said, "A book is not a platform for opinions. It's a place to tell stories."

Maybe that's the thing. Maybe my friend has discovered that he enjoys being a storyteller more than being someone who knows everything about everything. The nonfiction genre being a place where opinions, true or false, accurate or inaccurate, are tossed about more freely to suggest a piece that has possibly been thoroughly investigated, researched, examined, and maybe even fact-checked. I would suggest that such a hard and fast analysis be scrapped for something with more of a mucous membrane that allows for passage and modifications as needed. Look at John D'Agata's work. He makes no pretension that his nonfiction is fact-checkable and will stand someone's test of time. He doesn't care. That's not why he writes it.

How does my own writing fit into this discussion? As I've said many times in many places, I believe every word and sentence of my writing falls into the realm of fictography. Whether I have consciously dropped a piece of writing in my nonfiction folder or my fiction folder doesn't really matter. Yes, there must be some unwritten criteria which help me make a decision, but in truth, it all belongs in one large fictography folder. I enjoy my overabundant imagination. I like to fabricate, to tell lies, to make up stories and possibly have characters entering more rabbit holes than they should, going too sideways even for Ron Carlson to enjoy. But I also love to have my Google window open so I can be in mid-sentence when I need to jump over to the browser to find out the name of Ice-T's father-in-law so I can use some facts to talk about the issue of Covid.

Am I better at lying than examining? I'm not sure that I know the answer, and even less sure that I care about discovering an answer. Is my friend a better liar than an examiner? If it's true, then the whole assertion—"I lie better than I examine"—could just as easily have been written intentionally as a lie. Only he knows for sure.

All I know for sure is that my lies and examinations will continue to pair and merge and help me to create pieces of writing that other folks may need to figure out how to categorize, because like my friend, I'm not to be trusted.

Dear Sandra—8-1-20

GOOD MORNING!
Up at 2:38 a.m. mainly because the chemo makes me get up to pee so often.

There is so much to catch up on. It sounds like the pandemic urge of folks to move to the mountains is overtaking your working life. The good news and the bad news. More money, less free time to think and ponder the nature of the universe. Are you coming up with workable solutions to make sure your heart is engaged as much as your brain?

The Happy Valley Literary Society

I have attended some of the Saturday-morning sessions, but 80% of the discussion has been about Covid, and it wears me out. Having a third "C" in my life is too much. Cancer and chemo are plenty. One of our number has had some health issues. Stones in either the bladder or gallbladder. Needed surgery. Another needs a new liver. The Tin Man needs a new heart. The lion needs some courage. The scarecrow needs a brain. I need time.

Zoom Forward!

The day that Gavin Newsom shut down the state in March, I started thinking about the poetry reading of my new book, *Of Two Minds,* that I was supposed to have at Bookshop Santa Cruz and that had been cancelled. Half the joy of those readings was the gathering with folks beforehand and after to catch up. That week I organized a live reading through Zoom called *Zoom Forward!* where I had three local authors read from their work. I never looked back. We've had a reading every Friday since, just completing #23 last night. The good and the bad. The good is that it has really helped to keep a sense of community alive and it's great to talk to folks in the "lobby" before and after the readings. Also, we always invite folks to purchase books at Bookshop Santa Cruz to help keep them afloat. And it promotes local authors and their books. The bad is that this volunteer "position" has become a job that has a lot of moving parts to it. Bios. Photos. Rehearsals. Agenda. The herding of poets! I've hired my granddaughter Hannah as my assistant director for *phren-z,* Santa Cruz Writes, and *Zoom Forward!* She puts in about ten hours a week and helps with the Mailchimp campaign. I get lots of positive feedback from folks, which helps to offset the days I feel like "WTF have I done?" and feel overwhelmed. We have readings scheduled out into September.

The Writing Life and Related Topics

My writing has continued to be the core of my life. Three things have kept me alive this long (22 months since the 2018 diagnosis). My friends. My writing. My art. I have stayed up and positive throughout this journey. It's made all the difference. I have been on fire with the writing. *Of Two Minds,* which came out July 1, is the second book of poetry I published. I don't think you have a copy of it yet, so tell me the preferred address to send it to and I'll put it in the mail today or tomorrow. From November to February, I wrote a 430-page novel called *Pious Rebel,* about a woman named Lisa Hardrock who has to rebuild her life and self-worth after her partner of seven years is killed by a fallen oak tree on their property on Porter Gulch Road. I spent from March to June revising it, and now have it out to about twenty agents and publishers, rejections flowing in! If I don't get any bites, I'll have my poetry publisher publish it.

As I continue down this pathway toward my eventual fate, I have been thinking about and reviewing my "Writing" folder that contains almost everything I've ever written, minus the hard-copy journals I have kicking around. There is a ton of stuff, and most of it has been dormant for years. My friend Scott, who is kind of a strategic consultant and expert, helped me prioritize the seventeen projects that are unfinished. I now have a list and an order-of-completion map that drives me forward. I finished another project called *Smith: An Unauthorized Fictography* that is 204 pages long. A friend is currently reading it for copyedits.

The Happy Valley novel is on the list, as is the novel I wrote in 2018 called *Capture and Release,* one of the protagonists having experienced the capturing of her mother's soul as she was holding her hand at death, and then the same thing with her father at his death. She became interested in this capturing-of-souls thing, and joined hospice so she could continue that work, work that was both valuable and disturbing. Also on the list is a 400-page short-story collection that I need to narrow down to 280 pages for an upcoming contest.

I took a memoir/personal-essay class from a friend early in the summer. I had never been much of an essay writer, but came away with a few interesting pieces, as well as a desire to write more essays, so I started a daily writing process called Daily Fresh, where I wake up every morning and write something fresh and new. This morning will be twenty-seven days in a row.

Art

Because of all the time spent on writing and *Zoom Forward!* finding time for my art has been an issue. I've been thinking about and mapping out an art-project idea for a couple of years, and finally made a breakthrough a couple of months ago and am slowly moving forward on it. I've done research on thirty extinct birds, and am now working on a sarcophagus for each bird.

Photo credit: Karen Wallace

The containers I'm using are the antique treadle-sewing-machine drawers. I've downloaded the bird images from the web, modified them in Photoshop and Illustrator, and then cut them out on my laser cutter. I print out maps of where the birds went extinct and glue them to the inside of the drawers. I've completed one and have twenty-nine to go. I'm thinking when

I finish the last one, I'll contact the Museum of Art and History to see if they'd like to host the installation.

Mom

Jeannine Carlotta Post, born December 4, 1932, is having a hard time. On Mother's Day, we went over for dinner and, as we were leaving, she tripped and fell on some stairs and compound fractured her left wrist. Urgent Care, ER, the works. We brought her home with a temporary cast and were told that she needed someone living with her full-time. Given my condition, it didn't make any sense for it to be me, so my sister, Shelly, who has lived in our apartment for thirty years, has moved in full-time with Mom. She has fallen at least six times. We get the phone calls from Shelly, and Karen has to hustle down there to help lift Mom off the floor. I'm worthless, because I have no muscles left. Urgent Care, ER, Dominican Hospital. She spent five days in the hospital and of course none of us could visit her, and they tested her for Covid and didn't get the results back for five days. She continues to fall. It's really difficult for Shelly, who doesn't get much sleep, worrying if Mom is going to try to get out of bed to pee and fall on the way. And it's difficult for me because I feel so useless. Karen is the saint in the picture. Not only running most everything about our household, but also relieving Shelly of her duties a number of days per week. Sigh.

My Condition

Since the February CT scan that indicated metastasis to the liver, two lesions, I have been back on a full regimen of chemo for going on twenty-four weeks, twelve cycles. The twelfth cycle begins next Wednesday with six hours in the infusion center. I'll have another CT scan on August 11 to determine if there have been any changes. The last scan was two months ago, and as the oncologist said, "The results are mixed." The large tumor in my pancreas has not changed, has not changed at all in twenty-two months. One of the two lesions increased in size by two millimeters, the other one disappeared. The new CT scan next week will help guide us in determining if we move forward with more chemo. I continue to be somewhat of a poster child in terms of my side effects. Yes, I have the nausea and the diarrhea, I'm sure for as long as I live, but I haven't had any pain or vomiting, and I'm holding strong at 175 pounds for the past few months. My brain is more active than it's ever been, and chemo brain has never been an issue, almost the reverse, where these poison drugs have set me on fire and keep my fingers on the keyboard and ideas rolling out. For that I'm thankful. Ah, for so much I'm thankful.

Karen

And speaking of being thankful, let me talk about Karen. She is/has been/will always be a saint. I would have been dead and cremated ages ago if it weren't for her. Today is our anniversary, thirty-third year together, twenty-seven years married. What a lucky partner and partnership I found. She cooks for me, supports my writing, puts up with my rare bad moods, because in this new state of mind I tend to get pissy about redundancy and repetition.

Drama

My good friend Kathy Chetkovich meets with me every Sunday morning for two hours. We have been in a playwriting group together for four years now. We talk about anything and everything. A few weeks ago she had the idea that I should have a *Zoom Forward!* reading of three of my plays, and she has stepped up to produce the show. Two ten-minute plays and one

one-act play. Trying to figure out how to put them on in the time of Covid and sheltering in place has been quite difficult. It has been an added pressure this past week that just about put me over the edge. For the first time in twenty-two months I slipped into a little depression, which thankfully I'm digging out of now. Anyway, theoretically the show, called *Side by Side*, will appear on Zoom on Monday, September 14, at 6:00.

You

Okay. That was quite an early-morning dump about me. Tell me about you. How are you holding up? How is your body and health? How are Bobby and the grandkids? How about Mueller and the grandkids? What else? Do you ever get to see Tim live, or is that mainly a verbal and email relationship at this point?

Okay. I'm going back to bed now.

Love ~ Jory

Pressure

SO MANY KINDS. My unresearched first thought is that they all have to do with buildup. With some sort of tension or expectation. At least mine do. And those I observe in others. And not just people, but the planet and things on the planet other than people.

My sister, Shelly, suggested this prompt yesterday. Said we should both write about it. It's not a surprise that she mentioned it, given what's going on in her life right now. She is on the front lines with our mom, having moved into her house, being the one to worry 24/7 about her well-being, about her lack of eating, her dehydration, her independent tendency to get out of bed and seek out the bathroom without help, her wetting herself, her physical and mental reaction to new medications, her slurring of words and occasional unresponsiveness. The management of Mom's meds. The management of household modifications that will make life easier for Mom. The management of packing and moving thirty years of life out of an apartment that has been home to her. I've only listed a few of the responsibilities that Shelly has taken on to make sure Mom can stay in the home she's lived in for fifty-five years. The ones I can think of and imagine. I'm sure there are dozens more, all of which cause the tension that creates pressure. Pressure to succeed. Pressure to keep Mom alive and well and as happy as possible. Pressure to not be the one on duty when Mom suddenly fails and dies or falls in a way that makes her eventual end closer.

I believe all the other examples of pressure are secondary compared to that one. But for the sake of argument, no, for the sake of completion, for the sake of bringing this Daily Fresh in closer to 1,000 words this morning, I'll persevere, I'll talk and think about every flavor of pressure I can imagine before having my cup of Sillycow Chocolate Truffle hot chocolate. Take the last sentence, for example, the use of the word *persevere*. There is a goal implied, no, not implied, stated: 1,000 words. Such goals imply a pressure to succeed. To reach an end point. We put intentional pressure on ourselves to reach these goals, to feel a sense of satisfaction and success, which ironically helps to reduce pressure upon achievement. Ah, back to achievement and disappointment. It's like a toggle switch. Disappointment increasing the pressure, achievement decreasing the pressure. Or maybe it's like a beating heart. The inhale causing a certain pressure on the circulatory system, the exhale a release of that pressure.

I get tired of writing about the pressures associated with carrying pancreatic cancer around in my body, so I won't do so here, as I've already filled two books of poetry with those stories, working on a third.

But that brings up a whole new flavor of pressure which drives me forward to specific goals. This is a self-invented pressure to write every day and to complete seventeen unfinished writing projects as well as imagining and embarking on new projects. This pressure on myself feels like my lifeline, my blood, the pressure to stay alive and thrive as long as possible with and for the people I love by having a clear-cut purpose every morning when I wake up and begin my day. I'm happy when I make progress, feel more pressure when I don't.

For example, lack of progress infested my life over the past week. It coagulated my blood, clogged my brain, dropped me into a depression that would surely kill me if I let it. Multiple pressures occurring from every direction in my life: the difficulties with Mom, the nature of this *Zoom Forward!* project I've taken on, the pressures of thinking about the technical realities of producing a series of short plays through Zoom, the subsequent slowdown on my writing projects.

I know I just said I wouldn't talk about the cancer, but there are just too many good examples of pressure associated with it. Take the permanent neuropathy in my feet. It's a constant numbness, and that causes a lack of feeling and an oversensitive feeling at the same time. We have walked on our feet for a lifetime expecting a certain type of pressure from the gravity that holds us to the ground. But neuropathy changes the relationship of feet to ground, creates what initially feels like an unnatural pressure, especially when one wraps shoes around these hunks of flesh that occupy the ends of one's legs.

Then there's the bladder. The chemo drugs cause the need to pee all day and night long every two hours. So there's the physical pressure on the bladder that wakes one, and there's the mental pressure of knowing you need to drop your neuropathic feet to the floor and walk to the bathroom before peeing yourself.

There's more, but I'll quit talking about it now. I'll move on to something a little less animate. Take the tires on the car. With modern technology in the auto industry, there are dozens of colorful lights on dashboards that provide clues as to the state of your vehicle. For example, there's a little orange one on the far-right side of our Prius dashboard that suggests that the tire pressure on at least one of our tires is too low. It seems to be caused by a change in the weather. If we drive down to Steve's Union at the corner, we can use their air hose, complete with pressure gauge, to determine if we should add more air to any of our tires. PSI. Pounds per square inch. A definitive measure of pressure. If you look at the Prius manual, you'll find that 32 PSI is appropriate for tires. When our little orange light comes on, that usually means the front left tire has somehow fallen to 26 PSI. We attach the air hose and fill the tire, increase the pressure on the internal rubber until it reaches 32 PSI and is again safe to carry out its relationship with the pavement.

 Probably the strongest example of pressure under the roof of our house is our Instant Pot, a Canadian brand of multicooker. It's a marvel of a kitchen tool that has changed our breakfast life. Every day or so, Karen makes a new batch of steel-cut oats that we eat with bananas, blueberries, brown sugar, added protein powder, and cinnamon. The Instant Pot is fast, faster than typical pressure cookers. Ah! There it is: pressure cooker! The science and efficacy of this tool has everything to do with how it uses pressure to speed up the process of cooking. If you look up the PSI of the Instant Pot on the Internet you'll discover that it is 15.23 PSI. That's about half of what a Prius tire should be. That's a lot of pressure to be stored inside a small metal device tucked away in the corner of your kitchen cooking your breakfast every morning. But it's intentional. By design. So we accept it, because we want that quick meal and we trust that the manufacturer has run enough tests to ensure that the Instant Pot won't explode and shoot shrapnel across the kitchen and into our chest where it might puncture an atrium or ventricle and effect the inhale and exhale we have become dependent on.

Pressure (preSHer). The first definition given in the online dictionary is "continuous physical force exerted on or against an object by something in contact with it." So many things to think about in that definition. The first is "continuous." That means nonstop. That this action is relentless and has a job to do and will not let anything get in its way. Like an oil derrick in a Southern California desert, pumping away. Like the windshield wipers against your front window in a thunderstorm. Like the spray of water from a pressure washer that blasts sidewalks and deck railings clean. A continuous flow or movement that guarantees the job gets done. Then comes "exerted." So there's a conscious decision on the part of some person or machine to apply pressure in a situation to achieve the desired outcome. And the final phrase for consideration in definition one is "in contact with." Yes. Pressure makes zero sense if there is not some body or object that comes in contact with the exerted and continuous pressure. Like the wearing down of knee joints after sixty-nine years of walking, running, playing soccer and football, and square dancing, and having the 100-pound door in a bathroom at the New Teacher Center fall on your foot and hobble you for months.

The second definition of pressure does not disappoint: "the use of persuasion, influence, or intimidation to make someone do something." Right. We all know this one. During our long lives, we may have been the receiver of this type of pressure, or the perpetrator, depending on the moment, the situation, who was needing what, when, and why. This is the mental flavor of pressure that can throw one's week off, or longer if you allow it to. (Luckily, I've been able to throw this monkey off my back, get on with it, get back to writing these Daily Fresh pieces and attend to what's important.) "Persuasion, influence, or intimidation." Three different knives with blades of different thickness and sharpness. Persuasion appears to come in soft and gentle, and the pressure being used by the perpetrator might be missed by the victim. Influence is softer yet, but still there. "What writers have influenced you?" folks often ask writers in interviews. I think about what I would answer if I ever got asked that question. Just thinking about it causes some internal pressure that I put on myself. Should I say Ann Patchett? How about Proust? Carlos Castaneda? Kurt Vonnegut? There are so many. Will I embarrass myself if I say something that is unacceptable to somebody? The pressure slowly builds even thinking years in advance of something that may never happen. It's intimidation that is not soft, is blunt, smashes one over the head with a sledgehammer. The kind of pressure a loan shark puts on the neck of a hopeless gambler. The angry father demanding that the teenage boy marry his teenage daughter and raise together the child that she is expecting.

I know that I've barely made my way through the top layer of a pot of pressure soup that contains a hundred more examples. But I need to stop here, need to get on to the other demands of the day that I have laid out for myself on a To Do list, an agenda, a list of expectations that provides a continuous movement, an inhale and exhale that keeps me breathing and alive. Thriving.

I know I said, maybe even promised—did I promise?—that I wouldn't talk about the cancer here. But I need to end with it. Because there is one very clear example of pressure related to it that needs to be mentioned. Pancreatic cancer implies death. Eventual death. Of course, life itself implies death, but pancreatic cancer shortens the time frame, applies a pressure, of the mental type, that is ever-present. Not just to me, the one wearing the tumor. But more so to my family and friends who have to continuously imagine what life will be like without me. I see it daily in Karen's eyes, in her quivering lips, in the softness of the kisses she applies to my forehead. A pressure that raises her systolic and diastolic numbers, causes her to eat more Fritos and Cheez-Its than she should. I see it hidden below the surface in my sister and my mother. I see it in the actions and comments and eyes of my friends Kathy, Janie, Cheryl, and others. It's a specific kind of pressure that I don't have to endure. I'll be gone when their gauges reach somewhere between 15.23 and 32 PSI, where the pressure reaches its maximum, and finally bursts and releases.

    I don't look forward to being gone, but I look forward to the release of pressure on my family and friends.

The Lists

I WONDER AFTER TWENTY-EIGHT DAYS if my Daily Fresh thoughts will dry up and leave me tattered and withered in the yard, blown off the deck and down the mountain to be used by birds to build their nests. But then I think of Dixie Cox, who quite often in our improv writing group would write long, luxurious lists that simply fell out of her pen, her brain, and I think, "I can mimic Dixie, do my best to imitate her style and wit."

Or simply begin by imagining all the lists in the world, in my life, in my mind when I wake up with a To Do or start thinking about the agenda Kathy and I will use on Sunday mornings.

My most recent list occurred less than thirty minutes ago. Karen and I both start our days every morning by playing the *New York Times* Spelling Bee, a fascinating word game that keeps our brains active and fresh. We can both work on the same puzzle under my account and password. But if I am up at five cranking away, then Karen would see my words and wouldn't have the pleasure of discovering them herself. Unless, that is, I wake up, open an Excel worksheet, and as I find words, simply list them in a column, tracking my projected points for each word, and wait for Karen to wake up, go downstairs to grab a cup of hot coffee, and open her Spelling Bee. Then I can refer to my list and enter my words. At the moment, this is my most valuable use of lists. Well, at least my most recent use. There are many others that I may or may not remember to address by the time I complete this session.

There are other lists that come to mind. One I often refer to is the Modern Library list of 100 Best Novels. It's one I often return to, I guess mainly to see how my progress is on checking off these alleged masterpieces of fiction. Of course, you can't always trust lists. I mean, how was this ranking originally created? Who were the rankers? Were there 100 librarians around the country who each read thousands of books who made the final choice? Would I agree with them? If I walked into their living rooms and kitchens would I approve of their lifestyles? Would I trust their tastes in furniture, in art? After perusing their bookshelves, which I assume would be far and wide throughout the house, floor to ceiling, would I approve of their reading choices? I don't know, but for most of my adult life I've returned to the list a couple times a year, just a check-in, just a heads up.

As of today, it looks like I've read 70% of the top ten books listed. *Ulysses* is of course ranked #1, and I have read it a few times. *The Great Gatsby, A Portrait of the Artist as a Young Man, Lolita*. There are three I haven't read, and I'm not sure why. *Brave New World* by Aldous Huxley, *Darkness at Noon* by Arthur Koestler, and *Sons and Lovers* by D. H. Lawrence. (Notice that even in thinking about and writing about lists, I can't help but create a couple. This is not an apology, simply an observation.)

When I dig a little further into the list, I notice that I have to get all the way down to #15 before I find a woman author, Virginia Woolf for *To the Lighthouse*, which, to be honest, is probably my favorite book on the list of 100. Now I'm curious, so I skim down the list. Finally at #58 I find Edith Wharton and *The Age of Innocence*. Willa Cather appears at #61 with *Death Comes for the Archbishop* (which I haven't read). By the time I reach #100, I have found seven women authors. Seven percent. I now wonder what percent of the librarians who ranked the top 100 were men. Could it be 93%? I don't know. It's not something I want to spend too much more time on because there are other lists to consider, to create.

This fascination with lists began early for all of us, at least for all of us whose parents allowed a fanciful start to life with a healthy belief in Santa Claus. What an important list that was to create! At two we couldn't write the lists ourselves, but we had assistance from an older sibling or a parent who could guide us in our expectations, narrow our scope depending on their own financial circumstances. My list in the early 1950s was pretty simple: Mr. Potato Head, Fisher-Price Little People complete with school bus, Gumby, Play-Doh, and a pogo stick. Santa's list disappeared at a young age, especially when the bully in first grade told everybody that Santa was a hoax and that he had caught his parents putting out the cookies and milk last Christmas.

I don't remember at what age I was introduced to Benjamin Franklin's List of 13 Virtues or why. It probably wasn't in high school, where I didn't learn much of anything. Probably at Cabrillo College in a philosophy class with Sam Bloom. I wasn't impressed. As a nineteen-year-old I wasn't too concerned with temperance, frugality, moderation, chastity, or the other nine virtues that Franklin put forth as the guideposts to his life. He even created a chart so he could track which of the thirteen virtues he had achieved for each day of the week. For me, this was less about the list and more about obsession.

I had never heard about the details of Schindler's list until the movie by Steven Spielberg aired in 1993. I was thirty-three, finally growing into my brain as a teacher of eleven- and twelve-year-olds at Happy Valley School. The movie stirred up so many emotions, the severe sadness at what happened in the concentration camps in Germany and the overwhelming appreciation of Oskar Schindler and how he endangered his own life by helping his Jewish employees to be exempt from the camps. For me, one of the most important lists I had been introduced to so far in my life.

How about bucket lists? I had never liked the use or concept of bucket lists, what you would like to accomplish before you die. When the movie came out in 2007 with Jack Nicholson and Morgan Freeman, it furthered my lack of interest in the concept. I engaged in a bit of research to determine the origins of the phrase, and according to what I found, it's attributed to the screenwriter of that film, Justin Zackham. The only reference I could find was that it is rooted in the expression "kick the bucket," which we know means to die. While I still dislike the phrase, I opened up more to the concept when I was diagnosed with cancer. Yeah, maybe it is a good idea to make a list of the things you need to accomplish before you go. I've been living with my lists daily for the past twenty-two months.

Today we have Craigslist. A massive online list that replicates a massive regionwide flea market where you can find anything and everything you might ever want or need. I use it often, mostly for research. I think I've only made two purchases, a hot-mount press and another tool for our workshop. I will often look for tickets for shows that are sold out through normal avenues, check the going rate for office rentals or prices of old typewriters, or, more recently, hunt for antique treadle-sewing-machine drawers to use in art projects.

So many more lists, most of which I ignore, like America's Most Wanted Fugitive List, the Hollywood blacklist, the A-list. I'm more interested in lists that famous people have written and that have somehow made their way onto the Internet or into books so I have access to them. Recently I found one written by the architect Eero Saarinen to his future wife. It is a list of twelve items that explained what it was he liked or loved about her, #1 being "First I recognized that you were very clever." It goes on.

I love basketball. Love to watch good players executing the game well. James Naismith was the inventor of basketball in 1891. I discovered that Naismith began his venture by typing up a two-page list of thirteen rules, complete with handwritten corrections and notes. Basketball may never have found its way into the world, into my world, if it hadn't been for the thoughtful creation of his iconic list.

And now you can visit Wikipedia, where you can find a List of Lists of Lists, described as "a list of list articles that contain other list articles." You could spend a lifetime on these pages, lose yourself in an endless web of lists. I gave up after ten minutes. Because I'm somewhat deficient in my mythology education, I visited the List of Deities, which broke down further into twelve linked categories, including a List of Goddesses, which interests me. So I clicked and found another list of categories, nearly a hundred of them, by region. So I clicked on Afro-Asiatic, where I found another list of another 100 categories. So I clicked on Anahit under Armenian Mythology. Finally, multiple layers in, I found a page that provided everything I'd want to know about Anahit, the goddess of fertility, healing, wisdom, and water. While this was fascinating, entertaining, and might provide fodder for a future character, I couldn't waste my time digging through so many categories and levels to reach the actual content. So, I headed back to the main page, thought I'd try one more dive. This time, under the main heading of Society and Social Sciences, I clicked on Linguistics, another field that I'm highly interested in yet don't have any background in. Another list of 100 categories. I clicked on Word Lists by Frequency, where I learned that in a given corpus the word *the* occurs 3,789,654 times, first on the list. *He*, second on the list, occurs 2,098,762 times, and *transducionalify* occurs once and is 123,567th on the list.

This one just about does me in. I'm done with other people's lists. Though I must admit, I am fascinated by Houdini's Scene and Prop List, which he provided to his crew before his events. Or viewing pages from Galileo's notebooks, where he outlines supplies needed for experiments. Or even *Rolling Stone*'s list of the 100 best guitar players ever. But I have to stop now. Need to get on with the business of the day, as follows:

1. Drink one large mug of Sillycow Chocolate Truffle hot chocolate while finishing this essay.

2. Respond to an email from my sister that just came in.

3. Send Kathy an email to ask her for the names of home health-care folks she used, and ask her again about the wheelchair.

4. Take a shower to be ready for the landscape architect meeting at 9:00.

5. Put Emla numbing agent on my port to prepare for blood draw and doctor appointment at 10:45.

6. Continue to add character descriptions to 35 of the 45 characters in my novel *Capture and Release*.

Daily Fresh

7. Have a Zoom meeting with Scott at noon.

8. Prepare a 5-page manuscript for all three *Side by Side* plays to share with Kathy before directors and actors.

9. Create a spreadsheet list of all upcoming literary-magazine submission dates.

10. Send an email to the playwriting group with the Zoom link for tonight's 6:30 meeting.

11. Order dinner out from Crow's Nest. (Maybe the tempura prawns with rice pilaf and brown rolls.)

12. In bed by 7:30 after watching Jimmy Fallon.

13. Complete the crossword puzzle.

14. Read one chapter of James McBride's *Deacon King Kong*.

15. Think about tomorrow's list while falling asleep.

No, there will be no drying up of ideas as long as I have lists in my life, in my mind.

A Crumbling Cracker of Communion

THANKS AGAIN TO MY SISTER, Shelly, for providing another evocative prompt. I really have no idea how to start this one, how to put flesh around the bones, how to lower the landing gear and eventually set this one down for a soft and satisfying landing.

I guess I should begin at the beginning, or as close to the beginning as I can remember. That would be in 1953, when I was two years old and my mother had recently given birth to my sister, Katherine Lorraine Post. At the time of her birth on November 3, my parents and the rest of their families were probably best described as Methodists; just one reason why I'm not qualified to discuss the Catholic tradition of Communion. But by the time Katherine died of crib death in January, my parents had killed God, had turned their backs on an evil deity that could allow such a horrendous turn of events in their lives. Another reason why I'm not qualified to address this prompt with any fact-checkable reliability, given that I was raised in an areligious, atheistic family and environment.

We have a family joke around my sister supposedly asking what day Easter was on, in front of my dad's best friend and a Catholic, Dick, who laughed hysterically and said it's always been on Sunday, the day Jesus was resurrected from the dead. To be fair, I believe Dick misinterpreted Shelly's question and used it as the butt of one of his regular sarcastic jokes. The point is our family did not know religion. The first time I went to church was when a fifth-grade classmate invited me to attend services with his family at their Lutheran church. I liked David, told my parents about the invitation, and, though I could sense a coolness in their response, they nodded their assent. It was disgusting. Rigid, sterile, dogmatic, pedantic, not something any ten-year-old should ever be forced to sit through. The second visit was in Santa Barbara, when my cousins took me to their Catholic church. No crumbling crackers for me at this one because I was not a Catholic, and though the ceremony was a little more uplifting than the Lutheran service, I left knowing that Catholicism had not won me over.

I was married in a Catholic church, the old St. Joseph's in Capitola. I don't remember if I ever tasted a crumbling cracker during the prep or actual ceremony. Probably not. When they tore that church down within a month after our wedding, I should have known that the marriage wouldn't last, that maybe I should have agreed to the priest's suggestion that I convert to Catholicism to join my wife's faith. Too late. The lovely old church was rubble. So was my marriage. I can't say that my faith was also in rubble, because I never had any faith.

I'm sixty-nine years old. I have found some faith along the way. Faith in my friends. Faith in my family. Faith in the basic goodness of humanity, and the miracle of existence. Faith in my current wife (who was also once a Catholic). I've thought about heading down to Holy Cross Church downtown, walking in some Sunday morning, going through the motions, pretending to be a Catholic, just so I can make my way to the front of the church and have one of those wafers placed on my tongue, taste it just once, have faith in myself that I would turn around, leave the church, and never need to crumble another cracker in my mouth.

As is typical when I know nothing about a topic that I should have learned ages ago, I rely on the Internet, so I plug in "communion" to see what will come up. This will be today's self-imposed lesson. The first definition says, "the sharing or exchanging of intimate thoughts and feelings, especially when the exchange is on a mental or spiritual level." I'm highly interested in what this definition suggests to me, and can't wait to come back and dive into it. But because of the nature of this prompt, I have to focus on the second definition first: "the service of Christian worship at which bread and wine are consecrated and shared." Already my ignorance comes into question. Is it any Christian worship, or is it only Catholic worship? My whole premise could be off base. I dig deeper into the Internet. The first site I find is called Catholic Answers. On the page is an article titled "Why is Communion for Catholics Only?" Ah, I think. There's my answer in the title. But then I read the article that's framed as a dialogue between Catholic and Objector. There's a ton of information there, but by the time I reach the end I still can't tell if other Christian branches also have Communion.

I continue. I find a site called *The Mountaineer,* a newspaper centered in Haywood County, North Carolina. The title of the article is "Communion Ceremonies Vary Among Denominations." Ah. There we have it. Communion is not restricted to Catholics only. I feel like I'm in a catechism class, or should have been a long time ago, not to learn how to be a good Catholic, but to learn how the other side thinks. I considered saying how the "enemy" thinks, but that's not right. They aren't enemies. I do say that about my ultra-conservative right-wing high school friend who has gone over the edge. He is a Facebook friend. I only keep him as a Facebook friend because I want to keep the enemy close at hand, know how he thinks, how he supports and promotes his beliefs, beliefs which I believe are detrimental to a democratic society. I don't feel that way about my other friends and acquaintances who share different beliefs about faith and God and afterlife and a dozen other religious pathways. They all have good intentions and move about their faith in different ways.

The article in *The Mountaineer* says, "The celebration of Holy Communion is a thread that links all Christians." It's times like this when I'm sad I don't have a tribe I am linked to. It's also times like this that I'm thrilled I don't have a tribe whose beliefs I have to ascribe to in order to stay a member. The article continues to describe how Lutherans, Orthodox Christians, Reformed Christians, Presbyterians, Baptists, and others celebrate the sacrament in different ways.

I am so confused now I need to go downstairs and open the box of Stone Ground Wheat Thins and nibble on my own favorite wafer, wash it down with some cran-raspberry juice that I will pretend is wine.

I'm satisfied to know the only time I'll need to enter Holy Cross Church in the future will be for evening performances of the west-side choral group or Cabrillo Symphony, events that won't require me to deal with the crumbling cracker of Communion.

I lower my landing gear, see that the summer fog has hugged itself close to the runway, will make this difficult flight even more difficult to complete. I close my eyes, have faith that my wheels will touch the runway smoothly, taxi me in for a smooth arrival.

Ms. Bossy Pants—
Otherwise Known as CHETKO

Ms. BOSSY PANTS IS NOT A MONIKER I would ever have created for her myself, this Kathy person in my life. It's one she uses often to describe her own actions, actions that know how to get things done effectively using gentle prodding and persuasion. The proddings don't have an electrical shock attached to them, more a nudge of a shoulder, enough momentum to get a ball rolling, to get someone off his lazy ass and get to work on the business at hand.

What about CHETKO, you might ask? It's the first six letters of her last name, it's what follows her name in every email, capitalized, standing out, almost shouting itself to remind people who she is, from where she came, and where she's headed.

To me she's xok. The little "k" following the hugs and kisses in every email. While we have had dozens of visits over the past two years, most of which were in my living room in front of a warm fireplace, those since March in a Zoom room to avoid the potential transfer of Covid germs, the majority of our interactions have occurred through hundreds of emails over the past five years, where we discuss anything and everything. As I think and joke about a "literary estate" and consider the fact that I have no "letters" to speak of, my electronic communications with "k" probably do fit the definition better than anything else.

On one hand, probably the right hand, the one driven by the logically oriented left brain, she would probably dislike that I am writing this profile about her, would rather be the driving force in the background that makes important things happen, without a face, without recognition, simply satisfied by the fact that it works, that what some folks call bossiness is actually a soft assertiveness that is successful. In this right-hand mode, she would prefer being the wizard behind the curtain, the puppeteer guiding the strings.

However, the other hand is attached to the same body, is required along with the right to knit intricate designs that may end up wrapped around the wrists or necks of friends, or as a large afghan to drape across the downstairs sofa. So this left hand, this creative appendage, might appreciate a third-person view of her attributes, one person's accounting of his impressions of her. But probably just to keep to herself, to bury among the other emails and maybe highlight so it's easy to find when she needs a shot to perk her up.

Back to the knitting for a second. Kathy knew from the beginning that I was always cold, having begun my first doses of chemo in the middle of winter. It wasn't long before she showed up in my living room with a pair of blue wrist gloves to help keep my hands and wrists warm as I typed. Of course she knitted the kind with open fingers so I could still fit my fingers on the keyboard and type. This is what she does for people, helps to make the world a better place for them, helps them to be as comfortable as possible.

It's not just me. She has a whole herd of folks she attends to, folks who are scattered across the country from New York City to Bodega Bay to Felton to Santa Cruz. I only have a narrow window into how wide her swath is, but I often think that if there really are such beings as angels that she was sent here ahead of time to make sure all the other angels are doing as good a job as she does. She will be huffing and puffing when she reads this, will say "Poppycock" or "Tommyrot" or some other colorful term indicating that I'm off my rocker.

We met in a playwriting group maybe five years ago. The first time she opened her mouth to share her opinions about a piece of writing I knew immediately we were kindred spirits. She has the ability to read between the lines better than anyone I've ever known. She finds what's not there, what's missing, not those subtexts that we might want to keep hidden, but the words or ideas that make it clear why one sentence should follow another, how one character treats or reacts to another. She is able to pose a question succinctly that causes the playwright to consider what it is the character wants, needs, what motivates them to act or speak in a certain way. She makes us all better writers, better thinkers, better people. Well, most of us. Those of us who consider ourselves lifelong learners and are open to persuasion and new ideas, ideas we had probably never considered.

Before the Covid era, Kathy saw more plays in a month than anyone I knew. San Francisco, Berkeley, San Jose, Santa Cruz, Monterey, and an occasional jaunt back to New York to see everything she could. This itinerary, along with a lifeline to her director friend in New York City, keeps her steeped in everything theater. And since Covid, as theaters grapple with how to succeed with online venues and solutions, I believe she has watched more Zoom presentations than anyone and has opened her brain to the possibilities that will allow us to continue our foray into creative ventures that keep our minds fresh, our work innovative.

I won't share with you all the ways that Kathy has enriched my life over the past two years, because it would embarrass both of us. But I will tell you about the Companion Bakery coffee-cake rolls she brings, the ones that crunch and melt on my tongue. And I can tell you about the bunches of flowers she finds somewhere between her house and ours that brighten up a mantel, remind me that there is an out-of-doors with plants growing and people tending them. It's probably also okay to tell you about the exotic chocolates she brings back from New York City and shares with us. Then there's the introduction she made between her friend and hairdresser, Christina MacColl, and us, which enhanced not only my hairdo but also my life, another person who embodies the same qualities as Kathy. Or Claudia Sternbach, another of her close friends whom I was thrilled to meet. The list is endless, and would truly cause us both to blush if it were all written out here, because the pages would be way too long, the reading of it out loud causing us to lose our voices, our minds, to release the cords that ground us and allow the helium to carry us into another dimension.

If she were to return to the East Coast to continue her pursuit of Broadway and Off-Broadway success, the news would be almost as devastating as learning of the tumor residing in my pancreas. This time, instead of an intrusion of my body, I would be suffering from an exclusion from my mind, my life.

Luckily, I don't foresee that happening. She is firmly rooted in the landscape and community of Santa Cruz. Ms. Bossy Pants is here to stay, and that makes me smile and bow.

Side by Side

I HAVE BEEN USING TECHNOLOGY since the first Apple computers were introduced in the early 1980s. I purchased an Apple 2e in 1983 and would carry it back and forth between my home and my classroom Monday through Friday. At that point in time, Microsoft and Apple had a rocky relationship, and Word wasn't developed for the Macs until 1985. I discovered the Bank Street Writer word-processor program on floppy disk, and began teaching myself how to word process.

At about the same time I started writing grants to help me develop materials and trainings for both students and teachers. One grant allowed me to purchase two 300-baud modems, one that sat plugged into my computer in the classroom, and the other plugged into a computer at a sister classroom in Davenport. We created online pen pals between my students and the students in Davenport.

Daily Fresh

After twelve solid years working in educational technology, I received the National Christa McAuliffe Fellowship that paid for my full salary for one year to develop virtual field trips on the Internet for students and teachers. Eventually I was hired by Apple Computer to become the managing editor of a new program called Apple Learning Interchange (ALI).

These few paragraphs are intended to show the depth and breadth of my studies and projects in and around the uses of technology. Some thirty-eight years later I'm still at it, fingers on keyboard for many hours a day. I've become good at it, am a mentor to many, find myself as the primary 24/7 tech support for a few friends and my mom. I'm not bragging, but I want you to understand that I enjoy problem solving and am usually successful at reaching workable solutions.

My most recent venture into the deeper levels of technology has occurred around the Covid pandemic that the world has been facing since March. California was shut down initially by Governor Newsom on March 19. For those of us in the literary world used to heading down to Bookshop Santa Cruz a couple nights a week to hear readings, check in with friends, meet new people, the shutdown has been extra devastating. A year or so earlier, my friend Scott introduced me to an online communication tool called Zoom, where folks could see and speak to each other through their computer screens. Within a week of the shutdown, I was producing *Zoom Forward!* reading events where I invited local poets and authors, usually two or three per reading. We used a Mailchimp email campaign to invite hundreds of folks to attend. As of tomorrow night, we will have produced twenty-four Friday night readings. While there was a learning curve, it has been wildly successful.

And that brings me to the current venture. One of my very best friends who is in my playwriting group suggested that I consider presenting three of my short plays using the Zoom environment. Each of my three plays has only two actors. In the theatrical world, they are called two-handers. I started thinking about how two-handers might be produced, started thinking about the typical windows that participants appear in, and if it would be possible to have them appear side by side on the screen. Because of the general need, due to Covid, to have actors be on their computers in different locations, how to simulate what is seen on screen to represent the reality of the scene became a more and more challenging problem to solve.

For a couple of weeks, we experimented, and finally I decided that Zoom Meeting software was not enough, so I purchased the Zoom Webinar add-on. We continued to experiment, to research everything we could find on the Zoom site and YouTube and the sites of dozens of theater companies who were also trying to figure out the same issues as we were. All of the earlier mentions of my tech successes and savvy were leading up to my total sense of failure at figuring out how to have two actors side by side, using virtual backgrounds that made it look like they were sitting next to each other. I fell into a depression I haven't allowed under my skin in a very long time. It was a low point in my life, only because it was combined with a number of other issues over which I also felt a complete lack of control, a uselessness and helplessness I wasn't used to.

I eventually snapped out of it, and both Kathy and I began scouring the Internet and people we knew who might be able to help us out. Kathy contacted the artistic director of Santa Cruz Shakespeare, Mike Ryan, who met with us in a Zoom meeting and basically told us everything we needed to know to solve our problems. The next day, someone I had reached out to sent an email with the same information. Halle-fucking-lujah! Progress!

At last. While we haven't tested the truths of our new information, we will do so next week, and I'm confident it will work.

As it turns out, one person steeped in a lifetime of successes in the field of technology can be easily stumped and temporarily tumble into oblivion, feeling as if the end is near, as if it's time to check into a skilled-nursing facility and let someone else take control of the remote and flip the channels for you. But two, or three, or more working in concert to offer pieces to complete a puzzle is more valuable than the gold bullions of Fort Knox.

I'm so looking forward to these side-by-side productions that maybe even Sondheim would appreciate.

Style-ish

THERE IS A THEME that has been wading around in small puddles outside my sliding glass door, sometimes dances in the tiny feet of birds bobbing for seeds on my deck, suggests itself in the words and thoughts of others, appears as synonyms of itself in a thesaurus, flickers in the lit windows of houses on the hillside of Positano, Italy.

I don't want to label it yet, because application of a label is the opposite of what it intends to share with the world. When I try to remember when the thought first occurred to me, I'm unable to give a date, a starting point, as it has been unrecognizable as a concept to me, and I've had to get out of my own way, peel old layers of skin away to bare the raw flesh of where it lives. I know, this does not sound very transparent, too obscure, buried away like the puzzles that good poets hate. "Tell me what you see, what you observe, how it matters. Don't make me have to dig and pretend to understand what you are trying to say."

So I apologize that it may take some time for me to work through this one, to understand the double bind required to even think about it, to construct this piece, a framing of sorts that flies in the face of its very existence. To stay true to its message, there is no one definitive starting point at which all racers stand toe to toe ready to run this marathon. No starting gun that blasts at seven in the morning to get feet moving, blood flowing, inhales and exhales rapidly increasing. And likewise, there is no definitive end point, no finish line with adoring family and friends wildly waving their hands and screaming. Which I know is awkward. The idea of constructing this piece requires a starting point, an end point, a frame in which to think about the concept. But in truth, if I could figure out a way to portray this particular Daily Fresh in a circular fashion, I would do so, let you jump in wherever you will.

With all that behind us now, let me offer the word *style* as one way into this concept, an entrance that I'm sure you have already gleaned from the title of this essay. Before resorting to my Internet searches for a variety of definitions, I begin by thinking of style as a particular package that folks wrap themselves in. Styles can change over time, but there's a core learning that takes place over one's life that begins to carve wrinkles into foreheads that tend not to change, only deepen. Let me see if I can objectively stand outside myself and see if I can recognize and describe my style. I tend to be quiet, to be inside my head, to be paying attention to and observing what is going on around me, with other people, with sports teams, with animals that live in our backyard. At earlier points in my life I was a true introvert, preferring to hole up rather than engage. At a recent writing group one of the members said she had something to share, but that she wasn't sending us a hard copy, just wanted us to listen to it. Having been a classroom teacher for thirty years, I've researched learning styles: tactile, verbal, visual, and their hybrid combinations. I know that verbal learning by itself is not my strongest area. I actually prefer more of a hybrid, where I can be looking at a document while it's being read. I did this with George Saunders' wonderful novel *Lincoln in the Bardo*, bought the hard copy and the Audible version, and listened to a host of readers while I read along in the book. This style is not a choice, is not one that I can easily modify. I might say that it is innate, that I was born with a certain DNA that forced me in that direction.

During that same writing group, the notion of preference came up. Preference suggests that choice does play a role in determining one's style. One member has always refused to listen to or care about a certain mode of critique that involves the word *why*. Another member, who is also a martial artist, mentioned the notion of style as per Bruce Lee. In a subsequent email my friend went on to clarify Lee's ideas. He said that Lee didn't believe in style. That style was a crystallization, and that crystallization becomes dogma. Apparently in China, in the world of martial arts there is a Northern style and a Southern style. Early on in Lee's life he figured out that he wanted "no style as style." As a teacher, his students always wanted him to put a name on his "style." Eventually he was forced to give it a name: Jeet Kune Do, a formless form of Chinese kung fu.

Such a fascinating thought, that categorizing oneself in a certain style locks down an ability to be creative and spontaneous. Style causes us to build a world of expectations around it to support it, expectations we put on ourselves and that others put on us. In the extreme, it functions a bit like a straitjacket, keeping us restrained, unable to have a range of freedom that allows movement in a 360-degree fashion.

Last night I participated in a Poetry Society of New York Zoom presentation led by poet Kaveh Akbar. He was brilliant and all over the board and hard to understand, given that the presentation was primarily verbal, from a piece of writing that rambled on in many directions. Given my earlier stated learning style, much of it was difficult for me. But much of it was not, especially when he talked about the ideas of a few other folks. One such person was M. NourbeSe Philip, who has a ten-minute video of a poem she's written called "Discourse on the Logic of Language," in which she breaks free from the tyranny of the left margin.

Another phrase I heard during the presentation was "undoing the damage of habituation." Again, style, which has so often been thought of as a good thing, takes over and forces one to remain locked into well-formed ruts that guide one down the always-familiar pathways toward certainty. That we think of damage and habit in the same breath should be a sign. A sign that any sense of certainty should be avoided, that folks who use certainty to guide their lives, and often attempt to guide the lives of others, are ones to be watched. Not shunned, but observed carefully to understand how they are limiting themselves and falling short of their potential.

I love the idea of shunning the left margin. I don't know how to make it happen, but I have made it a light bulb to consider in the near future. It may have something to do with a circular presentation, writing in the form of a mandala where the entry point doesn't begin with a title, or a first sentence. Instead, a phrase or a word jumps out and guides the reader in to enjoy their own pace, their own pathway through the maze. I know. It sounds absurd. Sounds impossible. Much like some of my stream-of-consciousness ramblings that have received complaints from some reviewers.

But I will continue the grand experiment of humility guided by uncertainty, of attempting to capture readers by using fresh approaches to sharing ideas, by not being afraid to suggest expectations as possible foreshadowings, but then going sideways, jumping down a rabbit hole, and taking them and me someplace completely unexpected. Fresh.

The Urge to Submerge

I F I DIVE IN WITHOUT BEING PROMPTED, I worry that I will find myself on familiar pathways that I've forgotten I know, will rethink and rewrite topics that have already been dredged up and rung out in front of a live audience, even if that audience of one was only me.

I look back at the first sentence to determine if there's anything of value there, if one word or phrase might break something loose, a large wall of ice that cracks and falls from a floe and causes a humongous splash in the sea waiting to catch it. Third word in. The word is *dive*. I'll hop on its back and ride it forward into what's next, see if I find traction, listen to its whistle and smell its fumes.

I learned to dive in 1960 at the Dalkes' pool in San Lorenzo, a sleepy little suburb tucked in between San Leandro and Hayward. We lived on a quiet *cul-de-sac* across the street from

Evelyn Dalke and her pool. She was a bit crotchety but was an excellent swim instructor. The first thing she told us was that they used a special chemical in the water that would turn your pee blue if you dared to relieve yourself in her pool. We believed her, no blue monster ever seeping out of our swimsuits. We also believed her when she said diving was easy, fun, would liberate our minds and allow us to travel to the moon or walk on hot coals if we so chose.

At ten years old, I didn't understand her insinuations about the connection between water and fire and rocket ships blasting off from Cape Canaveral, but I believed her, the closest thing to faith I had in my life. The first time she led me to the diving board, I shook, wanted to run home and hide myself in my room under the safety of blankets and sheets in my familiar and cozy bed. But she wouldn't let me, stayed with me until my toes wiggled over the edge, her holding my shoulders firmly behind me. This would not be a running dive. Those would come later. She showed me how to lock my thumbs, raise my arms, and point to the spot where I wanted to land. She showed me how to flex my knees, how to create a springlike tension in my body that terminated in my toes and the balls of my feet, an uncoiling that propelled me up and out and into the water. The first few attempts resulted in belly flops that splashed water out of the pool and into Evelyn's flower beds, her screaming "No, no, no, no, no." Five of them. I remember distinctly that her chorus of Nos when critiquing a student was always five syllables long.

Within a week of lessons, my pointed fingers were making perfect entries into the glass-like surface of the water, my body following their lead with no splash, a sleekness, an accomplishment that made me proud. Sticking with the water theme connected to the word *dive,* my next venture was to the Hayward Plunge up on Mission Boulevard not too far from our house. Mom would drive us up, drop me and a friend or two off for the day, with lunches and towels and jackets. It was a huge facility with a number of outdoor pools, and a huge indoor pool. The diving boards were scattered about and varied in height, some rivaling Olympic-size jumps. I had gained my confidence at Evelyn's pool and was happy to show off my skill on one or two of the boards, but not the ones that were taller than me. When we'd become sufficiently waterlogged, we'd hike up the adjacent trail into the woods along a creek, find a bench to park ourselves and eat our lunches, knowing we weren't going back in the pools, so not worrying about cramps from food in our stomachs. Tuna-fish and egg-salad sandwiches with crunchy potato chips and pickles, Coca Cola in bottles, and a Hershey's almond bar for dessert. What a life we led.

I'd run into the word and concept of *dive* a few more times in my early education. From my sixth-grade teacher, Mrs. Hussein, I learned the nautical meaning of dive, like the submerging of a submarine, of which we had many examples in 1962 as the Cold War was heating up and many of our *Weekly Reader* issues shared photos and stories. From my seventh-grade teacher, Mr. Boynton, I moved out of the water and into the air, where I learned the aviation references explaining how pilots could achieve steep descents by pointing the noses of their planes downward.

In high school my father forced me to drive up with him to campus the summer before my freshman year to sign up for football. I hated the thought, but my size and ability kept me at it for all four years, making varsity as a junior. The coach had names for our plays. They usually had matching first letters. The two I'm thinking of now were Dive and Dart. They were designed to gain short yardage needed for a first down. The running back would get the handoff from the quarterback and plunge into the line off the center and guards' sides, hoping to gain a yard or two.

Daily Fresh

Back in those days before work and marriage, I'd sit with my dad on Friday nights and watch the *Gillette Cavalcade of Sports* broadcast from Madison Square Garden in New York. In 1965 we watched the rematch of the Mohammad Ali vs. Sonny Liston fight. Towards the end of an early round, Ali hit Liston hard, and Liston went down and stayed down. The crowd went nuts. The commentary after the fight and ensuing articles suggested that Liston had underworld ties and that he may very well have taken a "dive" in the fight for monetary reasons. I hadn't heard the word used in this context before. But it made sense, had a connection to a falling forward, a downward plunge, whether intentional or not.

I was not much of a drinker, but I loved to play games like pool and shuffleboard and darts, and would occasionally find myself in a bar or tavern that was known for having a seedy clientele, folks who were looking for a brawl, ready to cause a ruckus for little or no reason. I learned quickly why these types of venues were called dives. I wasn't quite sure of the connection to my previous understanding of the word, but when I thought about it, it had to do with the nature of the clientele who had made choices in their lifestyles to visit and support such establishments, that the dive had to do with those choices they had made, that their lives were on a downward trend that found them plummeting, plunging into a degree of darkness.

On September 29, 2008, the world saw the stock market take a dive, falling 777.68 points. The word they tend to use is crash, but it was clearly a dive, a plummet, a sinking, where individuals and companies lost everything.

The way I interact with dive these days is in a positive manner. I think of the successes I had in the pool across the street, of the success we had on the football field with the Dive and Dart plays, and today, my diving has to do with the desire to learn more about as many things as I can. A conscious dive into a research project, hands first, a sleek entry with very little splashing, sinking to the bottom of a pool and locating treasures for the taking.

Extracting the Fossil

IT BEGINS FIRST BY IMAGINING that there are real fossils buried in remote places or even in your backyard that are eagerly waiting for you to locate them, to free them from their encasements, their lifelong existence in straightjackets formed from erosion and earthquakes and rivulets of water that have surrounded them in hardened cake and frosting that require delicate tools for removal.

But let's not get ahead of ourselves. We are nowhere near leaping into the removal phase. Let me also say that this is no original idea. I'm stealing it from Stephen King, who mentions it in his book *On Writing*. I'm simply taking his idea and embellishing it. That's hilarious when you think about it. Me, embellishing a Stephen King idea. But he expects it, wrote this book so people would imitate him, be prompted by his thoughts, feel invited to steal whatever they like.

Let's go back to the imagining phase. What does that look like? What is it that we are trying to imagine with this endless supply of fossils? Even though calcified over time, each fossil wants to be touched, wants to breathe the fresh air of spring, wend its way through the seasons, be showcased and shared with those who are ready to see it, to listen to the crackle in its bones, to smell the years of decay, to hear the ancient battles that caused it to be buried away for so long.

These fossils are stories, or, if not complete stories, they are fragments, phrases, single words that incite riots and avalanches. They do not exist without our imagination. Or they may exist but without form, buried so deeply that no human, no writer, would ever be able to grasp or view them. Every novel, short story, essay, play, piece of flash fiction, exists solely to display the fossil on which it was founded. Or possibly more than one fossil, although well-aged and well-imagined fossils will usually not want to share the stage with others.

So how do we imagine, or identify, or create the fossils we need to use to grow our writing to fruition? Blueberries help. They call it a brain food. Drugs and alcohol don't work for me. I need to stay fresh and focused, set aside dedicated time to think, to crank the sometimes-rusty winch that squeaks open the hinges that expose my brain and allow whatever I hear, see, taste, touch, smell, to leap in and attach itself to brain cells. It often occurs as a conscious activity to take the time and energy to focus, to discover the locations where the fossils might be buried, might be hiding, might be my Easter eggs in waiting. It also happens in the middle of the night just before and after when I force my legs off the bed and walk to the bathroom to pee. The bladder is a signal. It lets me know it's time to wake up and relieve myself, but I'm not quite ready to move my numb feet, my thick legs, so I lie there, wondering about the size and shape and age of fossils. When I finally get my body to the bathroom, finish my business, I find my way back to the bed, the pillow, snuggle in, and watch the parade of potential fossils slide by as I regain my sleep. We use every waking and sleeping moment to scan the horizon for the aura of hidden fossils.

Once successfully imagined, brought to life in a way that convinces us that they do truly exist, we plant tiny luminescent flags with blinking lights in the spots where we believe the fossils reside. It becomes a large map of the planet with flags blinking everywhere. The next phase is a matter of choice. The map can be overwhelming, can lead to paralysis by analysis, with so many different fossils to choose from. It's now time to kick in that sixth sense, a little ESP that allows you to let loose of your conscious mind and allow the blinking lights to guide you, to prioritize themselves, to act like a Geiger counter or GPS that sucks you forward, brings you to your knees in front of the loudest, brightest, most active flag whose fossil wants to be found first.

There is one more phase to construct prior to the excavation phase: the toolbox phase. No archaeological dig has ever been successful in the removal of precious fossils without having a proper toolbox at hand. When the Coelophysis was unearthed in 1947 at the Ghost Ranch fossil site in New Mexico, you can bet that archaeologists had truckloads of the highest-grade tools available to successfully remove the gorgeous skeleton. We spend a lifetime reading how-to books, listening to lectures, reading interviews in the *Paris Review,* and now signing up for Zoom readings that are springing up everywhere and becoming requirements by publishers of their authors. When we hear something that resonates, we toss it in our toolboxes, save it in case it might be useful in the future. We overfill the toolbox, buy additional toolboxes, fill bookshelves and bookmark folders and order books from independent bookstores like Bookshop Santa Cruz, and we read, we study, we prepare ourselves, we work out, build up our mental muscle, get ready for the big dig.

Finally, on hands and knees, we pray to whatever gods we think might be able to help us through this next phase. We kiss the blinking light on the noisiest flag, remove it carefully and begin with small tools to displace dirt: toothpicks, cocktail forks, Q-tips, tiny tools from antique medical kits found at the flea market. When we see the first indication that a fossil might be near, we bring out the brushes, gently touch the surface, look for some sign of understanding, of how the fossil might be of use, if it even wants to be messed with, or if it would prefer to remain undisturbed, keep its secrets hidden for another millennium.

When we find one that is shouting for freedom, we work our way around its perimeter, lift carefully with salad tongs and velvet strings, set it carefully on a stand we have built specifically to hold it in place.

We now enter the observational phase. The examination. Depending on the individual nature of the fossil, this process could take minutes, or decades. It's in the examination phase that we may determine that the fossil may be useful to us. Or it may sit there on its stand in public view until it demands to be returned to its hole.

The fossils that have a heart, that breathe with insistence, will make their way into our lives, or work, will become the center of our stories, will uncover personality traits and locations and the complex texture of the words we are about to choose.

Every phase in the process provides us with usable information. We imagine, we map, we locate, we excavate, we observe, we write, and the fossils come to life in ways we never expected, they inhabit and take over our thoughts, our direction, the stories we must tell.

Mel Ott vs. Willie Mays

I DON'T KNOW YET WHAT FOSSIL is at the core of today's piece. It's a cold-call morning, doves already at the feeding tray outside, their calm demeanor wearing the shroud of fog well. I love their softness, how they don't flit their head around as much as the jays or woodpeckers, how they accept the chaos around them, even when the squirrel jumps up and edges them out.

Cold calls usually require a list of unknown names and phone numbers and a script containing what you are asking these folks, what it is you are trying to sell them, how much time is left before the offer expires. The closest thing I have to a list is seven pages of notes from an Anne Lamott workshop on Saturday paired with three dozen light bulbs gleaned from reading sections of Stephen King's book *On Writing*. It's possible that Stephen King himself could be the fossil I'm looking for today. At seventy-two years old, he is a bit of an ancient relic, though I expect him to continue to crank out best sellers until his nineties, like P.D. James, who published *Death Comes to Pemberley* when she was ninety-one.

What I am asking is for a fossil to appear. It need not be fully formed, can just be peeking out, expose just enough of itself to excite my interest. What I am trying to sell is myself, make myself seem worthy enough to accept the fossil's gift, its existence, its willingness to be mined and used by me for an hour or so, along with a clear deadline, which is now.

While taking notes on King's thoughts, I'm not sure why, but I recalled my fanatic love of everything to do with the Giants' baseball team. Maybe it was King talking about what his day looked like: writing something new in the morning, taking a nap in the afternoon, family and watching the Red Sox in the evening, and maybe some revision before going to bed.

For me, my addiction to baseball began early, when my dad took me to Seals Stadium in San Francisco on April 15, 1958, to watch the Giants beat the Dodgers 8-0, fueled by Willie Mays and Orlando Cepeda defeating Don Drysdale. It continued as games began being televised, and even more so when my parents bought me the Strat-o-Matic Baseball game in 1962. At eleven years old, I had never seen or heard of the game, so when I saw the long, flat box under the Christmas tree that year I assumed it was Monopoly or Clue, also games that I loved, but we already had them, so I wasn't sure why I'd need another. But when I ripped off the wrapping paper and saw the word *Baseball* prominently featured on the cover, I was ecstatic. Not much raised my blood pressure in those days, but I was thrilled with this gift.

Until that point in my life, as a young sixth grader, I had never really cared much about studies, about learning new things in school. My dad had been sick and was in the hospital for nine months without me being able to visit, and even though

Daily Fresh

it wasn't called PTSD in those days, I was suffering from it. But when Strat-o-Matic appeared in my life, everything changed. Not my tendency toward introversion and shyness, but my desire to learn everything I could about baseball players and stadiums and the math required to calculate batting averages and earned run averages and percentages. I was also not very organized, had never had a reason to be organized, until I cracked open the box and marveled at what was inside.

Half the box was filled with a cardboard replication of a baseball field. The first thing I had to do was take the lid off the box and slip it under the back edge so it would stand up at the back, providing me with reams of information that I'd need to play a game. There was a sheet of perforated orange split cards numbered from 1 to 20. These cards were used in certain situations to determine the outcome of an at bat. Every major league team for the previous year was represented, a pile of twenty 3x5 cards with every player having his own card. Batters' cards had three columns numbered 1, 2, and 3. Pitchers' cards had three columns numbered 4, 5, and 6. The numbers matched up with the numbers on three dice. The red die determined whether you played on the batters' cards. If you did, a 1, 2, or 3 number told you which of three columns to look at to determine what happened during an at bat. Each of those columns had possible baseball plays arranged 2 through 12, corresponding to the possible number totals of the two white dice.

Every card had been calculated mathematically based on the previous year's statistics for each player. The first game I played was between the San Francisco Giants, my favorite team, and the New York Yankees. The Yankees won, 7-2, behind stellar pitching by Ralph Terry. It became apparent that I would not be able to replicate a full 162-game-per-team schedule unless I was allowed to quit school and give up my household chores and lock myself away in my room 24/7. So, I had my mom buy me a supply of yellow legal pads at Woolworth's along with a box of #2 pencils and a pencil sharpener, and that was all I needed.

Instead of using all twenty major league teams, I chose the top five teams from both the National and American Leagues, and proceeded to build a schedule where each of the ten teams played every other team five times. Thus I had a fifty-game schedule, organized chronologically, with empty columns to tally results of each game. On a separate yellow sheet, I had one page that listed the standings in each league. Lots of erasing to update the standings after each game played, such that every few games I'd have to recreate the standings sheet to account for the erasure holes in the paper.

I also designed a team-statistics sheet for each of the ten teams, where I could track games played, batting averages, RBIs, home runs, wins and losses, ERAs, and everything else I could figure out using math to make these paper players come to life.

I never got bored with these games. However, on reading the materials that came with the game, I discovered that I could purchase sets of old-timer teams, the best teams ever assembled with the best records. As it turned out, I couldn't purchase the teams, because I had no money as an eleven-year-old, but I could mow lawns and do other assorted chores and have Mom or Grandma order the teams for me.

With ten more teams, I could now mix up my schedules, could have the 1932 New York Giants play a world series of seven games with the 1962 San Francisco Giants. The setup to this series and the playing of it was one of the highlights of my young life. I'd make popcorn with melted butter, cook up a couple of hot dogs, bring a tall bottle of Coke, close my bedroom door on a Saturday morning, and never emerge until the series was decided. In 1932, Melvin Thomas Ott, popularly known as Mel Ott, was right fielder for the New York Giants. He played in 154 games, hit 38 home runs, scored 119 runs, had 180 hits, knocked in 135 runs, and had a .318 batting average. He was tenth on votes received for Most Valuable Player. On the other side, Willie Mays played in all 162 games, hit 49 home runs, scored 130 runs, had 189 hits, knocked in 141 runs, and had a batting average of .304.

The stage was set. The concession stands were overflowing with hungry fans wolfing down their hot dogs and popcorn, washing them down with cola, waiting for the national anthem to trigger the events of the day. I couldn't sing, so I didn't try to replicate Bessie Smith or Mahalia Jackson, but I did find a way beyond my introversion when it was only me, and 40,000 fans. I became the announcer, the umpires, the managers for both teams, every player, and I had the necessary conversations with the players and myself to complete the series. There really was no way for me to manipulate the actions and outcomes so that my preferences ruled the results. There were the rolls of dice, the reading of results on cards, picking random split cards as needed. And I didn't really have a preference. I loved Willie Mays. I loved Mel Ott. I loved that I had created a venue where they could play on the same field and battle it out with each other.

By Sunday evening I was ready for game seven, the series now tied at 3 to 3. So far the stats had Ott ahead in home runs and RBIs, Mays leading with runs and average. Carl Hubbell of the '32 NY Giants had pitched and won all three games. I guess maybe I did abuse the arms of the pitchers by having them pitch every other game rather than have their typical three days of rest. On the SF Giants, Jack Sanford, Billy O'Dell, and Juan Marichal won one game each. Hubbell got the call again for the final game, along with Jack Sanford. The game went extra innings, and I felt a bit guilty about letting Hubbell and Sanford pitch into the extra innings, but what the hell, it was the World Series. I fell asleep in the middle of the fifteenth inning, had to wake up early before Monday-morning school and complete the series. Willie Mays hit a home run in the bottom of the eighteenth inning, leading the '62 SF Giants to a 7-6 victory over the '32 NY Giants. Ott vs. Mays proved to be as exciting as I could ever have imagined.

I continued to hone my research skills, my math abilities, my tendency toward organizing, and my undeniable love of baseball. I'm certain that Strat-o-Matic Baseball changed my life in innumerable ways. That I scored in the 99th percentile in math on the SATs can only be explained by the reams of accumulated yellow pads over the years. It could also explain why reading and writing lagged behind in the tests, as I spent all my time creating and living in these fantasy worlds rather than spending an equal amount of time buried in *The Chronicles of Narnia* or *Alice's Adventures in Wonderland*.

When I began my career as a classroom teacher, I bought a 1962 version of Strat-o-Matic Baseball and had each student pick a team. Rather than use textbooks to teach math, we ran a year-long league where each student had their own version of yellow pads, tracked all the stats, learned more about math by falling in love with their teams and players and tracking their successes and failures than they ever could by cranking out worksheets.

Six feet from my bed on a dusty bottom shelf my Strat-o-Matic game box still occupies a commanding spot. If I remember correctly, the Willie Mays card and the Mel Ott card are back to back on an all-star team created by me to play against my wife. They both hit multiple home runs in that game, jogged around the bases, waved at their adoring fans, and I waved back.

Another Good Week

TRYING TO DEFINE THE FEATURES of what makes a week good can sometimes elude me, find me holed up under an electric blanket on my bed at noon hoping to fight off the chill of the summer fog. It's sometimes easier to recognize and list the features of the bad week that occurred twenty or so days ago and compare those features to what has so far turned out to be a good week.

Strangely enough, the things that caused me to define the previous week as bad were not physical, as they can so often be, but were of the mental variety that drilled into my brain as if my dentist was trying to drill out a cavity or give me a root canal. The ensuing infection from his work blossomed into pulsating brain waves that wouldn't allow me to rest, caused a minor depression that pulled me away from my unstoppable trajectory. A long list of issues relating to my mom's continuing health problems and well-being rested at the apex of the list. Wheelchair and rollator and bed alarm and cutting a chunk out of a metal bathtub and hand railings and appointment scheduling and meals and her falling and having IBS and a dozen more factors that make her life difficult, and equally as disturbing, make my sister's life difficult, as she is on the front lines, living there full-time, having to deal with this list of problems every day, while I sit at home most of the time in a useless and helpless state of mind.

The uselessness and helplessness added to those mental brain waves that went out of whack in my head, sent me spiraling into a vortex that pulled me down. I'm good at what I do. Mostly on the computer. Writing, Word documents, Excel spreadsheets, Internet research, organizing, prioritizing what projects I might be able to do given the knowledge of a shortened timeline. But I'm no good at the tasks that need physical or in-person attention. I am mostly holed up in my shelter-in-place existence, and during that bad week, it felt claustrophobic and never-ending. In addition, in this pathway of becoming a writer, I have generally become good at receiving negative critiques of my work and rejections from publishers and literary magazines, knowing that it is one major part of the process that requires attention and also requires the ability to let it go and ignore it. During this bad week, I was less successful at letting it go, instead let it bore into my skin like a tick, felt it swell and heat.

I was able to break the spell, come back to the light, touch the head of a match to the tick and watch it leave my body, return to the focus necessary to proceed. And that has brought us to this new week, a good week, *another* good week, because regardless of everything else going on, I am looking at almost every week as being a good one. So what are the features of this good week?

- Terry finished another project for us, the sanding and staining of cabinets and doors in our studio so that it will be pristine when Georgia and AJ move in. And he did it quickly and reasonably. It's always a good week when Terry is in our lives. We'll need to keep finding projects for him to solve for us.

- We have solved the wheelchair problem, or nearly, or maybe doubly. I've ordered one which will be delivered tomorrow. And Kathy thinks she has located footrests for a chair she had given us. This is huge, as my mother lives on a hillside with lots of steep stairs and it's difficult to get her down to the car for appointments.

- The bed alarm I found, SafeWanderer, developed by a young Japanese man for his grandfather, works great and helps Shelly relax a little more, at least on that front.

- The rejections continue to roll in, but I smile when they do, know that it's part of the game.

- Then on Sunday, I was in my weekly Zoom meeting with Kathy when up popped an email from Paper Angel Press, saying they wanted to publish my novel *Pious Rebel*, and would have it out before the end of the year! I cried. The email from the acquisitions editor was glowing and helped me celebrate possibly the best day of my life. And she wants to read everything else I've ever written.

- Yesterday we had masked and distanced visits from our friends Dave and Maria, as well as our friends Woody and Jennifer, and our good buddy Janie.

What a great day! What a great week! I know I'll hit bumpy spots, go up and down depending on factors beyond my control, like the results of today's CT scan, like whether or not we continue to attack this adenocarcinoma inside my pancreas, like whether or not my mom progresses or fades.

I also know that I am driven, that I now have a relationship with a publisher who likes my work, wants more of it, and I am focused on a daily output to provide them and myself and my friends who have been by my side through all of it with evidence of progress and forward movement regardless of the results of blood tests and CT scans and the other inevitable roadblocks that attempt to slow me down.

As Gloria Gaynor first belted out in 1978, "I will survive!" At least part of me will survive. Lisa Hardrock will survive. Other pieces of writing, thoughts, ideas will survive well beyond my flesh and bones.

And that makes me happy, and provides the cap to another good week.

My Summer Fog

I CALL IT MINE even though I know that's absurd. The all-about-me view of the world that carries with it an arrogant sheen as the dawn sky stares at me through my bedroom slider. It's Anne Lamott's one-inch picture frame through which I view the world before I wake and remember there are others.

Of course it's not *my* summer fog. It's *our* summer fog. A hazy wetness I'm thrilled to share with you. A blanket that will toss itself aside by noon.

She cools our morning. We walk her to the beach and hunt for the horizon. Watch for the flocks of Arctic terns we know are hidden behind the veil, traveling from pole to pole and back, a 44,300-mile round trip. These red-billed beauties make our days, our whole lives, when we get a glimpse, when our fog chooses to release its grip and give us a snapshot of infinity, of what seems to have no end.

It's better when it's not about me, when it's us, forging a fire in a pit on Twin Lakes Beach, sticking hot dogs on coat hangers and dipping them into relish and mustard, as we begin to see the hills of Monterey bleed through across the bay. Will we hug, wrap a blanket around our shoulders and wait? Or stay six feet apart?

We are patient. We love seeing our summer fog give up its control, ease into the day, provide an opening for an afternoon of expected heat. The sun finally pokes through as we twist marshmallows over the flames, place them hot on Hershey's chocolate bars and graham crackers, remember our younger selves doing the same sixty years ago.

Youngsters with their parents toss off their shoes, their down jackets, head for the water. We watch. Smile. Nod our heads. Hydrate ourselves with gulps from our water bottles, can now clearly see the stacks from the Moss Landing power plant, and not the terns, but other flocks claiming their air space.

Together, we paint pictures of our pasts where we dipped a shoulder into a wave, tucked our heads and rolled until our feet touched the sand and the balls of our feet shot us out of the water.

We've lived here our whole lives. Have walked the beaches with her from Waddell Creek to Pajaro Dunes. Summers don't feel the same on days she forgets to appear. We feel abandoned.

At home again by myself in my room, I see her creep up the valley, bury Rodeo Gulch Road in her cloak.

And here is where I apologize. To you. To everyone. I reclaim *my* summer fog. Make her all mine once again. Just until I fall asleep. Just until I wake again and remember that I'm not alone.

A Deep Clean

A SIMPLE EMAIL THAT POPS UP in the corner of a screen while you are having your weekly Sunday morning Zoom meeting with a very good friend can make all the difference, can trigger a complicated Rube Goldberg contraption that sets your world in motion in ways you'd never imagined. After reading the first sentence your eyes moisten, you bare yourself to your friend, who has been with you since the beginning on this journey to turn your novel *Pious Rebel* into something someone might want to publish. After a few rejections over the past five weeks, this email changes everything, lets you know that you will be holding your published book in your hands before Christmas.

The moistened eyes act as a rinse, a cleansing of toxins, a river of emotions coursing through veins. Overly sentimental song lyrics appear that I haven't considered in decades, "Dawning" by Jay and the Americans.

The cleansing lays bare a platform, a space, a state of mind where you will begin building your Rube Goldberg miracle, piece by piece, inch by inch, idea by idea. You start by constructing an enclosure, a corral, a place to move around and give yourself room to dance, to breathe in deeply, get your life in order, where your wife can be with you and do her yoga. The fence that encloses you is made up of printed copies of emails between you and the publisher, you and the acquisitions editor, the ones you sent to every person who has assisted you on the journey.

It's beginning to look like an arena, one large enough to encompass the first and second stories of your house, the writing room overlooking your refurbished deck, the toolshed, the memory garden, the brass ensemble that lines your front yard with miniature succulents, room to expand the notion of a literary estate that you've been considering, room to spread things out, examine them, make decisions, move forward with specific goals in mind.

You take one comfortable chair into the center of the arena and sit, close your eyes, having left landlines and cell phones and audiobooks and how-to books and every other possible implement of distraction behind. You raise the screen inside your head and turn on a miniature projector that flashes videos and still images of your life and every other life and mind who may have been in a situation like this. Rube himself, Virginia Woolf, Proust, George Carlin, Frank Gehry, folks who enjoyed figuring things out, finding a way in, forging a pathway. Because that's exactly what you're doing, seeking the entry point that allows a smooth transition to what eventually will become the end point, the landing the achievement of the initial goal.

But you can't land on the beginning or end point until you imagine all the transitions and connectors and puzzle pieces and pieces of paper and binders full of critiques and reviews, all of it amid a cluster of dust and old books and detritus and clutter that might clog the pathways and block a smooth landing.

You sit in your favorite chair, eyes still closed, viewing and reviewing the layout of your foot-of-the-bed writing studio where most of your work has been created, the old writing room down the hall with file cabinets and containers full, full of stuff, decades' worth, which may or may not have value over time. But you are less concerned now with "over time," which suggests that it could go on forever, because your time is different than others, is more compressed, requires focus and intent. In a miniature helicopter, your videos take you to the writing room outside, to the workshop, to the crammed-full bookcases, the three printers, the whiteboards, and you hold up every book, every piece of paper, under an ultraviolet lamp, looking for hints, traces of worth, of what might be keep-able or toss-able.

In your mind, you complete the tour of everything that defines you, arise from your chair, open your eyes, now with a vision of what this contraption might look like, where it might be headed, how to get it started. And it's exactly like those plastic number puzzles where you have to slide one number up and over, rotating all twelve numbers, until you have moved them into the correct 1-12 sequence.

This puzzle begins with the table that sits on the right side of your writing chair. It holds years' worth of collectibles that you haven't looked at in ages, as well as those that you use regularly, like a bottle of water, two loose Tylenol, a tape measure, pens and highlighters, headsets, packets of Cialis, a pile of reviews from your fiction-writers' group, lots of dust, and you move down the hall and find an empty blue laundry basket and bring it back and load everything on that tabletop into the basket, roll the table out and set it aside, #1 now in its correct spot. The next pieces involve the emptying of a large bookcase full of books, putting the books on the bed, dusting, a little Lemon Pledge, and moving the bookcase to the spot next to the writing chair. #2 complete. Replacing books from the bed into the bookcase. #3. Selecting books to give away to Bookshop or Goodwill. #4. Back down the hallway to unload a four-drawer file cabinet full of writing-related materials, old stories, poems, other people's writing, stuff that may or may not have value. #5. Find a hand truck in the toolshed to help wheel the file cabinet into the bedroom next to the TV, where the bookcase used to be, put it in place. #6. Go back down the hall and one by one, bring the four drawers back and place them in the file cabinet. #7. This piece of the puzzle is huge. It's one of the primary connectors in this thing you're building, containing papers and letters and ways into your brain and thinking if anyone ever cares to do that in the future. Odds are that future relatives will haul it to the dump and burn it. But just in case, it will be in order, will lift its nose a little above sea level, say something like, "I was here," before the match is lit.

The color-printer cart is moved over next to the file cabinet. #8. There are stacks of papers everywhere. On bookcases, on printer carts. It's time to organize them, label file folders, place reviews for ten-minute plays in them, drop them into one of the file drawers, poetry in one drawer, fiction in another, plays in another, essays in the final drawer. #9. There's another file cabinet down the hall. Again, empty the drawers, move the cabinet, set it on the left side of the writing chair, refill the drawers. #10. Add new information and projects to the whiteboard. #11. Open your computer. Write the morning's Daily Fresh. Add more compelling reasons for Cody's pathology in *Pious Rebel!* Send a copy to the acquisitions editor. Dig back into *Capture and Release* and add more character descriptions. Revise plays for September 14 Zoom presentation. Read and critique Neil's stories before they visit next Tuesday. Open last versions of "Signage," "Nightlife," "Read All About It," and continue to polish and complete. Prepare for Zoom rehearsal and Friday-night literary reading. Continue to keep your fingers on the keyboard, activating your brain and thoughts to move projects forward, to oil the tracks of your Goldberg machine, to drop a one-inch steelie into the entry point, let it go, and watch it fling itself around the arena in a dress rehearsal, with no audience but yourself. #12. Puzzle complete.

This is the deepest clean you have ever engaged in. This preparation for a potential literary estate. This putting in order of things that may or may not have posthumous value. Minimally, your mind will be at rest, knowing that your afterlife is arranged, clean, free of dust and clutter.

The Moan of Lisa

HER LITERARY NAME IS ELIZABETH MCKENZIE, the name found on the cover of her books *The Portable Veblen*, *My Postwar Life*, *MacGregor Tells The World*, and *Stop That Girl*. To those of us who call her a friend, she is Lisa.

And I call her much more than a friend. I call her a confidant, a collaborator, a reviewer of my work, a supporter, an advocate, a brilliant light shining through a period of darkness, a soulmate, someone whom I can talk to about anything. I could continue with adjectives and superlatives until I reach the final line of this essay, but I won't, I'll stop now and dig in a bit.

The title of this piece was contrived primarily for the effect of the pun, to pull you into the story, to make you wonder if there is any connection between this Lisa and the one whom da Vinci called Mona. As Wikipedia says about the painting: "qualities include the subject's expression, which is frequently described as enigmatic, the monumentality of the composition, the subtle modeling of forms, and the atmospheric illusionism." I'd like to say I understood art critique enough to nod and say, "That describes my Lisa exactly." But I don't. I will say that when you spend any time with Lisa one of the first things that attracts you is her expression, a thin but reserved smile that holds an utter joy for life, a welling up of experience and success that can't wait to bubble out and influence those around her. As far as being enigmatic, absolutely! Not the difficult-to-understand part of the definition, but the mysterious side of the definition, yes! There is always a bit of mystery, puzzlement, that floats on the gleam that shines from her gaze. And she's not opposed to framing a question, making a comment, writing a paragraph or chapter or whole novel that showcases that tendency toward mystery, that keeps the reader, the friend, the acquaintance, on his or her toes to be able to glean as much as possible from this woman who has the ability to change lives.

Lisa has changed my life, as a true and dedicated friend, as a frank and glowing supporter of my writing and thinking, as a kindred spirit with whom I'm not afraid to share my most ecstatic accomplishments or my deepest regrets and failures, and as a writer whose work is a thrill to read. I have purchased multiple copies of *The Portable Veblen* to give to family and friends, to bring some excitement to their lives, to enlighten them to the literary skills and unique voice of Elizabeth McKenzie, a voice that continues to surprise and open new doors that showcase a keenly observed and shared view of the world. If you didn't know Palo Alto before reading this book, you will know it intimately after reaching the final page. You will also have been introduced to Veblen Amundsen-Hovda and thoroughly enraptured with her mind and life. And squirrels! So much about squirrels you thought you'd never know. I can't look at a piece of squirrel art ever again without buying it for Lisa.

Lisa as Elizabeth has been published in *phren-z* online literary magazine multiple times, accompanied by live readings at Bookshop Santa Cruz. She always has something new and fresh to share. She has a soft voice when she reads out loud, almost requiring the audience to lean in, pay attention, because what you're about to hear is like nothing you've ever heard before. The puzzle continues. She lures you in with a tenderness, a nestling in front of a hot fireplace with family and friends, before she delivers an enigmatic paragraph that turns your world upside down.

Speaking of fireplaces and nestling, before Covid Lisa would sit with me in the living room in front of hot fires. We'd talk about Stuart's or Nick's latest adventures, about her trips to Japan and Australia, about her famous conductor sister, about Steve's work on his novel about his uncle, about how her friend Terry was building her an amazing writer's room in her backyard, about the new projects she was working on or thinking about. I'd do the same, talk about new short stories, old short stories, the latest CT scan or CA 19-9 test results, a novel in progress, a ten-minute play about two people sitting on a bench on West Cliff Drive. Anything and everything. Since Covid, we continue a very similar routine, but now through Zoom meetings. Except for the lack of hugs, not much is different.

As fiction editor of *Catamaran Literary Reader*, Lisa was instrumental in getting one of my favorite stories, "Sweet Jesus," published, along with a live reading at Blitzer Gallery. The same is true of my first published essay, "Creek Views," excerpts read during a Zoom reading early this summer. In addition, as senior editor of *Chicago Quarterly Review (CQR)*, she helped me to publish an excerpt of *Smith: An Unauthorized Fictography*, as well as three poems.

Given her role at *CQR*, Lisa was the sole reason that Karen and I made our first trip to Chicago to read my poetry at *CQR*'s twenty-fifth anniversary reading in Evanston last December. We met Pete Ferry and other authors, got to spend time with Syed Afzal Haider, publisher of *CQR*, and his wife, Jan, lived in Syed's house for a few days, and got to see a part of the world I had been missing out on.

By now you're probably wondering if I'm going to follow through with the promise of the title, "The Moan of Lisa." I'll try, though I know it's a stretch, a result of my "overabundant imagination," as a friend recently described a piece of my writing. Given that my communication with Lisa is mostly through emails these days, her moans have taken the form of "Ahhhhhhhh!!" or "OMG!!!" The moans express not only dismay, such as when my scan results come back showing the lesions in my liver have enlarged some, but also thrill, such as when I learn from Paper Angel Press that they are excited about publishing my first novel.

A high degree of my small success as a writer has been due to my friendship with Lisa McKenzie. That I am still positive, thriving, writing fast and furiously has everything to do with the fact that Lisa has been with me as a constant companion throughout this journey. I enjoy hearing her moans of dismay and joy in relation to my life in the same way that I have enjoyed my own ecstatic moans when hearing of the nomination of *The Portable Veblen* for the Baileys Women's Prize for Fiction short list, or when she won a California Book Award for *Veblen* in 2016.

If I ever pick up a paint brush and try to emulate da Vinci, I will try to capture the enigmatic mysteries that reside behind Lisa's smile, that lift her moans above the rafters, that make my life so much more worth living. Thank you, Lisa.

Jory Post

Photo credit: Karen Wallace

A Shift in Focus

WHAT IF YOU USE THE COLD STEEL SHAFT piercing your brain behind the left eye with a constant throb as a focal point, an entry into creativity, instead of assuming it's a deterrent that will leave you empty and unable to produce? What if you spend some time twisting the shaft in a little deeper, turning and churning until the pain reaches an apex and has nowhere to go but down? Just a little more. Thrust it like an Olympic épée in the hand of a master. You can pay attention now to each pulse, feel the release of tension, adapt to its presence, observe your reaction for a minute before you move on. Touché!

You have options. You can crawl back under the safety of blankets and sheets and rest your head on the pillow, close your eyes and pretend nothing is there, close your eyes and hope to fall asleep. Or you can take more drugs, not the Tylenol, which you already took at 2:37 a.m. when you got up because the open slider let in not only the day's 93-degree heat, but also the incessant drone of the horny crickets trying to attract mates, but maybe a couple of aspirin, which you're not supposed to take because of its tendency to thin blood, which is not a good idea these days.

Or you can have your hot chocolate and Eggos a little early today, before your wife takes her morning run, see if the heat and syrup help to alleviate the discomfort, the distraction, the annoyance, see if eating and drinking moves the focal point to a different part of your body.

Or you can choose to jump into the shower early, blast a stream of hot water against your head and shoulders and just stand there, slumped over a little, just enough to never want to leave, and place your hands against the tile wall to hold yourself up as your knees and legs buckle.

Or as I suggested at the outset, use the invasion as a starting point, as a way to wake up your tongue, have it connect to your brain and begin spewing words and thoughts from your fingers until sentences form, ideas spill forth. Yes, this is really your only option today and every other day you have left. So continue. Look out at the deck and watch the blue jay who has just stuffed him or herself on seeds from the tray suddenly push off and fly a precise path around the corner of the house and into the oak tree on the corner of the property as if it's done it a thousand times or as if it has a built-in GPS system that allows its rapid speed and quick movements to navigate around edges and turns as if guided by computers and engineers sitting in hidden rooms in Washington, D.C., or Langley.

That's it. A new focal point. Another jay with no neck or head feathers pecking at seeds. It looks so naked, frail, as if it would lose all rights for pecking order if challenged. And then up pops the squirrel. With its size and herky-jerky movements, it scatters all birds to nearby trees and rooftops to observe the invader's behavior, to watch him or her gobble what remains, stuff its cheeks, keeping its head pointed toward movement of the large bodies inside rather than worry about the smaller birds in its world.

As it turns out, it's always about focus, if you have any, if you're able to fight off every type of distraction that prevents your productivity and pulls you into a specter of complacency. Whether you twist the telescope in for a tight view that shows the color of a dove's eyes or crank it in the other direction and give yourself a panoramic view of the universe, of planets and asteroids and meteors and space stations and extraterrestrial life we've yet to find. And all things and places in between.

Take, for example, the upcoming election, which you can find at a midpoint turn in the telescope. If you spend time thinking about it, you know in your heart, your mind, your wallet, that Joe Biden and Kamala Harris in the White House come January would be the best thing that could happen to the planet right now. There is no option. If Trump cancels ballots by mail, continues to send federal troops to bash protestors, steals the election, democracy will have completely vanished and will have difficulty ever making a return. Even though I believe in the Biden-Harris ticket, I am disgusted by the multiple emails and social media hits I already receive from a campaign only a few days old. It wears me down, makes me think on one hand that they are no better than the Trump machine that has already released promos bashing Harris. You have my vote. Don't make me regret it by inundating me with requests.

See how easy it is to change directions, to view the world from a different vantage point. I'm sitting in the same chair a few feet away from the birds, fingers on the keyboard of the computer where already two more Biden-Harris emails have flashed in the corner of my screen, not twenty feet away from the shower, less than ten feet away from the comfort of bed, and out the slider on the other side of the bird feeders I see the Loma Prieta peak in the haze probably five miles away. Now I've said five miles but that's a guess, so I open Google Maps and see that it is actually 20.8 miles by car, a 47-minute drive, or as the crow flies, more like ten miles. Two levels of distraction occur with this action. The first is the Google research that I so love. The second is remembering the times in my youth where I made the drive to the peak in the middle of winter when the blankets of snow would cover the mountain and we'd bundle up in parkas and make and toss snowballs for the better part of a day.

So much better to go sideways, as Ron Carlson would have you do as one of his writing students, to understand that there is a thread that moves from the entry point that proceeds to the end, but that along the way, it's valuable to take sideways movement into unknown canyons and crevices, to discover questions and answers never posed before, to encourage distractions that advance the productivity and creativity in ways you never could have imagined.

While the pain is not completely gone, for most of the past hour I've been able to avoid it, to concentrate my energies on other pathways, to move the work forward. I'll admit that I took two aspirin. I'll also admit that I'm really looking forward to the hot water pummeling my head and neck. That I may even crawl into bed for a half hour before getting back up and taking the next swipe at the day.

This is how we build retaining walls, brick by brick. This is how we construct a domino wall spiral, one domino at a time. This is how we use the pain to concentrate rather than debilitate.

The Defiance of Reliance

I'T'S NOT THAT I DON'T ENJOY COLLABORATION. I've benefitted from the results of brainstorms with friends and colleagues throughout various phases and projects in my life. During my college life at UCSC as a psychology major, I participated in Elliot Aronson's Jigsaw Method experiments in a class with Professor Bruce Bridgeman. We were divided into study groups of six and each week were given a lengthy hard-copy study dealing with the current topic of discussion. The documents were often forty to fifty pages long, and each of the six members was assigned one sixth of the document about which they were to become experts. We were not to read the other five sections. The study demanded two things: 1) that we take our one-sixth portion extremely seriously and prepare extensively to be able to share our understanding with the others in our group, and 2) that we learn to be reliant on the others in the group and trust that they would take their jobs as seriously as we did. Results were mixed. Not everybody could pull their weight and there were often gaps in what we needed to know for exams or blue-book essays. I don't remember that the official results of the experiment were shared with us, but I was quite aware of my own personal results.

Because we were graded through narratives, I wasn't able to compare a B with an A, but in reading my narrative it sounded like a B. I was pretty sure my narrative would have shined more if I had been allowed to read the full documents myself, but there was no way of knowing. What I know is that I had no choice. I was relegated to trust my group mates, most of whom I had met for the first time in the class. That I had to let go and rely on other folks to round out my knowledge and be determinants in my success or failure in the class was not an easy lesson to learn.

Other collaborations have been more successful, usually ones that involve two people rather than six. In 1988, Carole McPherson and I co-wrote *Learning about HIV*, one of the first manuals for middle-school teachers and students. We split up the duties, took on areas where one person's expertise was better than the other's, and, with the expertise of our publisher and editor, were able to deliver a high-quality product that not only provided teachers and students with state-of-the-art content and knowledge about HIV, but that also made Carole and me, along with ETR (the publisher), quite a good chunk of royalties. The issue of trust still loomed large, at least in my mind. Given the expertise of the ETR team guiding us along, we could worry less about it, because it was my responsibility to complete my half, and ETR's responsibility to make sure the other half was delivered.

About ten years ago my great friend Debbie and I decided to co-write a screenplay. We had met years earlier when I auditioned for an ensemble of plays with Debbie as co-director. I loved her writing, her direction, her sensibilities about life. At that point, I had a monster eighty-inch TV screen in our living room. Debbie and I sat on the couch across from the screen, and I attached each of our keyboards to the large monitor. This was a true collaboration! One person could write a sentence, and just for fun, the other person might hate the content and erase what had just been written. There was one word that Debbie used, "puerile," that I suggested was a little highbrow and folks might not understand. "Fuck them!" she said. "They should know it and understand it, so now's as good a time as any." The screenplay was called *Food for Thought*, and we developed the four main characters together, beginning with thinking which current actors we could keep in our brains as we developed details, traits, beliefs.

The lead was Janeane Garofalo, a literature professor with a low libido. The male lead, Carl, a wonderful chef struggling with his desire to own a restaurant, was played by Cuba Gooding, Jr. Their trust-fund somewhat-ditzy friend Ronnie was Lisa Kudrow. The fourth character, Brody, was a 70-plus-year-old retired professor whom we envisioned as James Cromwell. It was extremely helpful to move forward in this collaboration having these four known faces in front of us at all times. We didn't always agree on content, especially because Debbie's partner, who will remain unnamed here, was a huge proponent of the anti-circumcision movement as well as the recovering-one's-lost-foreskin movement, including the hanging of heavy weights on the penis to stretch and recover the skin. It's all in the script. I had to let go of my resistance to that one and trust that Debbie knew enough about it through her partner to deliver a logical and heartwarming portrayal of the process. We never did anything with that screenplay, but the process was highly successful and brought Debbie and me closer together.

Another example was when Apple Computer hired me to become the managing editor of a new project to be named the

Apple Learning Interchange (ALI), an online platform to deliver virtual field trips to teachers and students by partnering with content experts across the country. There was a team of six or so folks scattered across the country. Occasionally they'd come to the headquarters in Cupertino for a meeting. Usually, though, in the time before Zoom or FaceTime, we had conference phone calls to strategize our future. These were six very smart people who knew their own work well. And they liked to let you know how well they knew it. The work was often two steps forward, one step back. This collaboration required careful listening, restating the ideas of others, a willingness to trust the others' ability to complete their segments, and a certain degree of trust that you could create your own segments in a way that was appreciated and accepted by others.

This was not always easy in a company led by Steve Jobs, who had very specific ideas as to how to measure success and good work. He also didn't care much about the education department, given that his primary focus was the Switcher campaign, designed to have every PC user switch to the Mac platform. In our project, we cared about the content we were creating and delivering, not which platform it was viewed on. In the end, I moved on, realizing that no degree of collaboration would outweigh the company's emphasis on profit. It would take a lot more than collaboration to alter that mentality, and I didn't have the time or interest to stay for the long haul.

In my older years, I still like the idea of collaboration, of two or more brains working together, riffing off each other, finding new pathways and solutions that one mind couldn't work out by itself. But I also love to go at warp speed. Love to let my brain fling out ideas that I capture in my journal, in notebooks, next to light bulbs I use as prompts, regardless of how goofy or off the wall they may seem. I am often impatient, want to jump on an idea and let it roll without waiting for confirmation or jigsaw partners to give me their one-sixth interpretations and critique.

Thus I tend to rely on myself, not necessarily because I'm better than others, but because I have new restrictions and limitations in my life and I need to power forward when I can, without having to rely on others every step of the way, often defying the need or desire to collaborate.

My good friend Paola and I have been collaborating on a series of epistolary poems as instigated by our Catamaran Literary Conference workshop leader Dorianne Laux, who paired us together. We move forward slowly with our shared poems for each other, hoping to eventually have a total of twenty-six, thirteen each, that we will publish as a chapbook. This is a collaboration I love, one that is gentle, not in-your-face demanding, but with just enough inspiration to keep it going on a personal and mutual level.

Paola would also like to collaborate on a screenplay. I'm thinking about it. Have to decide whether I'm willing to let go of my egocentric defiance, fall back on a jigsawed reliance.

One Step Beyond

LIKE THE INFINITE COMBINATIONS provided through the twist of a kaleidoscope, the morning sky once again offers a view of the world that dazzles. When I see it, I quit trying to explain anything about the world we live in. Like the night before, when streaks of hot white lightning cracked everything wide. Like the gorgeous yellow bird perched on the hummingbird feeder trying unsuccessfully to stick his beak into the opening.

So many miracles we desperately seek to explain, to understand, to pack away into neat little boxes for future use, the primal need to know why.

Let's see if I can "change my world by changing my mind," as the Black Eyed Peas suggest in their song "Unity." Let's see if I can simply observe the miracles without caring why. Just watch the ring-necked pigeon staring at me through the window, dropping a pellet onto the deck. Let's see if I can avoid wondering if he or she is a sentry, a scout sent in advance to determine the safety of the feeding grounds for others in the flock.

Or lift my eyes to the corner where the black spider seems to have been resting for days now. Do I have the patience to watch without wonder? Do I care whether or not he or she is sleeping, or hatching eggs, or is possibly dead and waiting to fall to the floor to join so much other detritus?

So many little things strung together all day long. Like letting the next sentence fall freely from my fingertips in stream-of-consciousness fashion or slowing down, rereading, changing a word, changing the meaning of a thought by choosing "strung" instead of "connected."

When to make a choice to stand up, grab my floss, turn on the shower, bury my head under the hot flow, dry off with the luxurious Turkish cloth towel my wife bought me for Father's Day. Or whether to stay in the chair all day long and skip the shower, and which is the more sensible option?

I hear an engine in the distance over Soquel, a *chop chop chop* that identifies it as a helicopter. And I hear it closer now, hear it flying over the top of my house, feel the shingles shake, and is that enough, the undeniable sound, to hear it and savor it and track it in my mental journal, or do I need to think about the pilot? Did he or she serve in the military? Who else is in the copter? Is it a crash victim heading to Dominican Hospital? Will he or she live?

I turn to the bookshelf next to my chair, recently rearranged with new titles in view. I am overwhelmed by the brilliance of the authors: Russell Banks, Emma Donahue, Ann Patchett, Jonathan Franzen, Aimee Bender, J. M. Coetzee, Richard Ford, Haruki Murakami, John Steinbeck. Each name evokes an image, paints a biographical backstory, recalls stories of people locked in rooms, of professors, of a writer working at his trade. I focus on *Working Days: The Journals of "The Grapes of Wrath"*, which details Steinbeck's writing of *TGOW* along with "paranoia, self-doubt, and obstacles." I drift to the Salinas Valley, to his house off Highway 17 between Santa Cruz and Los Gatos. I lean over his shoulder, watch him work, try to crawl inside his brain.

And when my wife brings me a three-egg sandwich for breakfast, I'm thrilled to observe white and yellow layers laced together between slices of whole-wheat bread, and taste the inimitable flavors of eggs fried lightly in butter. However, I can't help but imagine the hens up at the Culvers' property in Happy Valley laying these eggs, Dave and Maria delivering them to us, Karen cracking the shells, ending up as my breakfast this morning.

Then an email clangs in the background and a friend mentions cornmeal pancakes, and I am returned to my youth, where such pancakes were a rare occurrence, usually shredded wheat drenched in hot water to soften and moisten, covered with melted butter and hot Karo syrup, my Grandma Esther's favorite meal to serve me when I stayed over with her. I smell it, taste it, could draw a picture of it, but what I really want to do is understand what made her fall in love with the meal. Was it simply the result of having grown up during the Depression and making do with inexpensive foods?

One more course of breakfast delivered by Karen: a Downtowner roll with sugar from Gayle's Bakery. I take a picture of it, so I can observe it twice, before and after I devour it. But it's not just about flavor, about bits getting stuck between my teeth, about describing the rolled layers of dough wrapped in cinnamon and sugar. It's about Gayle, and Joe, the business they've built in Capitola, the workers in the kitchen who prepared it, placed it in the oven. About the Covid precautions they must take to protect their customers and employees.

I'll end with one last example. The music in the background as I complete this piece. It's "Eleanor Rigby" by the Beatles. I love this song. I love almost every Beatles song. It should be enough to listen, to hear how the words flow together to tell the story, how it fits with the music. But no. I want to know about all these lonely people. What it is that makes Father McKenzie who he is. Why Eleanor keeps her face in a jar by the door. Who are these people? What happened in their worlds to cause their lonely lives?

I'm certain I could go on for days and weeks sharing the miracles of my world that I would hope to be able to observe and share without explanation. But my sampling so far suggests that my desires fall short. Yes, I can still observe and share well, but it's impossible for me to not dig in a little more deeply, to understand backstory, to know the whys and hows of what makes things tick.

I'm afraid I'll continue to do so and hope it doesn't come across as a giant example of navel-gazing.

The Failure of Immune Systems

SINCE I'VE BEEN SICK, I have steered away from politics, from Covid, from news and updates. I feel like it's better for my battered immune system if I avoid the plethora of negativity in the world right now. Last night, however, I tuned in to the opening of the Zoom-based Democratic National Convention to hear all of Joe Biden's former opponents line up to laud and support him. While they clearly threw their support his way to show a commitment and solidarity behind him, it was not because they agree with everything he says and thinks and believes in, but rather that the common enemy is large and on fire and needs to be doused.

Michelle Obama, a woman who occupied the White House for eight years, a woman who openly dislikes politics, gave the most articulate, intelligent, heartfelt speech of the decade. If she were the candidate, she would win by a landslide. But she's not. She is supporting a man with whom she shared governmental responsibilities, a man who she's hoping can defeat one of the most tyrannical leaders the world has seen in the past hundred years.

Much of her speech and the speeches of others were dedicated to denouncing the opponent, to pointing out his irresponsible, racist, sexist, elitist behavior and his role in downplaying the most devastating health event the world has witnessed in the past hundred years.

When I see posts on Facebook from high school friends who blindly support everything the current president says, my mouth falls open. How can these folks who I know are basically good people accept and support the package he represents? It is one thing to be conservative fundamentalist Christians who hope for a return to the values and morals they hold in high esteem, but it is another thing to close one's eyes to the anti-Christian, anti-humanity traits of this man. I fear that my friends have forgotten what it is they truly believe in at their core, a focus on family and friends and faith, none of which are important to the current president. Instead, they are simply riding the wake labeled "conservatism" that they think will restore their core values in a world run amok.

What has truly run amok is a nation that openly flaunts white supremacy, denounces the Black Lives Matter movement, seeks to devastate the electoral process by defunding the postal service that handles mail-in ballots, promotes racism, is homophobic, is male-centric, and does not believe that every American, that every human being, deserves a health-care system that guarantees them access to needed services and drugs.

Even though I call them Facebook friends it's only because that is the label Facebook has used since its inception. At this point in my life, I would have to call them former friends, could not imagine being friends with those who would support any of this president's comments, beliefs, inanities. And worse yet, that they are able to trick themselves into believing that a vote for this man will be better for the country. Maybe it would be better for them personally to see him devastating the tax base, that they could save some money if he is still in office. But the havoc it would wreak on the majority of people in this country who are barely eking out a living in this awkward time of Covid is unconscionable and flies in the face of every Christian tenet they have ever believed in.

Just writing this piece, trying to work myself into a final paragraph and sentence, makes me feel sick to my stomach. I can feel my immune system dwindling with every word, every time I use the phrase "current president." Every time I think of the good people in high school whom I knew and hung out with, who have become self-centered and refuse the notion that every person deserves the same treatment as they do. When I first noticed the hateful trends of their comments, I thought of defriending them. But no. It is better to keep the enemy close. Watch what they do, how they do it, how they phrase and mask their bigotries and racist beliefs. Try to understand what makes them who they are, and if there are any possibilities to break through their leaden armor to have them pay attention to who the current president really is, what he stands for, how our nation and the world that follows will erupt into unstoppable tyranny and fascism that will undo everything our nation was founded on.

I'll have to stop soon, knowing that in my current physical condition there is not a lot I can do to effect change. I can't walk the precincts, I can't travel to other counties and states to help get the word out, the vote out. I can send money, but I'm not sure money will win this election. I can sign petitions. I can write letters for Swing Left. But I doubt that anything I do will make a difference. I will vote for Biden and Harris. I will tell everybody I know that I am doing so, but for the most part, I will be preaching to a choir of fellow Democrats and progressives. What I believe is that the fate of our country lies in the hands of the Congress. Regardless of party, the fact that individuals are too fearful to step forward points to the greatest incidence of selfishness and blatant ignorance of what is good for humanity, the people of this nation, and the world at large. If they continue to allow a racist, ignorant president to send federal troops to cities where folks are protesting the inequities in our governmental policies, to slip people into vehicles and take them away to undisclosed locations, then we are close to losing all hope.

The upcoming election is critical to the arc of this planet. Given everything we know about the current president—his behavior toward women, LGBT folks, and immigrants; his elitism; his racism; his preference for golf rather than diplomacy—the planet is liable to lose its axis and fly off course if he is reelected (or rigs the results).

I believe a reverse in congressional support is our main hope, and I don't see it happening to any great degree. Those folks in Congress need to follow the lead of the former governor of Ohio, John Kasich, and step forward and denounce the current president for everything he stands for and believes. Only then do we stand a chance for survival. Only then might we be able to tackle the devastation of Covid and the resulting disastrous effects on our economy.

When Michelle Obama says to the nation that the current president's White House "operates in chaos and without empathy," she speaks from a compassionate place that cares for every human being in existence. It is this compassion that stirs in me when I do take the time and energy to pull my ostrich head from the sand and pay attention to what is going on even though it's not healthy for me to dwell on it for long. When I do allow myself to take the plunge, I might see the results of my next blood test deteriorate. But if I don't, I'm likely to see the results at the polls in November keep the same president in place, and I'll know my selfishness played a part in those results.

While I won't soon write another Daily Fresh essay on this topic, I will pay attention, send my financial support, sign petitions, put signs on my lawn and banners on my car, surround my Facebook image with the Biden-Harris logo, and share my support with others. It's one thing for an immune system to slowly fail, but a whole different thing to have a moral and ethical system fail along with it. Biden-Harris in 2020!

What's Next?

I TRY NOT TO SPEND TOO MUCH ENERGY thinking or worrying about what's next. Mainly because me worrying about the future will usually have zero effect on changing that future. The more likely effect is contracting an ulcer or increasing my blood pressure, neither of which I need to add to an already full plate of medical conditions. It is true that some forethought about some of what might come next could result in preparations that alter the effects of what comes next. But is it really worth the energy to imagine all of the possible "next" events that could alter one's life simply to gain an iota of control?

I think not. Let the chips fall where they may. However, to backtrack and recall a series of events that has affected one's life, that has brought one to the lively present place in which they live and breathe, that's another question altogether. I'm not able to ignore the journey back to help me understand where I currently am and how I got here, and if that also happens to touch on where I might be next, I'll accept that, though not dwell on it.

Let's drift back. How far to go for the first question? Do I roll back to when I was five and was left in the hospital to have my adenoids and tonsils removed? Do I flash forward to my dad's hospitalization and track the one hundred pounds he lost in nine months? Do I share my viral-meningitis story when I was a senior in high school? Do I showcase my marriage and divorce to my first wife? Or how long I smoked pot and when I decided to quit? No. None of that. Those were not earth-shattering or life-changing events for the most part. This is not a memoir that becomes novel length and tells the A-Z story of me. Instead, this is a series of dominoes about a specific period in a slice of life that leads to the obvious next question—What's next?

We'll use the beginning point of having stomach cramps and diarrhea that led to an appointment with my primary doctor, who scheduled a series of blood, urine, and stool tests followed by a CT scan. To shorten this piece and make it less memoir-like, I'll cut to the 7:15 a.m. phone call following the CT scan, where the doctor said, "I hate to drop this nuclear bomb on you," which is when I hear of the malignant tumor crowding the breathing room out of my pancreas.

Now is an appropriate time for the first What's-next question. It's a biopsy conducted by the GI-doc down at the corner office, where they stick a needle into my pancreas and send a piece of me to Stanford for analysis. As expected, the results come back as adenocarcinoma.

Okay. Next?

This part of the story is way too long to tell and keep interesting, though it does have embedded in it a series of What's Nexts. But simply put, fifteen months of chemotherapy and Cyberknife radiation treatments, with a CT scan by

Stanford that shows metastatic movement into my liver as two lesions. I'm given months to live by the radiologist.

Right. Next? Well, to be blunt, *live* those months as fully as possible. Which I do. But my oncologist is not happy with that diagnosis, and puts me back on chemo again, which I begin in February 2020, while I am busy writing, finishing a novel, short stories, plays, thinking about forming a literary estate for my unfinished work to possibly see some light posthumously.

Next? Covid-19. What the fuck is that? It's a deadly virus that primarily attacks elderly folks and those with weakened immune systems. It's airborne and has traveled across the planet to every country and is killing tens of thousands of people. Our leadership downplays it, calls it a hoax, but it isn't.

Next? Masks. We wear masks to prevent the spread of germs. We shelter in place to reduce the incidence of exposure. We stay out of gyms, sporting events, the beach, any place where crowds gather. The governor closes down the state in mid-March, and I am seriously having withdrawal symptoms from not being able to attend literary events and readings at Bookshop Santa Cruz and other venues, so I begin an online reading series with local authors called *Zoom Forward!*

What's next? A *Zoom Forward* every Friday night that attract from 70 to 200 participants. It becomes a part-time voluntary job. I bring my granddaughter Hannah on board as codirector. I continue to take Folfirinox for six hours on Wednesday and carry a pump home with me for the next 46 hours. I write feverishly. Life is fairly good.

Next? Mother's Day, May 9. I decide to break the shelter-in-place restriction and take dinner to my mom's house along with my wife and sister. As we leave, Mom falls on the stairs and causes a compound fracture to her left wrist. A hurried trip to Urgent Care, where she's told it will require ER treatment. Another hurried trip to ER, where my sister has to let my mom go at the check-in desk due to Covid restrictions. She stays in the hospital for five days of misery for all of us, mostly her. They diagnose her with Parkinson's and put her on a new med. The new med is devastating to her system, so when she gets home, she stops taking it.

What's next? We are told by Dominican staff that Mom needs 24/7 care. My sister moves in full-time. Lots of discussions about the future. Mom falls. We get calls in the middle of the night to come down and help. Luckily she's only a mile away. VNA gets involved. Neurologists get involved. Everybody gets involved. Except Mom. She mostly sleeps. Isn't too interested in food or drink. Shelly is extremely attentive and does everything possible to make Mom's life as comfortable as possible.

Next? My friend Kathy wants me to put on three of my short plays on September 14. She will produce. She puts up money. We start figuring out how to present two-hander, two-actor, plays through Zoom, because we certainly can't do them in front of a live audience. It becomes a monumental task trying to solve the technical issues. Not unlike Sisyphus pushing that stone up the mountain and watching it fall down the other side. Over and over. Mom has more falls, more fallouts. Karen relieves Shelly when she can. Shelly decides to leave her thirty-year apartment at our house and move everything out, which serendipitously leaves it available for our granddaughter Georgia and her boyfriend AJ.

What's next? Some excellent news! My novel *Pious Rebel* will be published by Paper Angel Press and will be launched by November 1. I cry when I hear the news. I am thrilled. It negates many of the negative What's Nexts that I've been dealing with.

Another next? A CT scan in early August 2020. (What a year!) The oncologist uses the word failure too many times when we discuss it. Result is two weeks off, then starting a different flavor of chemo, and having a biopsy to see if we can match my condition with any other trials or treatments. Definitely a bit of a downturn, knowing that the shortened time frame gets shorter, but also knowing that I need to crank on my writing to get as many finished pieces out into the world as soon as possible. Motivation. Inspiration. Even if the push is guided by mortality.

Next? An unbelievable dry lightning storm that lasts through the night and into the morning. The kind of storm I have only seen in the deserts of Arizona. The streaks of lightning start thousands of fires.

What's next? A heat wave that puts us into the hundreds and is debilitating to me, and which, along with my continual nausea, puts me horizontal more often than I like.

And next? The fires. The River Fire in Carmel. The Salinas Valley fire. The three fires just north of Santa Cruz. The call at 2:30 in the morning from Karen's sister, who lives in Bonny Doon, evacuating, headed our way in the morning. Karen's niece and family, evacuated, heading our way, with all their pets.

Next? We order tons of breakfast items from Silver Spur's take-out menu and have it ready when they appear—two kids, four adults, two dogs, one cat. They bring their own pet food.

What's next? Who the fuck knows? An asteroid? An earthquake? My mother dies? Aliens invade Earth? Or maybe I'll win the National Book Award! I won't put much forethought into it. I have too much work to do. That's what's next. Fingers on keyboard.

"They Got the Fire Down Below"

O CCASIONALLY IN THIS DAILY FRESH BUSINESS there's a transition from one day's essay to the next. I try to avoid it when I can, because it doesn't feel as fresh if it's a follow-up to the previous day. But today I can't help it. I'm already four hours behind my typical early-morning time at the keyboard, and the transitional topic is all that is being talked about, on news shows, in the newspapers, in my living room, where six evacuees from the Santa Cruz Mountains fires are concerned about their houses left behind in Bonny Doon and Ben Lomond, areas where the fires are known to have already reached.

Tuesday night at 2:30 our landline rang. We usually both pop awake and expect to see a call from my sister needing help with my mother who has fallen or soiled herself. This time it said *Alison Parham* on the LCD display before Karen answered it. "Fire," I said. Alison told us they could see the fire and weren't waiting for the evacuation demand. Their son Kyle, along with his wife Kelly and son Matthew, had already evacuated their Zayante home and headed to his in-laws' house on Glen Canyon Road. Their daughter Katie, her husband Joe, and their two daughters, Elsie and Eva, had packed up and left their Ben Lomond home. Did I mention the two dogs and a cat?

The four adults, two children, and three pets showed up at our house for refuge early Wednesday morning. We called Silver Spur and placed a large order for take-out food to have here when they arrived. Home fries and pancakes and French toast and four kinds of omelets, a half-dozen muffins, and a gallon of orange juice. When I walked outside to get in the car to pick up the order, large chunks of ash and debris were scattered everywhere, our front porch, the tops of cars, windshields, the sidewalks, and the roads.

There was not a lot of discussion when they first arrived, all of them in shock about the potential of losing all their possessions, other than the few they could fit in their cars, and their houses. I went online to look at the CalFire maps. The first one I looked at showed the four dominant fires, the ones in Napa, East San Jose, the Santa Cruz Mountains, and Carmel River.

After viewing the map of the fires, I thought back to the night the lightning storm slashed its magic wands across Northern California and left its mark in over a thousand locations. The Santa Cruz fire looked to be about the same size as the Carmel River fire, but nowhere near as big as the Napa and East San Jose fires. It was hard not to think about James Baldwin's book *The Fire Next Time* or the song "The Fire Down Below" by Bob Seeger and the Silver Bullet Band.

Joe works for the San Lorenzo Valley Water Department. He is now up in the midst of the monster, working, fixing leaks, doing whatever he can to help out. He has called Katie, told her he's driven by their house and it's still standing, but that the fire has reached the Three Poles peak and is bearing down on the town of Boulder Creek. We've heard that there may be as many as six hundred firefighters there trying to save the town, but it's often hard to separate fact from fiction. It's sad and pisses me off that Joe, with his asthma, is being asked to participate in this event, breathing ash with every intake. And yet it's nice to know that he gets to keep an eye on their house.

On the other hand, Chuck and Alison have to sit here and speculate, wonder if their house is already gone, think about what they will return to and whether or not they need to build a new house. They have a significant camper, so they would have a place to live as they figure out next steps.

My friend Gary Young and his wife, Peggy, live in Bonny Doon in a gorgeous house that Gary has built and remodeled over the years. They are directly across from the Bonny Doon Vineyards. Over the years, they have had to evacuate four times. I've heard from Peggy that they are in town and okay, but I fear that their house is probably gone.

My sister recited a line to me the other day that a friend had told her during a particularly rocky time: "God never gives you more than you can handle." It's hard to know if and how that advice can be used in a situation like this. Mostly, I think it's not useful. If I believed in a God, I would find a way to locate her and say, "What the fuck is wrong with you? Don't tell me to buck up and get ready to carry a heavier load. Are you serious? That's your lesson? On one hand, yes, I will handle whatever I need to handle to continue the process of survival and adaptation, but who are you to make those decisions for me? To load me, and the rest of the world, down with more than anyone should ever be asked to handle is brutal, insensitive, and satanic."

Daily Fresh

We are in a time of wearing masks and sheltering in place and worrying about Covid, given the 175,000 United States deaths that have occurred so far, with many more expected. And a heat wave that some benevolent God thought he would toss at us. And now we have these fires affecting the lungs of nearly everyone in the state of California, tens of thousands of evacuations, people expected to find places to live with friends or families or headed to shelters, all options that further the risks of exposure to others who have been exposed to Covid.

Part of learning the skill of adaptation has been figuring how to put fires out, how to douse the flame, rebuild, move on. The main phrase we have heard about this fire is "Zero-percent containment with no end in sight." Adaptation takes on a whole different flavor with that mantra running through your head. It means making an evacuation list, finding critical papers, packing suitcases, deciding on sensible shoes and jackets. It means knowing where you will go when the evacuation alert finally arrives. It means thinking about Mom and Shelly. It means imagining a world that has never entered a dream or nightmare.

It's too late to buy a fire safe or update the home insurance policy. But not too late to help our family, our friends, to reach out to those in need, help them battle the fire down below, the fire in their brains, help them plan for the new future in front of us.

A Matter of Principal

I'M DRAINED AND IT'S LATE—8:00 p.m. I spent my usual morning writing block finishing the reading of my novel in progress, *A Matter of Principal*, so Daily Fresh! has been pushed to its limits. After forty-six straight days, I find myself in danger of skipping a day, letting loose of my unwritten desire to write for sixty days in a row. But I let myself get lost in that fiction writing, the threads and characters that were dormant for seven years coming back to life. So much of the writing felt like it was written by someone much better than me. That felt good. I didn't feel so good when I couldn't remember that I had written everything I did.

I had forgotten about how much sex I included. I had forgotten about how dark I got with Jake's father, Lester. I had forgotten that at the end of the paragraph on page 380 there is a comma, an incomplete sentence and thought. I had forgotten that Delia was about to reveal a huge lie she had told about herself that colored the nature of their relationship. I had forgotten that it was just about time to assemble the hiring committee to hire the new principal. I had forgotten that my label for the new principal was the Motivator. I had forgotten so much but was thrilled at how much I already have, how many interesting characters there are. Now, to dig back into the electronic copy and make the changes I marked up over the past few days, then continue on to write the next 100+ pages, probably reaching a 500-page novel. I'm looking forward to this. Looking forward to the influence the new principal will have on Jake, how Jake will turn his life around with her help.

I'm also very interested to determine what I will do with Jake and Delia's relationship, how his friendship with Serena will continue to develop, whether or not or how his relationship with Roger will crumble, what and how he will teach sixth graders about photography. And who will step forward as the primary protagonist. Paula and Oswald have probably played out their roles. Roger could take on some of it, but it probably needs to be Bill Mullen, who will come at Jake and the new principal hard. Also maybe a little bit of Walter, but he has to get over it. Jake's life will shape up, fewer drugs, less tequila, less casual sex, enrolling in the Master of Education program with the Motivator's help.

Using this as a Daily Fresh feels a little like a cop-out, but given that I just finished reading the manuscript, these ideas are fresh in my head and I need to have some pointers for how to move forward. So I'll force myself to stay horizontal, keep my fingers pounding, open the valve in my brain to allow words to keep flowing through. Ideas. Thoughts. It's interesting to see how many of the ideas I included have made their way into other pieces since their initial inclusion in the novel. What I discovered while reading it was that it is one of those perfect examples of fictography I'm always talking about. Jake is definitely me, or much of him is me. So many of the activities and events and ideas are me and mine. But then I toss in so many sideways twists and rabbit holes and odd behaviors that I don't recognize and I'm happy, happy that it's not completely predictable, happy that when my Happy Valley friends read this one they will recognize so much, some will see themselves, and others will say "Who the hell is that supposed to be?" Or "I don't remember that!"

So this is turning out to be better than expected. Rather than get up early in the morning and hope to write two essays tomorrow to make up for one missed today, I'm making important progress, and in so doing moving *A Matter of Principal* higher up on the priority list. And what I have been lacking for a few months, writing new fiction, will be automatically addressed after I spend a few hours tomorrow cleaning up copy edits and consistency and redundancy issues. I will forge forward into describing the hiring of the new superintendent/principal and her reign at Rodeo Canyon Elementary School. One hundred pages of it. Followed by a chapter or two of Jake taking over as acting superintendent/principal when #4 takes a year off to have her baby.

I'm excited about it. I want to set myself a five-page daily deadline, which means the first draft would be complete by the end of October. Ready to send to Paper Angel Press. Onward!

Evacuees—What Is Left Behind

EMPATHY ONLY GOES SO FAR. It requires an understanding of the emotional states of other people. Under normal conditions, achieving that understanding can be difficult. During times of stress, that understanding can be buried behind layers of trauma and worry. So while I open my heart and mind to attempt to inhabit the world of those under more stress than I am, to inhabit their world from a distance, it's the distance that makes a difference. We talk about walking in someone else's shoes, but that's so easy to say, much harder to do, to fit my size-eleven foot into someone else's size-ten shoe.

As of 52 minutes ago, there are 64,000 evacuees from Santa Cruz County forced out of their homes, having had to make lists, pack suitcases, remember to bring dog and cat food, if necessary, decide which papers other than passports and birth certificates and living trusts are essential. How much will fit in the car? Do you take both cars? How do you prioritize a houseful and lifeful of memories? Not easily. But quickly.

The trauma begins with the lightning bolts. It grows the following day when reports of the thousand small fires trickle out. It deepens when the fires grow together, form a massive front, move south from the Santa Cruz Mountains. And even though the official evacuation notice has yet to be received, the trauma wraps itself around hearts, squeezes them, increases blood pressure, when the flames can be seen a couple ridges north of one's property.

Official or not, it's time to leave. To drive away, look out the window of your car for what may be one last look at your house standing tall. A couple with their dog and cat driving down Empire Grade into town, pulling their camper, full of treasures and essentials, heading for the home of relatives. We the relatives, opening our house to them as if it was theirs. The empathy. What we feel for them makes us weep for them, makes us weep for all 64,000, makes us consider our own list.

By 9:00 a.m. we have six human evacuees along with three pets occupying our house and property with us. We are probably a good ten miles from the front lines of the southern edge of the fire. The past few nights it has burned 700 to 1000 additional acres each night. It's currently up to 67,000 acres. Empathy is one thing, when it's for others that you love, and moves into something else when the whole county is warned to prepare to evacuate. That preparation begins when you look out the back window to the new deck built from con-heart redwood, when you look beyond the deck and see solid vegetation and trees in every direction you look. The tinderbox leads northwest back toward the fire in a solid mass of flammable wood and brush that translates into personal concern rather than empathy.

It's our turn to imagine flames engulfing our two-story home, ripping through walls and decks and reducing everything to ash.

This is what has been going through the heads of our evacuees since they arrived. All six of them not able to avoid imagining what is happening at their houses in the direct line of fire, in Bonny Doon, in Boulder Creek. It's post-traumatic stress disorder (PTSD) in the making, more in the pre stages that is carving its way into brains, into memories, into the cardiovascular systems that move blood from one part of the body to another.

The adult evacuees in our house watch the news and press conferences when they come on TV. They listen closely to the updates. The zero-percent containment, the "no end in sight" professed by every newsperson. The ninety-seven structures gone so far. The five teams of investigators who will drive up into the fire zone to identify additional structures that have been destroyed. This is the trauma that grips them. Knowing that the odds are extremely low that they will be able to return to their property and find a home still standing.

We can only imagine. We can only begin to write out our list of essential items. To prioritize. Documents first. Living trust. Birth certificates. We don't have current passports. But for me, medical stuff related to the past twenty-two months of being under the influence of adenocarcinoma. Maybe a few folders of short stories or other writings. Ten-minute plays. It depends. On the capacity of our suitcases, or the back end of our Prius. If we take the old Honda as well. Tech stuff is next, maybe even more important than the documents because our whole lives are nestled into the bits and bytes of electronic files and folders. The computer, the iPads, the cell phones, all the chargers. Flashlights. Tools is another category, but I don't know what we would take. A hammer? Two screwdrivers? Clothing is a key area of concern. How much do you need? Will wherever you end up be anywhere near laundry facilities? Underwear, for me, pads. Two pairs of pants, t-shirts and button shirts for the infusion center. My

George Foreman diabetes socks. Maybe a hat or two. One belt. Not sure what Karen's priorities would be for this one. Maybe two pairs of shoes each. Maybe three. Things of value. Here comes the rub. How do you prioritize this one? And what is meant by value? Sentimental value? All of the photo albums and cards and gifts from the heart? Or are we thinking monetary value? Which would mean the two Daniel Owen Stolpe art pieces. Probably none of our own art. Well, maybe one. Maybe the Norfolk Island Kaka sarcophagus. Just because. To have as a memory of what might have been.

There are a few boxes of coins under the bed that have monetary value. They need to go. What else? Food. Whatever we can fit into a couple of shopping bags. Cheez-Its, water, soda, some canned goods. Cash and checkbooks. All the checkbooks that are current. Shred the others before we leave. And the cash. After Karen's trip to the bank yesterday to grab $1,000 we now have $2,500 in one of our fire-safe cash boxes. The fire-safe cash box. We need to bring it. Meds. This is probably one of the highest priorities. The daily meds and those taken as needed such as Imodium, Zofran, Compazine, and those are just mine. Karen has a few of her own. And make sure we have prescription information for the meds. I should bring a few copies of my poetry books. Other books. Try to figure out my favorite ten books and drop them in another shopping bag. *To the Lighthouse*, if I can find it. *The Art of Voice*. *On Writing*. *Zen and the Art of Motorcycle Maintenance*. A few more. This is one of the most difficult areas to prioritize, but I should let it go, can order new books if needed. Oh! My first-edition copy of *Views of Jeopardy* by Jack Gilbert. I have to save that one.

I haven't even started loading the suitcases and am already feeling the pangs of remorse that our houseful of evacuees have been feeling for days. Again, I feel for them, try not to throw myself into a deep depression that makes me useless to everybody, keep myself detached just enough to be able to stay up for them, provide them with a homey atmosphere as best as we can.

In my mind I'm cramming the suitcases full, shoving in one last book, maybe Morton Marcus's ivory pipe, maybe the pink glass heart Cheryl gave me, maybe the nice letter opener from Artisans gallery. But I have to stop, imagine jamming the last case into the Prius, strapping myself in behind the wheel, Karen by my side, ready to back out of the driveway, look at the brass band hanging from the courtyard fence, Terry Kvenild's mosaic monkey in the front yard. The red mailbox with POST on it.

What are we leaving behind? Thirty-one years of life together on this property where Karen's kids and our grandkids have carved memories with us. I'm envisioning us as evacuees, stopping at my mom's and picking up Shelly and Mom to take them out to Gary and Cheryl's 100-acre sanctuary south of Watsonville on San Juan Road.

But it's really too soon. As of this morning there is 5% containment, there has been a degree of success at creating a construction line or fire break from Highway 1 to Highway 9. At least too soon for us to be imagining life as an evacuee. All we can do is dredge up our empathy for Ali, Chuck, Katie, Joe, Eva, Elsie, their dogs Annabelle and Gracie, and a cat in the camper whose name is unknown to me. I ache for them. I say things like "Just imagine the mansion you'll be able to build from scratch with the insurance money."

I know my empathy falls short of what they need right now. But I'll continue to pretend I know how they feel, that I can squeeze my feet into their shoes, try to visualize what it is they've all left behind.

Magical, Mysterious, Magnificent Art Workshop

BEING COOPED UP IN SOMEONE ELSE'S HOUSE, worried whether or not your own house is still standing, having to wear a mask when you're indoors, not being allowed to go outdoors because of the unsafe smoke levels, and becoming frustrated with your younger sister who seems to be even more under foot given the closer proximity of your living conditions, is enough to drive any eight-year-old girl into uncontrollable meltdowns.

All that, and Eva is not just any eight-year-old girl. After five days with her, I have become privy to her moods, attitudes, beliefs, huge heart and compassion, bossiness, and a vocabulary that surpasses most college students.

All day long, every day, the people around her are talking about the fire, about whether her uncle's house on Bear Creek is still standing, about whether her grandma and grandpa's house is still standing, about whether her house and her bedroom and her stuffed animals and drawings and everything else are still there.

At one point during the day I'm by myself in the living room with my head buried in a novel, making revisions. Eva walks in, sits down in the chair across from me, looks at me and says, "Uncle Jory, I'd like to have a conversation with you." I feel like I'm about to be lectured to by my second-grade teacher who didn't like me much.

"Okay," I answer. In the background I have the golf tournament on the TV with the sound on low.

She looks at the TV, then at me, and says, "Can you mute that while we talk?" I want to show a big grin, want to laugh at this eight-year-old going on eighty. But I know better. I feel like I'm back in the classroom with some of my old students who held themselves like Eva. I often worried about those students, knew that their too-articulate way of thinking and speaking always landed over the heads of their peers and made them stand out as odd ducks. I wonder about Eva and how she fits in with her teachers and fellow students. Wonder if she used the same know-it-all behavior with them, or if she has enough common sense to catch herself.

Karen shared an example of Eva's behavior that she experienced yesterday. The grosbeak birds that we so love were perched on the bird feeder and Karen said, "Oh! Look! There's a grosbeak." She pronounced it the way we have always pronounced it—*grows–beek*. Eva corrected her, told her it was pronounced *grahs–beek*. One of my pet peeves is that if you're going to step up and correct someone for their behavior or vocabulary, you'd better be right. Later I went to the Internet, and both pronunciations are correct, with *grows–beek* usually listed first.

Back to the talk I'm about to receive from Eva. I mute the TV, set down my pen and the paper I've been revising, and give her my full attention.

She begins. "So, Uncle Jory, I don't know if I should be talking to you about this, but I figure it won't hurt if you will allow me to tell you about something I learned. I was watching this program about how therapy dogs help people who are sick." Eva is highly aware of my cancer and has seen me diminish over time from 230 pounds to 175 pounds. She has empathy, compassion, would do anything in her power to make people feel better.

She continues. "The therapy dogs can make people who are sick feel a whole lot better. For example, there is a dog named Lark who lives with Logan, and Logan sometimes has trouble bending over or moving very well, so he will ask Lark to help him. Maybe he drops a pen on the floor and Logan says, 'Lark, get my pen please.' And Lark bends over, gets the pen, and hands it to Logan. I was just thinking that it might be nice for you to have a dog that could do things for you and make you feel better."

Part of me wants to cry. Part of me wants to laugh. Most of me wonders where the hell this young girl has picked up the ability to think and talk and feel like this. I also want to be careful not to be too glib, not to have her think I'm making fun of her.

"Thank you so much, Eva," I say with sincerity. "I thank you for thinking of my well-being." Then I can't help it, need to throw a touch of humor in to lighten the mood. "If Lark was my dog, or some other therapy dog, I would ask him to go into the kitchen and make me a chocolate milkshake."

She laughs. We laugh together.

Every day for the past four days Eva has suffered some sort of meltdown. It's certainly not hard to figure out the causes. She says, "Everything is so hard since *she* has come along." Eva's talking about her five-year-old sister, Elsie. Eva loves Elsie. But at the moment, in the middle of so many life-changing events, Elsie is soaking up some of Eva's limelight, gets in the way of Eva getting to do whatever Eva wants to do.

The day continues with fire updates on the TV and her dad, Joe, who is working up in the middle of the fires, calling in with reports, running out of water, new walls of flames, that he hasn't been able to get close enough to Boulder Creek to see if their house is still standing. We are all in command mode, listening for every new piece of information and sharing it with each other. Eva and Elsie run up and down the stairs, choosing one room or another to roost in, to work on art projects, to eat a sandwich, to stop and join in and listen to what the adults are saying, and Eva fashions herself as much an adult as everyone else in the room, and as a former teacher, I would probably place a hefty wager that her IQ far surpasses any one of ours.

Karen and Ali hatch an idea to have a family Zoom call and invite a dozen or so folks to give them an update on the fire, its proximity to us, odds of whether or not houses are still standing, if we all might have to evacuate and head south. Eva and Elsie and her mom and dad are upstairs in Georgia's studio on their computer. We see them on our Zoom screen even though they are only fifty or so feet away. The conversation is nearly 100% about the fire. Folks from out of town want to know details, want to hear things that we've been saying over and over to each other, things that Eva has been listening to and thinking about.

The call lasts for about an hour and eventually there's nothing more new to say. By this time Eva has come downstairs and is sitting under the table in the living room where we put puzzles together. We conclude the Zoom meeting and idle chatter begins. Mostly about people we hadn't seen for a while or had just met. There is a bit of talk that continues about the fire.

That's when Eva speaks up.

"I get tired of hearing about all this bad news about the fires and our house and everything else that you all talk about all day long. Can't we just try to be happy and talk about happy things?" It went on. Silence in the room except for the fifty-year-old Eva telling us how to act and think and feel. Eventually I had to respond.

"I understand how you feel. I have something like that, too. Two years ago, when I got cancer, I thought of it as the two 'C's, cancer and chemo. And then along came Covid. I couldn't stand to think about or hear about Covid in my life when the other two 'C's were so prominent. And I'm a writer, but I have refused to write about Covid, didn't want it taking over my life. So I understand that you feel that way about all the fire talk." Then I went into the "but" phase. "But everybody in your family is worried about losing all the possessions and memories and photos and things they've loved and cherished their whole lives, so it's natural for them to worry nonstop about it, to think about it, to talk about it, to watch the news to see if they get a glimpse of their houses either standing or as a pile of ash. And every person thinks and deals with these things differently." I said more, in my teacherly fashion, in my undergrad-psych-degree fashion.

We went to bed. I got up at 6:00 to watch the CalFire briefing. Eight percent contained! That was good news. I wanted to tell everybody. But I didn't. Instead I drove to Home Depot, bought some supplies to build Eva and Elsie their very own "Magical, Mysterious, Magnificent Art Workshop" in our workshop, put up two easels, one for each of them, got out the acrylics, color pens, glue, magazines to cut pieces from, screwed the canvases to the wall, then went to Gayle's to buy a pile of food for breakfast and lunch.

Now that's a good way to start a happy day and have enough activities scheduled to forget the fire and smoke and other not-so-happy things that come along with it, for a little while.

December 7, 1932—Santa Catalina

MY MOTHER WAS BORN ON DECEMBER 4, 1932, in a hospital in Oakland, California. Three days later the *Catalina Islander*, published weekly in Avalon on Santa Catalina Island, distributed their December 7, 1932, issue.

There is no connection between my mother's birth and the *Islander* issue that hit the newsstands and was delivered to doorsteps in Avalon. The closest connection I can make is that today is day fifty of my Daily Fresh essays and I need a topic to write about.

For a number of years I have been fascinated by the website titled smalltownpapers.com, a website that has archived more than 250 newspapers from forty-seven states. I've written poems and short stories that originated in these small-town rags.

This morning while hunting for a way in, a topic, I clicked on "California" and found fourteen cities with archived newspapers, including Gualala, Westwood, Burney, and Avalon. Thus my discovery of the *Catalina Islander*, a twelve-page issue, Vol. XIX, No. 49. All I need to do is read the masthead and I'm in love and addicted.

In the right corner of the masthead: "Year round mecca for tourists and travelers. Boating, bathing, golf, tennis, baseball, riding, fishing, hiking, marine gardens. Unexcelled accommodations." I've never been. I want to catch the next flight down. But then I read a sentence on the left side: "Baseball training field for Chicago 'Cubs.'" What?! I scour the rest of the issue hoping to find more about the Cubs and their training field. I know I'm going to find buried treasures among these twelve pages, enough to fill more than a 1,500-word essay, but my attention has been waylaid, and I open a new browser window and search for "Chicago Cubs Avalon training field."

Photo credit: Love Catalina, Catalina Island Tourism Authority

Bingo! I find an article on a site called *lovecatalina.com*. Apparently in 1919, William Wrigley, Jr., and his wife, Ada, began a lifelong love affair with the island. They purchased everything they could, including hotels, restaurants, and other attractions. Within a year and a half, Wrigley had a spring training facility built that matched the exact dimensions of Wrigley Field in Chicago. He also constructed a clubhouse that eventually became the Catalina Island Country Club. This relationship between Wrigley, the Cubs, and Santa Catalina Island lasted for thirty years. The tagline "The Cubs Are Here, You Should Come Too" was used widely to promote both the island and the Cubs. In 1952, the Cubs moved to a new training facility in Mesa, Arizona. The training field is gone, but a commemorative plaque still exists. I need to get there, take a photo of the plaque, feel the auras of Smokey Burgess, Hank Sauer, Dutch Leonard. Another time, after Covid and fires and heat waves.

I dig back into the December 7, 1932, issue. December 7 won't take on its infamous recollection for another nine years, so for these reporters it was just another week of regular reporting. Page One news includes a short article on Avalon Night, surrounded with a flashy border so it will stand out, so all the town's residents will remember that on Thursday night, the Hotel St. Catherine featured upgrades to the dining room, Spanish dancers, dinner dancing, and a buffet for $.65. In another article it doesn't go unnoticed that the regular meeting of "Business Men" was held, and that they were in fact 100 percent males.

The other front-page item that fascinates me is titled "Sunshine Psychology—Motivation" by the editor. The sentence that first captures my eye is a quote from another article in *Psychology Today*: "The main and most curious connection between the pituitary gland and telepathy is found among the Hindus."

What?! In 1932? It continues: "The sea of emotion and mind in which we swim, like psychic fishes, innocent of the medium that suspends us, has ripples and waves of unimaginable fineness. These penetrate not only stone and lead, but the solid matter of the human cranium. We are immersed in these seas of sensation all the time, penetrated with sensation, but for the lack of positive attention and knowledge, the psychic world goes by …"

I'm flabbergasted. First a training field for the Cubs and now telepathy. It goes on to talk about salt blood and electrical forces, the similarity between boiler pressure and blood pressure, internal parasites and secretion.

I move on to Page Two, where I find an inch-and-a-half column listing the Game Fish of Catalina:

- Marlin swordfish
- Broadbill swordfish
- Dolphin
- Giant Bass
- Yellowfin
- Albacore
- Bluefin Tuna
- Yellowtail
- California Bonita
- White Sea Bass
- Ocean Bonito

I'm curious about why this list garners Page Two space. I'm certain the residents of Avalon are already aware of the game fish they've been living with for most of their lives. And how many tourists would be visiting for a little game fishing in December?

I'm engaged by the advertisement on Page Three for Gerard Food Market, who delivers. The two-pound jar of Rose Brand peanut butter for $.20, the small leg of lamb for $.17 a pound, the dozen cinnamon rolls for $.19, and the avocadoes for $.05 each. Just to the left of the Gerard ad is a Wrigley's Gum ad. Hah! Mr. Wrigley once again. It says, "Great between smokes. Keeps the mouth cool and moist. $.05. Inexpensive. Satisfying."

Page Four is edited by the journalism class of Avalon High School, an insert titled "The High School Sugar Loaf," where we learn that the junior girls beat the senior girls in the final basketball game of the season; that *The Bold Dragon and Other Ghostly Stories* by Washington Irving has been added to the school library; that

Florence Chasse left Avalon to attend school on the mainland; that Howard Bailey was appointed to hall guard as a result of the departure of the former guard, Florence Chasse; that more than 1,100 youngsters graduated from the Juvenile Traffic School in Los Angeles; and that the touch football series was continued in spite of the slight drizzle of rain last Wednesday.

On to Page Five, where one item stands out, an ad for Mrs. C. B. Parker, a taxidermist who offers "careful mounting of Catalina fish." I want to skip Page Six, but I read about the Catalina Island Treasure Hunt scheduled for December 24 and 25, where a real pot of pirate gold can be found at "the end of the rainbow."

I slow down again on Page Seven when I see "Social and Personal" at the top of the first column. Tidbits. "Mr. and Mrs. John Barrymore and children left for the mainland on Thursday last, aboard their beautiful yacht 'Infanta' after a week's stay." "Thursday evening, while on her way home, Mrs. Wm. Orr was knocked down and seriously bruised by a large dog which was apparently chasing a cat or other animal. Mrs. Orr had to be taken home in a taxi. She is gradually recovering from the injuries. This is another reason why dogs should not be allowed on the streets except on a leash." "Mr. Pete Vulch is out again after an attack of the flu." "Lyman and Thomas Smith of 122 are entertaining Bruce and Wayne Ripley of Los Angeles."

I'm ready to turn the page when I see "The Islander Adlets" in the bottom-right corner of the page, things for sale in Avalon:

- A cottage at 228 Metropole for $2,500.
- Bridge Score Cards for $.25 or $.50.
- For Rent – comfortable ground floor flat, neatly furnished, $25 per month.

My main interest on Page Eight is a poem posted by R. V. Vaughn:

Creation
I sat upon the mountainside and watched
A tiny barque that skimmed across the sea,
Drifting, like humanity upon
A world of hidden peril; then she sailed
From out my ken, and mingled with the blue
Of skies unfathomed, while the great round sun
Weakened toward the waves.

          Ch'ang Ch'ien

Before I turn the page, I glance at the ad by Mrs. Anna M. LeFavor, who has canaries for sale on Metropole (just a few doors down from the cottage for sale).

Based on what I find on Page Nine, I'm guessing the islanders don't engage in a lot of reading, as the Avalon Public Library is only open every other weekday from 2 to 5 and 7 to 8:30.

Page Ten grabs my interest with an article titled "Economy and the Next Legislature," where the key concept is "A unified public opinion is necessary if any program of retrenchment in government is to succeed. Every person in California must do his part to make possible the reduction of the cost of government." So glad to see that this is the responsibility of the men and not the women. There is also a two-inch column dedicated to the bacterial diet of sea worms as studied by a Hopkins Marine Station's scientist named G. E. MacGinitie, who fed sea worms nothing but bacteria for 68 days.

The key headline on Page Eleven states "H2O Scores Victory," where the California "civilization" is compared with the Mayan civilization. "The investigations tend to show that the ruined Mayan cities were destroyed by erosion. This same factor is a major menace to our present California civilization."

One last note on Page Eleven: "Catalina Island—the place where quietness and repose soothe ragged nerves and renews health and happiness."

Daily Fresh

Now on to the final page, Twelve, where the majority of the page is reserved for a column titled "Refined and Crude," which is an attempt by the *Catalina Islander* editors to leave their audience with a bit of humor. I had hoped to include one example here, but they are all awful.

After reading through the December 7, 1932, issue of the *Catalina Islander*, I feel like I was born there, have lived my whole life there. I know where to buy canaries, where to rent a room or buy a cottage. I know what kind of fish to expect if I book an expedition, and I know where to get that fish stuffed if I want to hang it over the mantle. I know to stay away from Pete Vulch if I want to avoid the flu.

But more than anything, I know to return to *smalltownpapers.com* to dig into pathways of history that make me love communities and the folks who inhabit them.

Reset

So many of my prompts originate in discussions with my friend Scott. I'll write them down next to a light bulb after a conversation, let them sit in my journal until proper gestation has taken place, then pluck them out and drop them into an initial paragraph, like this. This morning I skimmed back through the journal and found this one inspired by Scott, the notion of *reset*.

I like to start with definitions, so let's see what Wikipedia has to say: "In a computer or data transmission system, a reset clears any pending errors or events and brings a system to normal condition or an initial state, usually in a controlled manner."

Hmm. I wouldn't have gone there first, but I do like the idea of clearing "any pending errors," suggesting that we might use a reset to avoid extremely traumatic or devastating events in our lives. It's worthy of consideration, but focuses on the negative rather than the positive. Clearly if I was using this definition as my guiding light, I would drop back before my father died and spend some extra quality time with him. Or I would go back twenty-two months prior to a negative health diagnosis.

Merriam-Webster's definition is terse and to the point: "to set again or anew." This is what Scott and I imagined with our brief foray. If we were going to start anew, fresh, at what point or event in our lives would we do so?

This is one of those mental activities that requires props, a concatenated series of home videos that takes one back to being slapped on the butt by a doctor and proceeds to being stuck in the chest by a nurse some sixty-nine years later. So much footage to consider, but at least we're limiting our choices to positive events in our lives that we wouldn't mind revisiting, reliving, possibly even freezing in time.

Remember, this is an edited retelling, a sampling of events, of good times that I wouldn't mind having my DeLorean time machine drop me in for a day or a lifetime. The viewing of episodes is chronological, not yet ordered, so you will see I am doing my homework first, delving into the research to understand the continuum in front of me. Later, maybe I'll prioritize, maybe not.

"Roll the footage, please!"

The film rolls by, yellowed and aged. The reel makes the little popping noises I remember so well. It looks like I may be spared having to relive the negative aspects of my life as it appears that parents and others didn't tend to film those events. Which is good. I see Christmas trees and presents and half-eaten cookies and half-empty glasses of milk. Pretty good times, but not where I would want to be stuck in a *Groundhog Day* loop, because my brain was not yet developed enough to appreciate things. There's a BB gun under the tree which excites me, for a day or two.

The film races through the days and years on Seminole Avenue in Hayward from ages three to eleven, with my dad's darkroom set up in the hall bathroom, his '67 turquoise-blue-and-white Chevy sitting in the driveway, our dog Zack digging holes in the backyard, my dad and me making homemade box kites and flying them in the empty field at the corner.

Then we zoom forward to Keller Street in San Lorenzo where my strongest positive memory is playing Little League as catcher for the Arroyo Giants, where I threw runners out at second base, hit two home runs, and loved the refreshments in the food stand after the games, especially the frozen chocolate malts we ate with wooden spoons. I know I said I wouldn't prioritize yet, but it's hard not to as I revisit these segments of my life. I will say that nothing so far warrants a reset.

But next comes the family's move to Santa Cruz, where my father lands a job. I stay with Grandma Esther in San Leandro playing Little League All-Stars while the family settles into an old Victorian behind the Casablanca Hotel and Restaurant just up from the beach and Boardwalk. I love Grandma's house, love the RC Colas she buys by the case, the weeping willow tree in the backyard, the avocado tree, the shredded-wheat breakfasts.

The film begins to track the changes in our lives, puberty setting in, a summer steeped in fishing off the wharf and playing pinball in the Casino. This was a good summer. I had one friend at Mission Hill Jr. High School, Jamie MacAdams. He was a good friend, a very nice and caring person, and he taught me how to play a game called Stocks and Bonds.

I know I've touched on many of these memories in other pieces I've written, but I have no control over how this chronology rolls out in this film spliced together by a technician who knew nothing about us. So I'll keep watching, move to Soquel High School, have my first girlfriend and sex and play football and graduate. The pool table in our garage is a place where friends come to hang out after school and on weekends. I love the math and physics of pool balls traveling over green felt. I love the feel of the cue sliding through my fingers. My dad opens an auto-supply store and four druggies open a pool hall next door called Fast Eddy's and I hone my skills on the snooker table, the billiards table, and the regular Gold Crown tables. I'm not the best in town, but I'm in the top five for a while when I focus and put in the time.

At Cabrillo College the film speeds up, shows me playing football, hating the statistics class, loving the Philosophy of Nietzsche class, the first intelligent discussion I can remember myself participating in. I fast-forward the film through my first marriage because I am focusing on the positive, rushing ahead to my time at UCSC. I majored in psychology and education and then began my career as an educator at Happy Valley School, where I met lifelong friends whom I still see today.

A parade of people fill the film: people who changed my life, opened me up to think of myself and life differently than I could ever have imagined. The reading of auras against white sheets hung in living rooms, collaborating with others interested in writing, learning how to become a better teacher, write and implement successful grants. There's Kitty at the New Teacher Center, and Jon Silver, and Robbie Jaffee, and Lynn Kepp, and then along comes Scott, who helps to open my brain, expands my possibilities like LSD might have done if I had ever used it.

And here I am at thirty-eight years old, taking the elevator to the second floor of the Cocoanut Grove Ballroom, just above that Casino where I spent so many Mercury-head dimes in pinball machines, arriving in the large ballroom in 1988 for our twenty-year

Soquel High School reunion, which is where I am reunited with Karen after twenty years, where we eat together, dance together all night long, and I have one of the best nights of my life.

The film shows a drive-by of a white, two-story house with green trim that we buy together, move into along with Jeannie and Ali, Karen's daughters. And now I notice that the technician has spliced the film together out of sequence, as I now see the hiring committee at Happy Valley selecting a new principal back in 1980. That's where I meet Cheryl Morris, possibly the most influential person in my life. She is bubbly, friendly, dedicated, and we hire her. And she rocks my world. I sign up for a Master's in Education program at USF. I quit using drugs. I win the National Christa McAuliffe Award to develop virtual field trips on the Internet.

We come back to 1993 with a wedding in our backyard with 150 people in 99-degree heat, and I love seeing this footage. My dad and cousin Kent are both still alive, slaving over a hot Weber barbecue, cooking skirt steak. My aunts and uncles are there, still alive. We fly to Maui for our honeymoon, friend Annie putting us up in a gorgeous little cottage 4,000 feet up Haleakala with a view of everything. We stay for three weeks, island hopping to Kauai and Oahu.

The film brings us back to the mainland and Santa Cruz where we continue to live a charmed and loving life.

Much of the remaining footage shows me sitting in one of my favorite chairs with fingers on keyboard, typing. It shows the launch of my first book of poetry, *The Extra Year*, with nearly 150 people in attendance at the Food Lounge in downtown Santa Cruz, where Gary Young, Danusha Laméris, and Farnaz Fatemi read poetry with me.

More fast-forward that shows my fairly rapid weight loss from 230 to 175 pounds. Completion of the second poetry book, *Of Two Minds*. Nonstop writing on one project or another. A steady flow of friends who come by and visit with masks, or on Zoom. The fresher footage brightens up, shot more recently, full of light, easy to see the miracle bleeding through the hazy skies. As the film slides off the reel, I see the miracle flapping, make itself large and clear.

I haven't shared everything I've seen in the footage, everything that was either visual or implied. Just enough to frame my choices, help me make the priorities needed in case I'm ever given the gift of reset. The short list includes the first day of chemistry class Karen and I had together in 1967 at Soquel High, the dancing together at the twenty-year reunion, the backyard wedding, meeting Cheryl, meeting Scott, launching the first poetry book. Those with Karen drift to the top, but they're all important, make it impossible to prioritize.

When I think about it viscerally, I might not accept the reset if offered. I've got the film now and can revisit all of it whenever I want, though from a distance. Maybe the distant view is better than reliving it. Instead of a reset, I'll simply stay set where I am. Right here. Knowing what I know about where I've been, the excellent times I've been lucky enough to have lived during this miraculous journey.

So keep your reset. I'm fine.

Apologizing for Priorities

WHEN I PUT MY HEAD ON THE PILLOW AT NIGHT, usually no later than 9:00, I'm thinking about what I might find to write about the next day, tossing around a few ideas from the day that could sprout into something in my dreams, like hearing Jimmy Fallon say something about people planting seeds sent to them from China. I have no idea if this was a joke or real, but it rolls around for a bit. The notion is gone by morning, but I open my computer and find an email from a friend which erases all thoughts of China and seeds and anything else that may have wanted to take center stage in today's brain dump. (But wait. I couldn't help myself. The seeds thing is true. Unsolicited packets of seeds from China have been delivered to many folks in the U.S. and other countries. This may be the item of interest in tomorrow's writing, but onward with today's topic.)

The email is long—463 words. Not the typical breakfast email. This is a friend I have had for nearly a decade. I will try to be discreet and keep his/her identity as hidden as possible (because I know he/she will read the book when I publish it), and more importantly, mutual friends will read it and will wonder who it is. To aid in disguising this person, I'll use a technique I generally dislike in others' work. I will use a combined pronoun and call this person he/she, use him/her when I need. Within the first two sentences he/she says, "I apologize for not being in touch for so long." Thus pops the theme of the day. In the following sentence he/she says, "I can imagine you might feel hurt and pissed."

I respond to his/her email and say what I've been thinking for a long time: "I don't know that 'hurt and pissed' describe my emotions, but your scattered check-ins do evoke thoughts and feelings. Given that you brought it up, let me be honest. If you looked back at nearly every email you've sent me over the past two years, you'll find a consistent thread of apologies, telling me why you haven't stayed in contact, often making your partner the bad cop, so at least it's good you have a dog now to transfer those bad cop tendencies to. :-) Please stop with the apologies. We all have a ton of stuff going on in our lives, good and bad, so establishing priorities is critical to our individual survival. I have a mental continuum in my head of the people in my life. I pretty much know where they fall on that continuum. No judgments. It's just a study on human nature and how people respond to illness and other issues in their busy lives. Hearing about what's going on in your lives is enough."

It's true about the continuum. I sometimes visualize it as a straight line, an A-Z timeline where occupants of the far left never make contact, and occupants of the far right may be in daily contact, in one form or another. At other times I see it as a dartboard, with concentric circles surrounding the center hub that is me. It's a matter of proximity. Karen and a few others occupy the circle that hugs me closest. Those who I have never heard from occupy the thin outer circle. There are other models, but it's not so much about the model or frame, but rather about the sentiment that causes placement within the model.

It is true about the judgment comment I made to him/her in my response. In my own life, I've occupied different circles on the board or spots on the timeline depending on who the sick person was and my then state of mind. How we prioritize our attention toward others is based on a whole bag full of mysterious and twisted histories that plunge into our own backstories as well as theirs. There have been times in my life when a fellow teacher got breast cancer and I organized food deliveries to her house in the mountains. There have been other times where I had to turn my back, move forward with my own life for fear of skidding and veering over a cliff.

The he/she above and his/her partner visited occasionally in the beginning, were helpful with their advice, and occupied a spot between M and N on the continuum. As time went on, they slowly disappeared, but for good reasons. Children with difficulties. Covid. One of them with a highly stressful job. It's the apologies and excuses that bothered me. No need for either one. I cherish them both, as caring and loving people, and as friends that I may not hear from as often as I might like.

I have twenty-one friends who crowd the XYZ end of the continuum, who are there for me so much, and I in turn am there for them—four of whom I have written about so far as topics of a Daily Fresh. I will get to all twenty-one of them before I'm done, and will compose a document I'll title "The Twenty-One Gun Salute", or possibly something without the gun in it. We spend time with each other when we can. Phone calls, FaceTime, Zoom meetings, socially distanced and masked courtyard visits. When we can't, we don't apologize or make excuses, we know we'll find mutual time soon.

Some of these friends read to me from their work. Others read poems written by other poets. I read to them. We talk about Covid, the fires, the heat. We talk about what's currently important in our lives. We talk about our kids, our grandkids. Anything and everything we can while we can, because we all know what's coming, and even though we do, it's not the center of our lives, the core of our discussions, because the clock continues to tick.

There are a few friends who can't stand the thought of death, in general, and specifically, can't stand the thought of my death. As Janie says it, "I can't imagine a planet without you on it." I understand. I can't imagine a planet without my dad on it. But he's gone. I can't imagine a planet without Kobe Bryant on it. But he's gone. I can't imagine a planet without 400,000 Americans dead from Covid on it. But they are all gone.

When I spend rare time at the far edges of the dartboard I am often baffled. I don't spend much time there because I'd rather focus on folks who are closer. But when I drift there, it's not with judgment that I stare into the eyes of one person, just one, who has been a friend for nearly sixty years. It's more about being baffled by his disappearance, his abandonment. Okay. Using the word *abandonment* sounds a bit judgmental. But he's never been one whom I've been able to figure out and categorize. It could very well be that he can't stand the thought of being around or thinking about sick people. I know that's the case for many. I have a feeling I'll never know. I'll probably pass before he's able to break himself out of his concrete mold.

But I don't think of him much. There is some sort of magic connected to spending time with someone who knows the time frame is short. Some folks know that and flock to be around it, to breathe it in, to remind themselves how precious time is. It's sad to me that he will miss out on capturing some of it, carrying it with him into his future.

And I am so thrilled that the others have been with me throughout this journey. No apologies. No excuses. No second-guessing. Simply a straight path forward with eyes wide and focused.

The Compound

TWO OF OUR EVACUEES LEARNED TODAY that their house on Empire Grade in Bonny Doon was gutted by the CZU fire in the Santa Cruz Mountains. The days before found us all looking at the map provided by CalFire showing which houses had been destroyed, designated by a tiny red house, and which houses had survived, designated by a tiny green house. The status of those that were simply grey was unknown. One of us would check every hour or so to see if there had been any change. Yesterday morning my sister called and had just looked at the updated map and told me the house now had the little red house. I told Ali about the bad news. The biggest tell was a silence, hard-pressed lips trying to keep everything locked inside.

It was a devastating realization. When the house looked grey, there was hope, there was a positive attitude, the "I feel good about our house still standing." This news ended all that, sent them into the what's-next frame of mind. Chuck was a manager at Big Creek Lumber for most of his career, retired recently. The talk quickly moved into assessing what was gone, what had recently been purchased, making a mental list of what would need to be replaced. Chuck was on the phone in a hurry, talking with friends at Big Creek, talking about current cost per square foot of building a new house.

Life in our house has undergone radical changes in the past few years, beginning with my diagnosis in October 2018. At that point four people occupied our house. Karen's daughter, Ali, lived in the guest bedroom for a couple years upon returning to town from Los Angeles. Shelly occupied the studio that she lived in for thirty years. In February, Ali's father died and she moved into his house. Then Covid arrived and sequestered us even more than usual. And finally, my mom fractured her wrist and Shelly moved in with her full-time, slowly removing everything from the studio. We now had a true empty nest in our 2,300-square-foot home for the first time since 1989. Until the fires. That's when our evacuee family moved in without question. Six of them with two dogs and a cat. And in a few days, Georgia and her boyfriend, AJ, will move into the studio full-time. The nest has suddenly become overflowing with eight adults, two kids, two dogs, and a cat. Oh, and Georgia has two cats.

I know it's not a great time to be smiling about anything, but I am, I'm laughing hilariously inside about what it is we can never predict that can change our lives dramatically with the snap of fingers, with a bolt of lightning. It is sickeningly funny, makes me want to create a stand-up comedy routine containing a bunch of jokes told way too soon. But I won't. Instead I'll sit in my room and ponder, put on paper what I can, reflect on the truths and absurdities of our lives. Or like this morning, I'll slip out of my closet, my cave, make my way downstairs to the living room that has been the hub of our existence for the past nine days, where everybody gathers to watch the morning and evening updates from CalFire. We play a guessing game with each update, trying to predict what percent of containment has been reached. Last night we were up to 21%, which stayed the same this morning.

It's more difficult to focus and write while downstairs, but I pay attention to the dialogue, mostly between Chuck and Ali, decide to use it as the core of today's reflection. I'm sitting in the midst of their "what ifs" as they walk through the memories of their burned-out home, listen to them wonder if they can find any hand tools in the rubble, doorknobs and other pieces of memorable metals that may have survived. They walk through each room of the house taking mental inventory, happy that the fireplace was gone because they never liked its location. They begin a handwritten list of things to replace: the stove, the refrigerator, the couch, the chairs, the art supplies, it goes on and on. I try to imagine doing the same with our house. I believe Karen and I both have fairly good photographic memories, or at least good spatial-relationship skills, so the virtual walkthrough itself would not be difficult, but the task at hand, the thinking about a pile of ashes that used to be possessions, treasures, antiques, photos of parents and grandparents, that part seems so overwhelming that I can barely stand to think about it.

They continue. Will the Honda Accord still be there? What about the tractor? Will the swimming pool have melted into a mass of plastic? What about the cinder blocks in the workshop? What will it be like to walk through the rubble, hunting, a scavenger hunt like no other they've been on in their lives?

Chuck is on the phone talking with contractors, architects, insurance folks, right on top of what needs to be done as quickly as possible. He has already secured his contractor of choice who tells him he might be able to have the house rebuilt in three months. That seems overly ambitious but who knows? Chuck is good at this, uses his management skills from Big Creek to quickly become his own general contractor. They are going to be fine. By Christmas, they are going to have a nice new house and can wrap it in a big red bow. Forethought. Action. Delivery. All it will take now is access to the property by CalFire and the sheriff's department. Access to the insurance money by State Farm. Dumpsters to haul things away. Expedition by Santa Cruz County to waive the usually tedious permit process, and they will be on their way. I'm guessing a month to get the process moving and the property ready to build. Then three to five months.

Which brings me back to the not-so-empty nest. I predict that Joe and Katie and the girls will be allowed to return to their house still standing in Boulder Creek within a week or two. At that point, Chuck and Ali can move into the guest bedroom, relieve themselves of the cramped life of living in a camper. They have been told by insurance that they will cover rental fees for up to two years. It will make more sense for them to move in with us full-time as long as they need, as long as they are comfortable with that, as long as Karen begins treating me as if I'm still alive and that I have equal say in what we do around here. This might sound a little harsh, but at the rate things are going related to my health, I don't imagine I'll be around to see the completion of the new house in Bonny Doon. But, while I'm still here, I plan to continue to live as full and active a life as possible, so I don't want to be ignored, coddled, or kowtowed to.

So, I'm envisioning a life in the near future where we share our home completely with Chuck and Ali and Annabelle, partially with Georgia and AJ. For me, the only question is Spotty, their cat. Will they leave him or her—at least I now know the name if not the sex—in the camper full-time, or will he/she also occupy the house before long?

Daily Fresh

It becomes difficult after fifty-three days to keep topics clean and separate. With so many life-changing events affecting everyday life, they clearly overlap, twist together, pop up even when I'm intentionally trying to avoid them.

But we are an adaptable species. We make room for new ideas, new people, family, friends. We look forward once we clean up the rubble of looking backward. We can't wait to see what is just beyond our immediate vision. Show me something new, fresh.

Perspective

THE FIRE IS 74% OUT OF CONTROL. The fire is 26% contained. The fire grew to 82,540 acres. The fire only grew by 500 acres last night. Evacuees from Ben Lomond, Felton, Boulder Creek have not been allowed to return home. Evacuees from Scotts Valley have returned to their homes. It goes on. All the way to the proverbial glass and determining its level of fullness.

It begins with the eyes and the amount of light in the room. How much can the eye actually see? What is let in and what is kept out? And what makes it to the communication center in the brain, where ideas and opinions are formulated and distributed?

There are always at least two perspectives, e.g., the half full and half empty. Yesterday I saw a comic on Facebook that gave a third perspective, not so much about the interpretation of fullness, but rather about the content of the glass, suggesting that in the wake of 2020 the yellow liquid was urine.

Last night on the news a woman who just celebrated her 102nd birthday was interviewed. She was articulate, uplifting, not complaining about her aches and pains, not complaining about Covid or the fires or smoke. Instead, she focused on the miracle of her life, the miracle of all life. For a minute I wanted to be her, but just for a minute, before I remembered I didn't want to be carrying my bag-of-bones body around the planet for another thirty-three years. She was born in 1918 during one pandemic and was now living through another. I wanted her attitude, her bubbling spirit, her here-and-now minute-to-minute living of her life.

It doesn't matter whether you use a telescope, binoculars, reading glasses, a small pinhole in a piece of cardboard that lets you safely view an eclipse, or simply watch a shadow expand and shrink on the sidewalk as the sun moves. It's more about what you see when you close your eyes. What you imagine surrounds you, what you see as your immediate and long-term future.

There is always the obvious that can pull you forward, sometimes into a negative plunge, but it's the hidden, the implied, that interests me more, that keeps me positive and looking forward. Through the walls and down the halls I hear the screaming of young girls living in a house that's not theirs, making the best of it, having some fun, ready for a new day of exploring and art and discoveries. I'm not used to the noise in our house, used to the quiet of my own brain interrupted by the occasional grosbeak or dove eating seeds off my deck. At first I tend toward the screeching causing my glass to appear half empty, but I quickly smile, find myself laughing and watching the glass spill over with an abundance of liquid as the girls dance and spin and chase the dogs around the yard.

It is not rarefied air that I breathe or a delusional mask that I wear to achieve a relative sense of calm in the face of so much that can pull one into the muck and quicksand. It is simply a choice, because in the end, it's always about how we choose to view and live in the world in which we find ourselves.

Even if that world is filled with hurricanes battering the Gulf, fires eating up California, white policemen shooting black men and women, seventeen-year-old vigilantes killing protesters, metastatic cancer in the liver, the lives of black folks seeming not to matter to so many, 180,000 COVID deaths in America, and dozens of other examples of issues that could lead to severe depression and even suicide, I choose to observe and celebrate the miracles, when and where I can find them:

- In the face of a white orchid
- In the wet tongue of a loving rescue dog
- In watching the nationwide solidarity toward Black Lives Matter
- In the fried-egg sandwich my wife makes me for breakfast
- In the daily CalFire updates indicating progress on the fire
- In my fingers on the keyboard
- In knowing that our granddaughter Georgia will move into our studio on Sunday
- In the whine of a mating mountain lion in our backyard
- In the memories of my charmed life
- And the thoughts of what lies ahead

We can choose to wear the dark mask of tragedy or the wide smile of comedy as we make our way through this one-time journey. I will choose to laugh whenever I can, to watch stand-up comedians and *Saturday Night Live* and Jimmy Fallon and Stephen Colbert rather than the Republican National Convention or even the Democratic National Convention.

Am I tricking myself with this ruse? Probably so. But every ruse becomes a trick, and I'd rather be tricked into believing the miracles, expecting them to continue, whether in my face or implied, whether woven from the feathers of quail or lifted from the words of saints.

There are times when I'll need to walk away from the ranting of others, remove myself from the middle of their negative views of the world, rather than stay and fight with them, fall into their traps and let them trick me into a view that's not mine. I'll disappear into my soundproof booth, record *Goodnight, Moon* for my grandson, think about recording *Pious Rebel* for my wife, record my own thoughts in a journal that has tracked the events of a wild and crazy 2020, a vision that none of us could have predicted, and yet we shuffle through the rubble and find the shiny objects that give us joy.

Just one little plunge into Merriam-Webster—"the capacity to view things in their true relations or relative importance." This is where we run into trouble. Both the pessimist and the optimist can hold views that are true though opposed to each other. Is one more true than the other? Not necessarily, but when I choose to play the role of the optimist, to choose that ruse to live my life by, I carry with me a sense of hope, a piece of the miracle in my pocket, a guide to carry me into the unknown future.

A Little Bit of It in Everyone

WHEN NEIL YOUNG WROTE *The Needle and the Damage Done*, he could very well have been writing about drugs and junkies and the tendency to lose. Or, he may have simply forgotten to include a hyphen between the "e" and the "d."

I don't remember when I first saw the word *née* in my life. It may have been just prior to Lee Hanson and Coraly Brose's wedding way back in the early seventies when we were younger and mostly stupider than we are today. It would have been on the wedding invitation, reading something like: "Lee Hanson and Coraly née Brose invited you to attend their wedding on …" I can't remember when or where, but I do know that even though Brose was a prominent name in our county, there would have been no question that Coraly would take on Lee's last name, another prominent name in our county.

Even then, seeing it written out, I still didn't know what it meant, didn't take the time to care, was busy with a life that didn't care much about being well lived or paying attention to detail. I have a series of Junior League cookbooks and I'm guessing that every woman's name in the book either has a née in front of her original surname or uses the surname as a middle name.

I have learned of *née* in my life due to other interests. I play crossword puzzles and Scrabble and Words with Friends every day, and have for decades now. Like *enya* or *uta* or *eton* or *uma*, *née* is a crucial word to know and remember if you are going to successfully solve puzzles or achieve high scores. I only learned of its meaning through the implied clues in the puzzles, "born" and "formerly known" or "Norma Jean Mortensen."

When I finally looked it up, I discovered that the French word was first recorded in the mid-1700s, and that there is a male version, *né,* both emanating from the past participle *naitre,* meaning "to be born."

If my first wife had changed her name to Janice Post, she could have been referred to as Janice Post *née* Crooks. If my current wife had changed her name to Karen Post, she could have been referred to as Karen Post *née* Wallace. I personally am happy to see the trend where women keep their original surnames and identities that connect to centuries of history and ancestry. For me there is very little reason for women to only be associated with the surname of a man, or woman, they happened to marry.

It turns out that *née* as it's defined can be used in instances other than marriage. For example, in the National Football League, the Houston Oilers became the Tennessee Titans, so saying "The Tennessee Titans *née* the Houston Oilers" is perfectly acceptable and makes sense.

I woke up with *née* in my head and I knew the frame was weak, that I would be lucky to pull 500 words out of it, so I'm happy to have reached 510!

Every Hug Is a Small, Soft Jail

THE FIRST TIME I SAW this Richard Powers sentence in *The Overstory* it floored me. It did so again last night with a second reading. It may be the last sentence I ever need to read or write, or maybe say out loud three times quietly to an absent audience.

"Every hug is a small, soft jail," I whisper to myself. Here we come back full circle once again to the intent of the action. Usually there is a giver and a receiver when it comes to the hug in question, the initiator of the movement, the one who opens arms and moves in, and the acceptor or rejector of the often-subtle request.

If it's mutual, then there is no issue, no second thoughts, no questions of refusal, simply a merging of desire that culminates in the collaborative clasp. There may be a release of tears, a sigh of something just beyond relief that drains one from skull to sole. It's not unlike a basketball team before the tip-off, arms locked around shoulders and backs in group embrace, appreciating each other, glad to be alive, to be in this arena, this game, with these mutual huggers. That's when it's good.

Like when the army sergeant returns home from a one-year stint in Baghdad or Kabul and his wife and two kids rush him as he debarks the plane at San Francisco International Airport, and the wife grabs him first, he drops his bags, grabs her back, and the two kids wrap themselves around their parents, as if they've been missing him for 365 days and nights, counting every day, checking them off on calendars hanging on the walls next to their beds, one day at a time until this eventual embrace that has invaded their dreams, driven their nightmares, captured their needs like nothing they could ever have imagined.

Or when the soprano Fanny Salvini-Donatelli, who was playing the lead role of Violetta in Verdi's *La Traviata* and had been jeered by the audience at the premiere for being overweight and too old for the role, belted out the final lines to the final song, took her bows, then rushed backstage to find the arms of anyone who would hold her. Not so much out of desire, but out of a crushing need on Fanny's part, an empathetic acceptance by the receiver, whether a backstage hand, a husband, a lover, or a cast mate.

Then again it could be the type of engagement that is made wholly of desire, a clutch that is intended to be the precursor of something more, arms wrapped around shoulders with hands roaming around backs, agitating skin, arousing excitement, removing clothes and falling naked together into a waiting bed where the hug is maintained when one rolls on top of the other, and vice versa, their grips tight, until the release, the rolling over on backs and staring at the ceiling with deepened breaths.

But these mutual examples are not what Powers had in mind when he penned that jewel of a sentence. Once again, a little louder this time, just enough for the birds at the feeder to raise their beaks and wonder if they are at risk, I clear my throat, and for the second time say: "Every hug is a small, soft jail." And I say it like I mean it, like I've lived it more than once. Like I've experienced the crunch of someone who wants it more than me. I try to remember instances where it's occurred, but my vision is blurred, blocked by a thick fog that chooses to avoid a clear pathway to memories.

I persist. Feel the embrace of a former girlfriend wanting to continue. Me pulling away, resistant. The wrap of relatives who want consolation at the memorial of a loved one, of a grandmother or father, me wanting to resist the sympathies of human touch, to back away from the maudlin hands of death reaching for someone new. Or the more mundane approach of someone you went to high school with who finds you on Pacific Avenue while home for the holidays and getting in some Christmas shopping, who rushes you, mouth open, kisses your cheek and says, "It's been so long! I've missed you!" An embrace you try to remove yourself from as quickly as possible when you remember how she made hurtful fun of people behind their backs when she was a cheerleader in senior year.

But none of these examples are what Richard Powers had in mind when the arms of Adam Appich's mother found their way around his body, and though with the gentleness of swaddling a newborn baby, made it clear that she was in charge and that the hug was not done solely out of love for her awkward son. This is me pretending to dig into Powers' mind and imagine what it is he was trying to say, what he wanted me as a reader to understand from the eloquence of his language. That Adam often felt caged in his life, that he was more human than the other humans in his life and on the planet. That the reasons why folks seemed to not understand him and his way of thinking and living had more to do with them than it did him. That when his mother pulled him in for a hug, with his painting clutched between them, that he did in fact feel like his mother had installed a wall of bars around him that made him feel imprisoned, locked in a jail solely of her making. The bars were not only crafted by his mother, rather by every member of his family except the one sister, Jean, who cared for him, seemed to understand him.

I lean away from my keyboard, recast myself as the actor chosen to play Adam in the reenactment of his life, try to feel the bars pressing against my back, the claustrophobia of being trapped in a space created by others, knowing that there is some degree of softness in the creation, but not quite enough.

For the final time, I say out loud, into the mirror, this time with a fist clenched, "Every hug is a small, soft jail." And this time I mean it, I live it, I feel as though I am serving a life sentence and need to appreciate the softness with which the bars were crafted.

Quietude

WHEN YOU'RE USED TO IT, and it disappears, you slide into withdrawal, need a fix where you can find it. You might jump into your car, drive to an isolated park at the end of a cul-de-sac where you do nothing but sit, eyes closed, hoping no one sees you, hoping a neighbor doesn't start their engine, rev it up, honk at you on the way to work.

When did it begin? Probably in the womb, but I don't recall. I imagine the lack of noise surrounded by amniotic fluid, floating for nine months, an occasional soundless kick, maybe the soft voice of Nat King Cole or Billie Holiday working its way through the uterine wall.

Or the time I was left in the hospital to fend for myself at age five, awaiting the removal of tonsils and adenoids, refusing to talk to nurses, doctors, my parents, a self-imposed silence that stayed with me almost forever.

Locked away in my bedroom at a young age with all of Robert Louis Stevenson, the *Mutiny on the Bounty* trilogy, Archie comic books, Tom Sawyer and Becky Thatcher, the voices were in my head, talking in stage whispers under my pillows, under sheets illuminated by flashlights and an active imagination. And Strat-o-Matic Baseball, the make-believe crowds cheering mutely, the three dice thumping lightly across cardboard. The noise I appreciated was always inside my ears, never outside.

When forced into situations where noise was the primary medium of interaction, like every class I took from kindergarten through college, my preference was to listen and take notes rather than to speak and hear my own voice try to compete with others. I would find ways to reduce the external noises whenever I could, when appropriate, like buying bags of a dozen foam earplugs, like buying ever-more-expensive noise-cancelling headphones throughout my life.

As a classroom teacher for over twenty-five years, I had to get creative in my attempts to feed my addiction. Because of my philosophy of education—to instill a love of learning in every student—my classrooms were always noisy, active, required collaboration and dialectics. To counter this necessary din, I had daily silent reading periods, where the whole class, including me, buried our heads in books and kept our mouths closed. I held regular writing sessions where the only rules were to stay quiet and keep your pen or pencil moving on paper. I always joined in these sessions, shared my work with students when we slipped into workshop mode.

I have always loved the stillness of libraries, spend time in them whenever I can. While an undergrad at UCSC, I had a favorite table on the fourth floor of McHenry Library that was always vacant, where I could spread out, sit for hours, never hearing any sound other than the inhale and exhale of my own breathing. The pensive walk to my car over the bridge the perfect ending to a day.

Writing began to take over as a key avocation in my life, and with it came an ever-increasing need and desire for an environment conducive to the production of ideas. I never listened to music when I wrote, never have, most likely never will. I've usually preferred quiet rooms with comfortable chairs with a view of birds, quiet birds, not blue jays or woodpeckers. It's not that it's impossible for me to write with a noisy background, but it slows me down, makes me have to stop and remove splinters from under my fingernails or small pebbles from my shoes, makes me focus on something other than what I should be concentrating on. I did write one novel in two and a half months in the middle of an office downtown complete with buses and cars and jackhammers and noisy office mates and conference calls and every other imaginable noise, but I used them, incorporated them into the story to trick myself into thinking I didn't care and it didn't bother me. But it's certainly not my preference.

Put me in a chair for three or four hours and let me hear nothing but my fingertips clicking on the keyboard and the internal voices in my head making their presence known. This is what I am used to. This is what drives me on through every other obstacle. The ability to be alone with myself and my characters until I reach a final period. It's what keeps me alive and thriving even inside a body that naturally wants to do otherwise.

But life changes outside the parameters of one's specific desires and needs. The priorities of the world push preference aside and one's selfishness must take a back seat, or at least pretend to do so. Cancer quieted my mind down, but sped up my fingers. Chemo seemed to do the same. Covid brought with itself a required isolation that was just fine with me, forced me to stay put in the chair for hours on end, a perfect result.

Unfortunately we are in the throes of a 2020 vision that demands us to consider what's next, and when the what's next includes a heat wave, thousands of lightning strikes, historically devastating fires in our backyard, we look outside ourselves and offer support to our family members who have suffered loss at the hands of fire and heat, evacuation, lost possessions, displacement, trauma and stress like they've never seen or felt before. Which translates to us opening our house to four adults, two children, and three pet evacuees fleeing the fires, needing a place to recover and dig in.

What comes with a houseful of humans and animals, each with their own set of needs and desires, is a whole new lifestyle for them, and for the original occupants of the home. This is where the issue of noise begins to take on a life of its own, and the addiction to silence is overwhelmed by a house full of sounds that are not conducive to the writing, or even living, style one is used to.

Some things are small, don't really make much of a difference, like sitting on the toilet while making sounds required of constipation, and realizing that on the other side of the wall someone else is sitting on another toilet making different sounds. The number of flushes heard on any one day approaches a dozen. The two dogs race up and down the stairs, barking at each other, barking at every noise or perceived noise on the other side of the front door. We haven't seen the cat, who lives in the camper parked in the driveway, so there are no associated noises with him/her.

The most persistent and insistent noises fall from the mouths, or more accurately from the lungs, of the two young girls, five and eight, who are out of their element, worried about their house, their grandparents' house, life in general, and it's not clear if these noises are something they always emit, even at home without fire raging outside, or if they are new and needed in their altered lifestyles. But I can tell you, it drives me a little crazy. Sometimes the screeching and squealing can go on for thirty to sixty minutes and I wonder why they are allowed, maybe even encouraged, to do so. It wears me down, it makes me feel selfish, even though I know I am overly generous in this situation. It's not something I can talk with anybody about, Karen just a little, but she's not in my camp with this one. She will try to please everyone else before herself and me.

Thus, I consider the earplugs again, the latest headphones, or getting in the car and going to our friends around the corner and asking if I can sit on their back deck, close my eyes, and maybe fall asleep. I feel guilty even writing this. But I know four of our loving lodgers will be gone in a week or two, and the other two will be living with us for four to six months while their house gets rebuilt. If I ever publish this series of essays, it will probably take at least six months to hit the market, so by then, everyone will be either back in their homes or in a new one, and will be thrilled they made it through, so reading these words written secretly by a host will be less jarring to them than if they were to read them now.

So I will take my fix where I can find it, will slip into a meditative mantra to block out the sounds of the world as needed. Will crawl under my covers and wrap my ears in a pillow. Will hide myself away in isolation and fill my ears with insulation, block out the new sounds that have inhabited and taken over my world.

Night Walk

I AWAKE TO A PHOTO posted on Facebook by my friend Barry Vitcov, titled "Night Walk."

Barry lives in Ashland, Oregon. He writes haiku, other poetry, fiction, just about anything that will bleed out of his fingertips and heart onto the page. While Barry and I have known each other as educators for close to forty years, and while we have always been friendly, I've never had a drink or meal with him, so he might consider it a stretch for me to call him a friend. But I believe that our Facebook connection has allowed us to break through the friendship barrier. He has shared many of his walks through his neighborhood, photos of flowers he finds along the way, and photos of dinners that he and his wife Shirley craft in their kitchen.

This photo blasts me open, with its red flame of headlights, sky on fire, ready to hide the remnants of the day, dip below the horizon, guide me into my own night walk.

I wake at 11:10 on a Monday night, *Midsomer Murders* halfway through an episode, the eerie music drifting through the background, Barnaby and Jones on the edge of another breakthrough that buries red herrings, brings hidden clues to the forefront. Karen is in deep sleep. I slide gently from the bed to avoid unnecessary movements that might wake her, touch my numb feet and toes to the carpet, slip on my ever-present grey nylon Costco pants, step into my Altra walking shoes that they no longer make, find my black Patagonia jacket and zip it to my throat.

I make sure I have my money clip—not that I'll need it to purchase anything or drive, but more that my ID is there, just in case somebody needs to identify me—a small flashlight, an eight-ounce bottle of cold water, a small bag of roasted cashew nuts, a knit Warriors cap to pull down over my ears, a mask—just in case—a handful of Kleenex, my keys, and the black-and-blue Paul Smith gloves that Janie bought me when I started feeling so cold. I think that's it. I'm not really sure, because I have never gone on a night walk while living in this house. Thirty-one years later, I'm ready, thanks to Barry, thanks to the circumstances of my life. I put my hand on the front doorknob, stop, go back upstairs, open a dresser drawer and remove a scarf given to me by Jon and Kathy on New Year's Eve 2018. I wrap my neck, and now I'm ready, back to the knob, which I turn and lock as I proceed across the brick courtyard, past the quiet brass band serenading me from our front fence, laced with succulents, good humor, and the ability to thrive.

I avoid the sidewalks, wanting to skip the rise and fall of each driveway, would rather hold the flat and steady pace of the middle of the road, not expecting much traffic at this time of night. I turn and peer into the homes and lives of each neighbor, as if I deserve the right of a Peeping Tom having lived so long with them side by side in this community of ours. I see a few lights, the flash of TVs, no people, all hunkered down in easy chairs watching late-night shows with their bowls of popcorn and mixed drinks, and at the corner I veer left up Winkle and pass our sister house, same Tara-like posts in the front yard leading to the second story, same dangerous arched concrete walkway leading to the front door. I approach the end of the cul-de-sac and prepare to loop myself around and head back toward home, but then I remember, this is my first night walk ever in this neighborhood, and could very well be my last, so I go sideways, dip under the chain blocking the fire road and make my way onto the dark pathway that leads out to the cliff that looks west over Monterey Bay, looks down at my mother's house below. Because it's hard to see my shoes touch the ground, I want to pull out the flashlight, steer myself forward in safety, but this walk is not about safety, more about exploration and experimentation and an acceptance of what I might find. The piercing cries of coyotes guide me to the edge of the cliff, the crater-like indentation that I've known since I was twelve years old.

 I sit, stick my gloved hands into my jacket pocket, snuggle up under my scarf and try to generate my own body heat. In one pocket I find the cashews, remove the bag and toss a couple of fistfuls into my mouth. From the other pocket I remove the bottle of water, drink half of it in one gulp. After a couple of sweeps of the panorama, I remember this is supposed to be a walk, so I push my palms into my knees, force my body to stand, shake out my legs until I feel blood moving. I circle back in a different direction, check out the new multimillion-dollar homes being built on upper Winkle, hear the coyotes following me, a couple of night owls asking who I am, ground squirrels and rodents skittering about through underbrush. As if I'm a pied piper, I seem to have a following, a herd of nocturnal beings reminding me that I am not one of them, that I'm a pretender on this blackened pathway, that I'd better be careful and watch what I do.

Again, I want the security of the flashlight, to shine it in the eyes of my companions, but I resist, instead tighten the scarf around my neck, pull my cap over my ears, make myself warm behind the trails of breath leading through my nostrils. I'm back on the pavement of Winkle and choose not to head home to the comfort of my cul-de-sac life, veer down the hill, work my way through neighborhoods, houses, and TVs I'm not familiar with, a few people with noses to windows wondering whether or not to alert the police, but I walk on, don't slow to view the paintings on their walls, Jimmy Fallon on their TV screens, smell the contents of their cocktail glasses.

I walk through the parking lot of the elementary school, view the finger-painted drawings on the kindergarten-classroom windows, the replications of famous pieces of art by the sixth graders, the bulletin board with flyers for rooms to rent, missing cats and dogs, Saturday yoga classes, golf lessons, $50-per-hour tutoring lessons, and two students who as a team will mow your lawns and whack your weeds at a reasonable rate. Past the administration offices, dropping into Hidden Park behind the school that is mostly invisible, tucked into a bowl behind a few homes, playground equipment, a water fountain, benches for picnics. And on the other side, I find the gate, the entrance my wife has told me about, where she runs into the Chaminade land, carefully paying attention to the whines of mountain lions who are seeking mates if not dinner. I'm listening, almost wanting to hear the low hissing, wanting to see one or two of the big cats leap onto the trail in front of me, quietly stare me down, forcing me to decide if I want to remember everything I've heard or read about how to protect yourself in the face of an attack, to spread your arms wide, make yourself taller and bigger, but I can't remember if I'm supposed to scream, to make noises intended to cause retreat in these muscular beasts. But that doesn't matter to me now, as we gaze into each other's eyes, them wondering what I'm doing out here in the middle of the night, me wondering the same thing.

They eventually lie down in the middle of the pathway, snuggle into each other, ignore me, and I turn away, my hand in my pocket tightly gripping the flashlight, wondering now if I thought the thin ray of light might have been able to save me if they had been hungry.

I approach my driveway, open the side gate, walk into the backyard and pull a chair over to my new deck that wraps around the back end of our yard. It's con-heart, it's gorgeous, and I haven't spent much time with it since its completion. But I'm here now, elbows resting on the arms of the chair, hands clasped lightly in my lap. I look across the canyon at a few speckled lights that lead up the foothills to Loma Prieta. Although my feet are firmly planted on the deck, and it appears that my walk is over, the fact that I am out here, feeling the chill in my ears, the numbing of my cheeks, reminds me that this is simply the cooling-down period for this night walk that I am attributing wholly to Barry and his photo.

Another owl querying me. I answer softly, "It's just me." I hear the sliding-glass door to the deck of our bedroom slip open.

"Honey? What are you doing?" Karen asks in a half-asleep voice.

"I'm finishing up a night walk."

"Oh. I love you." The slider shuts.

I finish the cashews, wash them down with the remaining water. I'm about ready to place my palms on my knees once again, help propel myself to a vertical position, find my way back to the front door, when I hear what sounds like a bird chirping, or a human whistling. Maybe a wailing child. I stay seated, remove the flashlight from my pocket, shine it into the thicket of oak trees just beyond the deck. I don't see anything, but the noises stop.

I believe they followed me here. Not to eat me. Not to harm me. For companionship. Someone their size for a change, out for a night walk, side by side.

The Next to Last Supper

WE BEGAN AS A HANDFUL OF WRITING GROUPS thirty or so years ago. Two or three of us would gather at what was then the best Chinese restaurant in town, O'mei. By the time O'mei was forced to close down in August 2017, due to public outcry over the owner's donations to David Duke's U.S. Senate campaign in Louisiana, our group had swollen to twelve, and to mourn the loss of Red-oil dumplings, Jiao Yan sweet potatoes, Yuxiang pork, Sichuan Gan Bian string beans, and the large round tables with lazy Susans, we had to locate another spot for our monthly gatherings.

This was no easy task, to get twelve free spirits to agree on anything, especially as our taste buds suffered through the loss. Eventually we decided to rotate our eating venues. At a planning meeting held on the beach behind the Crow's Nest, we watched the volleyballers, tracked the sailboats coming in and out, named our group "The Next to Last Supper," because even though we had lost O'mei, we never wanted our group to end, so next to last allowed us an infinite run. We alphabetized our first names to map out who was responsible for selecting the next restaurant, which was not easy, as will become evident when you see the list of names. We limited our geographical boundaries to north of the Pajaro River, south of the Boulder Creek Golf Course, Davenport to the west. The list looked like this: Cheryl, George, Janie, John, Jon(1), Jon(2), me (just another "J" word), Karen(1), Karen(2), Kathy, Lisa, Paul, and Scott. We desperately looked for a Ringo to round out our John, Paul, and George, but it never happened.

Three years later, on the anniversary of O'mei's closing, it was Paul's turn to choose the venue. We had never eaten together at Laili, across the street from Abbott Square, so we looked forward to it. Paul, the oldest in the group, was worried about Covid, so his choice was influenced by the outdoor patio and his reservation of a long table that allowed us to sit six feet apart from each other. As the host, Paul sat in the middle, six women to his left, six men to his right. We tried to keep the balance. If a woman moved to Idaho or died, we replaced her with another woman who had been waiting for years to join us. Same with the men. Twelve apostles and our monthly Jesus.

As we arrived, waiters filled wine glasses with 2012 Savigny-Lés-Beaune Bourgogne Pinot Noir, and when the thirteenth person took her seat, Paul raised his glass, said, "One of you will betray me."

Kathy quickly rang in, "But not tonight, because this is not the last supper. It will always come later, much later, infinitely down the line. So, salud." She took a sip. "Damn! This is good wine. Are we all going to need second mortgages to cover this check?"

We never ate lunch on our appointed supper dates, so we all arrived hungry, meaning we ordered all five appetizers: the

Mediterranean Plate with hummus, tabbouleh, baba ganoush, and cucumber yogurt; vegetarian Maush-awa soup; Bolani, crispy flatbread filled with spinach; and Kadoo boranee, with butternut squash, garlic, qurut yogurt, and mint. That was the easy part. Wading through the entrees with thirteen folks was a half-hour job, but we didn't mind, always thrilled to be spending time with each other. My favorite had always been the trout with basmati rice and salad, so I stayed with it. Others went for the pomegranate chicken kabob, salmon pasta, braised lamb pasta, and roasted cauliflower. In between the appetizers and entrees we managed to devour orders of naan and other flatbreads. But enough about the food, at least until we make it to dessert a couple of hours later.

There were no set rules about the content or agenda of the meetings other than lots of wine and food. Given that the roots of the group were formed with writing, occasionally folks brought something to share. An informal check-in gave us all a chance to catch up on reactions to the heat wave, whether or not we or anyone we knew had been tested for Covid, and who had been evacuated or lost their homes in the CZU fire. Three families had been evacuated from Scotts Valley and Davenport, but luckily no one had lost their home. Janie talked about the death of her husband's son, at age forty-three, from liver failure. Cheryl shared that her son Jonathan was planning a big wedding on their acreage south of Watsonville. Jon(1) had finished a novel he'd been working on for a couple years. Jon(2) said his back was better and he'd been able to ride his bike a little more often. Karen(1) was typically quiet, laughed at other folks' stories, sipped her fine wine, while Karen(2) was just about ready to lock down a book of short stories she had been developing for years. George shared about his latest trek to Pear Lake. Scott shared that he had just taken his daughter to the airport to return to school at Rice in Houston, just ahead of

Hurricane Laura. I stayed quiet. Everybody knew my story and I didn't like being the center of attention, especially when it was Paul's turn to play Jesus.

The third bottle of $115 Pinot Noir was cracked open and poured just before entrees arrived. Just enough alcohol had been imbibed to loosen folks up enough to offer pieces of writing. The delivery of these pieces followed three styles. The first style was what the anal folks liked to do, print thirteen copies and distribute it to each participant. Scott was first. He defended his method by slipping into a dissertation on learning styles and why it was better for folks to both hear and see the work at the same time. When everybody had their one-page copy in front of them, Scott stood, and read:

"I went to the refectory of the Convent of Santa Maria delle Grazie in Milan, Italy, with my family last summer. Very little of the original painting remains, but seeing da Vinci's work in person was a highlight of my life. The point in the lives of the apostles depicted by da Vinci comes immediately after Jesus speaks of the eventual betrayal. We see the expression on each of their faces, reactions that may very well reveal the actual betrayer. Judas Iscariot, hidden in shadow, is surprised by this revelation of his plan." He raised his glass and continued: "I recommend that all my fellow apostles get to Milan while you can to see this marvel." John tapped his knife against his wineglass, and others followed.

As waiters appeared with plates of food, Lisa stood up, held a half sheet of paper in front of her, using the second method of performance, reading directly to her audience. She cleared her throat to get folks' attention. She was a soft speaker, so waited until all food had been delivered, until she had everyone's attention, then said, "I don't usually write much poetry, but this came out yesterday without me understanding why or how." She coughed twice to prime her vocal cords again.

"This mobius strip of our lives
Provides a never-ending slide
Into the bowels and mysteries
Of the vortex.
A ride I wouldn't trade for gold or candy
These friends whose memories
I can trace with one index finger
On this next to last supper we never eat."

    She sat down, bowed her head as everyone flashed their jazz hands, those sitting on either side of her wrapping their arms around her shoulders, somewhat of an unsafe hug.

    I plucked my fork into my whole trout, pulled a bite out, combined it with a bit of basmati rice, slid it on my tongue, one of my favorite flavors in life. Others dug in, lifted pomegranates, bits of lamb, cauliflower in ginger sauce. The room grew quiet as chewing took over. After a few minutes, John stood up, using the third method, no paper at all, a memorized recital.

    "These majestic birds of the Ventana Wildlife Society's Condor Sanctuary who have been through so much are once again being affected by the forces of nature exacerbated by uncontained wildfires. Wildlife biologists are looking for a dozen or so condors and their young. Please help their efforts by visiting their website and making donations to their efforts. Thank you."

    Folks opened their wallets, made out checks, passed them down the table to John, asking him to make the donation as their proxy.

    It went on. The wine, laughter, bad jokes, more naan, and finally another set of decisions with the dessert menu. Cardamom *crème brûlée*, rose meringue, baklava, chocolate mousse with sabayon cream, flourless chocolate torte. We ordered them all, shared them, passed plates around the table, hoping we'd be lucky enough to keep avoiding the exposure to and transmission of Covid.

Paul stood, raised his glass one last time. "I want to retract my opening statement about one of you as betrayer. After careful fact-checking, I was amiss with my suggestion that any of you could commit such a betrayal. It may have been one of the waiters, or a misplaced nightmare trying to bring itself to life, become the center of discussion. I apologize, and so appreciate you all in my life. Here's to just one more Next to Last Supper."

The History of Fried-Egg Sandwiches

I'VE NEVER REALLY BEEN SURE if the chicken or the egg came first because it is one of those dialectical loops that could keep a pair of philosophical types locked in circuitous conversation for weeks. Of course there had to be a chicken to lay that first egg and likewise there had to be an egg to produce that first chicken. It's that type of endless argument I've had to let go, because it has so little to do with my goal, the telling of the story about how fried-egg sandwiches made their way into my life and diet.

I have no proof of the first incidence of fried-egg sandwiches on the planet, meaning I'm certain that rigorous fact-checkers would be successful at blowing holes in my recounting, but I'll proceed as if I know what I'm talking about anyway. It would be my best guess that the ominous event occurred near the end of the sixteenth century, in Shakespeare's time, though I'm more than a little surprised that he didn't include mention of it in at least one of his plays. It was most likely in an outdoor kitchen where freshly baked loaves of bread were being removed from an oven, set aside on a wooden table to cool, platters of fresh churned butter sitting next to them, when the hens were frightened by some large unknown animals in the area which may have been bobcats, wolves, foxes, or even the dreaded mountain lion. Suffice it to say that the stress of the lurking beasts was enough to send the hens cackling and flying away from their roosts, not allowing the proper time for the brood to fully hatch to fruition, thus the fluttering and dismay causing eggs without correctly formed shells to drop from the hens onto the hot grills in the kitchen, thus frying them almost immediately, and when the hungry beasts intent on having fresh hens for breakfast arrived on the scene a bloody battle ensued that ripped open loaves of bread, spilled runny butter onto them, and flung runny fried eggs into the mix. The chef, who had been relieving himself behind a tree when the foofaraw began, emerged to find the beasts with hens in mouths and fired his rifle above their heads, not wanting to kill any of his layers. Once he had shooed the beasts off, returned the hens to their cages, he assessed the damage to his bread. He picked up two ragged slices, now adorned with melted butter and fried eggs, and took a big bite. He nodded to himself, sat down on an old wooden chair, and devoured the eggs and butter and bread, and from that day forward, fried-egg sandwiches became a major staple.

At first he didn't tell others about his newfound delicacy, worried that as soon as they tasted it they would be flocking to his kitchen, diminishing all his supplies. But he was a generous man, and also liked to show off a bit, so before long he shared the meal with a girlfriend or two, and the news spread. Folks started bringing him more layers, supplies for breadmaking, until he finally opened a breakfast shop that served only fried-egg sandwiches. Travelers to England heard about his establishment, now named "An Egg in Hand," and before he could control it, unauthorized franchises sprang up all across Europe, in France, Belgium, the Netherlands, into Spain and Portugal, where they added a few more spices and sauce to the menu.

My research goes sideways about thirty years after Shakespeare died in 1616, with no further mention of fried-egg sandwiches until three hundred and thirty years later when meat sandwiches virtually disappeared because of rationing during World War II. Because of the disappearance of meat from most menus, a White Castle restaurant in St. Louis began making the first fast-food fried-egg sandwich that the modern world had ever seen. The dish was not appreciated by patrons whose addiction to meat had been well entrenched. When the war was over, the dish disappeared, replaced by ham and pork and ground beef. Not until 1971 did the fried-egg sandwich reappear in a franchise of a restaurant chain in Santa Barbara as the McDonald's Egg McMuffin.

As they say, the rest is history. But not really. My father's love of fried-egg sandwiches, which in turn inspired my love, had nothing to do with Egg McMuffins. In fact, I am guessing that he may never have tasted one in his life. No, I'm certain, again with no hard facts, that for my ten-year-old father, part of a lower-middle-class family of eight during World War II, cheap eggs made for a fairly healthy meal—a loaf of bread, a dozen eggs, a slab of butter.

My family was also not wealthy as we grew up in the '50s and '60s, so my mother was always coming up with clever menus that provided us with inexpensive dishes that satisfied our taste buds and hunger. In addition to chipped beef on toast, minute steaks on Langendorf bread, tacos, banana and corn fritters, ranch beans, Armenian rice pilaf, liver and onions, and grilled cheese sandwiches, every couple of weeks a fried-egg sandwich would appear, mostly through my dad's requests.

It stayed with me throughout my life. I have continued to eat all of our discount meals, with the exception of liver and onions. I always loved the onions, but hated the liver. My intake of fried-egg sandwiches over the years has ebbed and flowed depending on the current research about cholesterol and eggs and how many a week should be eaten. As that research changed, so did my intake of the fried-egg sandwich, especially over the past twenty-three months, when the egg and soft bread and slight dab of butter seems to ease my erratic and demanding digestive system.

I probably eat three sandwiches per week now. I imagine my late grandpa Harold probably also loved them with his houseful of kids in Oakland in 1942, which led to my dad's love, and eventually mine. I have no kids of my own, so I believe the legacy ends with me. Although maybe this short essay, possibly published and read posthumously, could start a revival of homemade fried-egg sandwiches to rival those of McDonald's and Starbucks and Peet's and a hundred other ma-and-pa eateries across the country.

A couple of slices of whole-wheat bread, a dab of soft butter, some pepper and salt, three large eggs cracked into a small skillet and fried to the perfect consistency without crispy edges, slid from the pan onto the bread, sliced in half, ready to make my day.

.

The Golf Fade

I JUST COMPLETED A SEARCH of my 342-page 2020 journal for the word *golf*. There were nine occurrences, mostly having to do with balls, shows on TV, Trump, my friend Scott, and a small course my friends Dave and Maria have on their property.

Prior to October 2018, you would have found closer to a hundred entries, dealing with my golfing, my scores, my addictions, new clubs and putters, in my journals. Adenocarcinoma of the pancreas goes a long way toward creating an unasked-for diet that not only causes the loss of seventy pounds but also strips muscle from bones.

I have loved golf for a long time, over thirty years. In some ways, this is an elegy to my life as a golfer. My scores on an 18-hole course, usually DeLaveaga, have ranged from 105 to 78 over the years, usually in the mid-80s range. The mantra that feeds the addiction is "I can do better!" Every time you step on the range to hit a bucket of balls before your early-morning round, you are thinking about that elusive round in the upper 70s. Until you walk up to the first tee, step up to take your first drive, and superstition takes over. If you nail one and it stays in the middle of the fairway, it's going to be a good day! You can do it on every hole, every swing, make every putt, break 70 for the first time in your life. Until the second shot slices off your five metal and flies into the trees on the right, where you know you'll need to play a lofty wedge to pop it out and get you a little closer to the hole. Lying four on the green, if you can make the lengthy putt, you could start the day with a par, but you don't, you two-putt, bogey on hole 1, and you do the quick math and know that if you bogey every hole you'll shoot a 90, and 90 is not what you want in front of you.

The ability to control the flight of your ball is what determines success and failure in golf. The hook and the slice, the fade and the draw. Luckily the terms are alphabetical. When you hook, your ball is veering out of control to the left. When you slice, that ball is flying off to the right into another fairway or pond. The draw and the fade are less radical, more contained, somewhat intentional. Again alphabetically, the draw moves to the left, the fade to the right.

It's the fade I want to concentrate on here. I was never much good at controlling the intentionality of a fade or a draw, which gave me fewer tools in my bag to shoot a sub-80 round. Never knew how to adjust my swing, my wrists and arms, shoulders and follow-through in a consistent fashion to repeat what appeared to be something I'd like to do again, like when I did shoot in the 70s, but had no clue why. I just knew it felt good, that my body didn't ache as much at the end of the round, and that it was nice to look at the scorecard a few times again during the week.

But it's this double meaning of the word *fade* I need to concentrate on here. I refer once again to Merriam-Webster to help me reach the end of this piece. 1. "To lose freshness, strength, or vitality (wither)." 7. "Of a ball or shot: to move in a slight to moderate slice." I'll stick with definition #7 for a bit, because that's what the game is about, as I've said, being in control of your swing, your ball, having a focus and the skill. Rare times during my golfing years I slipped into an accidental groove where everything went right for a few weeks or months, where my handicap came down, where my accidental draw and fade aligned well with the features of the course.

Now we'll come back to definition #1, to lose freshness, strength, or vitality. The effects of a pancreatic diagnosis lead directly to all aspects of this definition. The effect of the tumor in the body clearly blocks the pathway to freshness. The addition of chemotherapy drugs to the routine zaps strength and vitality. Not so much in the brain, as my mind has been functioning well throughout, in some cases I would argue even better than before. But in the body, the lack of muscle and depletion of core strength make it nearly impossible to imagine ever swinging a driver again and hoping the ball will travel 200 yards down a fairway, regardless of hook and slice, fade and draw.

Because in my mind I have achieved a sense of focus and determination related to writing and getting thoughts on paper, because my ability to focus feels so much stronger than before, I've often thought that if I could ever get back onto the golf course with my early-morning buddies, I would be able to better think my way around a course, around my way into the elusive 70s. I've never really had the core strength of Larry, who is able to coil, release, and snap through the ball, and never had the brute strength of Chris, who muscles through the ball. But if I could get back out there, I could think my way through it, remember to make each swing count and not think ahead to the final score on the card.

When I was playing golf three or four days a week, for a year or so I would wake up early on golf mornings, sit in my chair, take myself into a meditative state, and play the round in my head before getting into the car to drive up to the course. Occasionally it helped, but not consistently enough to call it a solution. Something about the focus got lost in translation between the range and the first tee. I did go up to the course once after I began my chemo routine, got a cart, took only my putter, and drove along with my friends until they reached the green. I dropped my ball on the green just inside the farthest ball away from the pin, just a point of reference, a place holder. That person would putt first, so my putting wouldn't give them a clue about the distance or breakage of the putt, then I would putt. The focus wasn't bad, but it was only a partial satisfaction. I only did it that one time as my strength and vitality diminished.

I watch a ton of golf on TV, listen carefully when the seasoned announcers talk about the precision of the draws and fades of the players. I watch their backswings, their follow-throughs, the complete swing from shoulder to shoulder, a completion that ends in a freeze, as they watch the flight of the ball and hope for the ideal distance, landing, spin, proximity to the hole.

In my head, I know I can emulate them. Know what it is I need and have to do to shoot well, to hit the 70s regularly. But that's my head. The body provides the true obstacle to success. The true fade. The loss of freshness, vitality, and strength. I'm not sure I could carry my bag of clubs to the car anymore. Or walk up the hills, climb into canyons to retrieve sliced or hooked balls, much less swing my clubs the way they need to be swung.

I doubt I'll ever make it back to the course, ever complete another round much less make it to the 70s. Instead, I turn on the TV, watch Dustin Johnson or Jon Rahm drive the ball, chip, and putt the way I imagine I would do so myself. They are my mentors now, my instructors in a game that has been relegated to a chair in front of a screen. But I still love doing so, and can't wait to flip the remote in a half hour to watch round two of the Tour Championship.

The Gamester

EVERY DAY OF MY MEMORABLE LIFE I have been engaged in some form of gaming. By "memorable life," I mean those activities I actually remember participating in, not those that a parent or friend reminded me about.

The first I can remember was when my cousin Terry stayed with us for a while in Hayward, California, and he taught me how to play chess. He was a seasoned ten-year old, and I was only six, so it took many years for the intricacies of the game to set in.

There were many board games that made it into my life in the mid to late '50s, given by Grandma Esther as Christmas gifts. Chutes and Ladders, Candy Land, Parcheesi, Sorry, Touring, many more that brought me into the gaming way of thinking, an activation of the brain in ways different than daily life, even different from school activities. Beginning to understand the value of strategy and futures.

I learned to play poker at a young age, mostly through watching my dad's home game, and quickly discovered that a straight flush was much better than two pair. Even though they played a variety of wild and crazy games, the relative value of hands was always the same, unless they played jokers wild or baseball with threes and nines wild. Poker has lasted a lifetime for me, both at casinos in Tahoe and World Series of Poker tournaments, and at a fifty-year home game.

Cribbage was a game I played first with my dad, just a two-person game that allowed a bit of bonding between father and son. A very different and distinct set of rules applied to the cards in your hand, tracked on a race-track-type board with metal pegs, with the phrase "Fifteen-two, fifteen-four, and two is six" a common refrain throughout. In later years, I'd play with roommates or friends, girlfriends, wives.

Canasta was another game I loved to play from a young age, usually at Grandma Esther's house, often when Aunt Irene visited. They were both good opponents, though Aunt Irene usually had a tumbler of MacNaughton whiskey in hand as she played. I loved getting the extra hundred points for red threes, the stopping power of black-three discards.

At my parents' house in Santa Cruz there were a number of games played at the kitchen table with three, four, or more of us—Mom, Dad, Shelly, or neighbors who would come over to play Tripoli, Monopoly, Careers, or Touring. Tripoli was a fun game that had a mix of mini-games built in, everyone having a chance to win something, like the best poker hand, whether or not you had the ten, jack, queen, or king of hearts.

Even though I've already written a whole piece on the role of Strat-o-Matic Baseball in my life, I'd be remiss to not mention it here in this chronology of games in my life. So, once again, I bow to my love of the game, to my grandmother for buying it for me.

In 1964, we moved to Santa Cruz and I met Jamie MacAdams at Mission Hill Junior High School. He and his family were from Canada, and when I visited his house over by Santa Cruz High, Jamie would bring out a game called Stocks and Bonds that I'd never heard of. It was a great game that taught us more about money and percentages than any classes we had at school. One memorable evening at Jamie's house we had burgers and fries while playing Stocks and Bonds and watching the Beatles' first U. S. television performance on *The Ed Sullivan Show.*

Scrabble has slipped a bit in this retelling, probably because I still play it every day now that it's available online through Facebook. In truth, I started playing it back in the days when the boards were cardboard instead of plastic, the letters made from wood, pieces now collectible as vintage items. Karen and I used to play it in bed at night, and then when it became available online, I played with multiple friends, and especially my mom, because it was a daily way I could check in on her to make sure she was still doing okay.

Physical games, otherwise known as sports, came in more in junior high and high school. Football, baseball, racquetball, a solid six years of activity that took me through Cabrillo College. Golf started about this time but didn't take off until later.

In 1967, Milton Bradley came out with a boxed version of Battleship, complete with two game boards and pegs to represent ships. The game was okay, but because it was first invented in 1930 and made it into our lives around 1955, we were already hooked on the pencil-and-paper version, goal being to sink your opponent's fleet before yours were destroyed.

In high school I had a couple of close friends who were far ahead of me in their gaming minds. We would meet at Craig's house after school, and one of the three of us would pull out a joint, and we'd listen to "In-A-Gadda-Da-Vida" and play Risk, one of the best strategy games I had ever played. We did this our whole senior year, until the one time that a lion jumped out of the speakers during "In-A-Gadda-Da-Vida" and tried to put its teeth around my throat. But what a great game, stoned or straight.

While at UCSC in 1974, I discovered the text-based strategy games offered only through UNIX systems that college students used to take their minds off studies, to visualize the venues of the game only by translating the white words seen on a black screen. I loved it. It opened up a new world to me I didn't know existed or was even possible. About five years after I discovered the UNIX environment, the Miller Brothers designed and released Myst through Broderbund, an adventure-puzzle video game.

When I worked at West Foods Mushroom Farm in Soquel, I had the opportunity to travel with one of the drivers to Lake Tahoe to deliver a truckful of materials for a monster house that Rowland West was building just north of Stateline. On the return trip, me just short of seventeen, the driver and I stopped at Sahara Casino, I won $100 and have been hooked for life. I read Edward Thorp's *Beat the Dealer*, which entrenched me even further. My next few trips to Tahoe I also learned the ins and outs of craps, keno, roulette, and slot machines. Most odds were always against the player, in favor of the house, but not when you read and understood Thorp's book, which I had.

In my twenties and thirties, while I was married and working full-time, a number of new games made their way into my evening and weekend entertainment. Probe was a new word game that we all loved, another game that required a good amount of strategy and a decent vocabulary. Then came Mastermind, color-coded pegs hidden behind a wall, the guesser trying to determine the colors of the opponent's six pegs, very similar to the strategy behind Battleship, a search-and-destroy mission. Then came Connect Four and Rummikub, less about strategy and more about fun with plastic.

Because I have played them for much of my life, I have left out the crossword puzzles that made it into my life when I first started buying my own newspapers in my early twenties. I have probably worked on puzzles nearly daily for the past forty years, either in the *Sentinel* or online through the *New York Times*.

New addictions came about through eating at restaurants that used rolls of white butcher paper for their tablecloths. We created a game called the Four-Letter Word Game that required only a pen or pencil and a four-letter word hidden from your opponent. Though only four letters, the rules and strategies are pretty much identical to Mastermind. Later, in the past few years, I began playing the same game with five letters that Jon Franzen told me was called Jotto, which had rules available online. More word games. More strategy.

And as the Internet ramped up, Words with Friends, online Scrabble, Spelling Bee, Letter Boxed and other word games popped up and allowed me to mainline them straight into a vein.

Oh. And how could I go this long without mentioning pool, snooker, billiards, that took their toll on my attention, focus, sometimes wallet, and a lot of time? But that's another story.

Every day I touch at least five of these games, either through direct play or reading about them in the newspaper. I often wonder what type of person I would have become if I had spent those hundreds of thousands of hours of game playing reading every novel on the Modern Library's Top 100 List. Speculation and futures, Stocks and Bonds. I could probably design a game to calculate the odds, but I haven't become a Queen Bee yet today, so I'd better put in another hour before dinner to get there.

World Series of Poker, Lake Tahoe—5-4-2005

YESTERDAY'S WRITING ABOUT GAMES kept me awake most of the night, or in that twisted sleep pattern that keeps replaying one event that stood out from the day's activities. Last night it was Texas Hold'em poker that got the nod. Thinking back to a trip Karen and I took to South Lake Tahoe to stay in our favorite casino and hotel, Harveys. We only planned to stay for part of the scheduled 2005 World Series of Poker, not stick around for the $10,000 main event held later in the week with a projected first prize of $500,000. I knew how to play risky poker, but always played within my means. And $10,000 for an entry fee was well beyond my means.

I first learned to play Texas Hold'em at the Cal Neva Casino between Crystal Bay and Sand Harbor on the North Shore. It was the casino that Frank Sinatra owned part interest in before being forced out. It was a homey spot, good restaurants and bars, a big showroom where Sinatra and friends performed, and a relatively small card room, where newcomers learned the intricacies of Hold'em. I never made a killing there, but I held my own, occasionally winning a few hundred, losing a few hundred. But it became my heroin of the decade. I'd seek it out wherever I could, whether it was North or South Tahoe, Las Vegas, or eventually a little closer to home at Bay 101 in San Jose. It took a while for the first Hold'em games to appear in Santa Cruz so I could just drive the three miles to town and play.

The year before the South Shore tourney at Harveys, we had taken my mom and dad with us and gotten them a great suite with a view out over the lake. Dad was not healthy, didn't take well to the altitude, but he loved to gamble, loved to play keno and blackjack. His third cancer in seventeen years was spreading. When it was time for us to get ready to head to Harveys, his health had declined and he was pretty much sticking around home. But we made arrangements to keep in touch with him and Mom, keep them in the loop, let them play along with us vicariously. We made the long drive from Santa Cruz, wound our way up through Sacramento, not yet too hot, over Echo Summit and down Meyers Grade, where we always received our first glorious view of the lake. Making our way east on Highway 50 to Stateline was always a thrill, always a lot of traffic, gamblers and fishermen and families jammed into cars too small, working their way towards their desired destinations.

We hit the stoplight at Stateline on 50 that gave us a view of Harrah's Casino and Hotel on the right, Harveys Resort on the left. After checking into a room near the top floor of Harveys, we plopped onto the bed for a short nap, then made our way down the elevators to Hard Rock Cafe for a burger and fries. Next stop for me, the poker room where I registered for Event #1, a $200-buy-in for a no-limit Hold'em tournament, to be held the

Daily Fresh

next day at noon. I spent the day playing in a series of no-limit games where I broke even by the end of the day. Karen was playing her favorite poker and Wheel of Fortune slot machines that kept her happy, especially when she hit a straight flush. I don't remember if we ate dinner at the high-end restaurant on the 19th floor, which may very well have been called "19" by then, or if we went for the decades-old standby on the first floor just outside the craps tables called the Sage Room, where you could order large chunks of T-bone or filet mignon off rolling carts. After a filling meal, we were off to our room, tired and gritty with the sweat of playing games all day long, ready to put our heads on pillows, knowing we'd be awake early and ready to start again.

Which we were. We had room service deliver vegetarian omelettes and oatmeal with large glasses of orange juice. We brushed our teeth, combed our hair, emptied the safe into our pockets, and headed downstairs for another day of hard and fun work. I signed up for the small, daily 10:00 tourney, with the big tourney scheduled for after lunch. It's a $25 buy-in, which is similar to taking batting practice before a game. I finish third, win $75, and by lunch, Karen is down $100, so we walk across the street to Harrah's and eat at the buffet on the top floor, return just in time to get my ticket, find my seat. Karen watches for a while, but quickly needs to get back to her bank of poker slots. There are 253 entrants to the tournament, which makes the odds pretty steep to move forward. But I play tight, try not to make ignorant calls based on hope rather than statistics. At one point as they rearrange tables, I'm sitting next to a young man, maybe in his thirties. The dealer says to him, "Jory, are you in," and he nods affirmatively, giving up no clues from his voice. I turn to him and say, "Jory? Really?" He answers, "Yeah, I know. It's a weird name. My mom found it somewhere along the way when she was pregnant." I remove my money clip, hand him my ID.

"No way!" he says. "I never find people anywhere with my name. It must be a sign." He smiles and winks at me.

A few hands later I question his premonition as he busts out of the game, aces and eights beaten by trip threes. He high-fives me as he walks away.

By that evening we are down to two tables, and I'm still in, squeaking by with weak hands and strong bluffs way too often. With only eleven players left in the tournament, I go all in on three kings, get beaten on the river by a flush. I finish in eleventh place, and am presented with a rack with $1,155 in chips. Funny how they do that. Have it right there in your hands so you can drop a few hundred back on the blackjack or craps table. But I avoid the trap, go right back to the poker window, inquire about Event #3 coming up in two days, $500 entry fee. This is the time for a parlay, when you're using house money, out in front so it's a good time to expand the streak. I get my ticket, still $600 ahead for the day, and look for Karen, knowing exactly where to find her in her halo of machines. She's up a few hundred, and we head back to the room for some room service and much-deserved sex. We sleep, take a drive around the lake, stop at a little restaurant on Highway 89 we've never eaten at before called Evan's American Gourmet Café. As soon as we see the menu, we know we've stumbled into a slice of heaven. There are only a few appetizers listed but they look like this: Scallop Quenelles with sherry-lobster cream; Savory Chili Cheesecake topped with Maine lobster salad and sautéed white corn fricassee with a duet of avocado and chipotle aiolis; Hoisin and Orange-glazed Prawns with Asian-style slaw, served with tangerine reduction, chives, and sesame seeds. We split the prawns and cheesecake, and order a butter lettuce salad with julienne of apple, blue cheese, candied pecans, and walnut-oil vinaigrette.

We're not sure our eyes or stomachs can take the full extent of entrees, but Karen chooses the Peppered Grilled Pork Chop with bacon-horseradish potato cake with maple apple chutney, applejack demi-glace, and green beans. My mouth is drooling waiting for the Rosemary and Garlic Marinated Rack of Lamb with raspberry wine demi-glace, parsnip mashed potatoes and minted zucchini curls. There is no way we can fit dessert in, but we order it anyway, a frozen white-chocolate mousse and a dark-chocolate crème-brûlée tart.

We slowly make our way back down Highway 50, have the car valet parked, and head straight to our room to enjoy the sunset on the lake, fall into our bed, and revel in the successes of the day.

Next day we head downstairs to the breakfast restaurant near the craps tables. We order omelettes and French toast, some fresh-squeezed orange juice, then I have to spend a little time at the craps table before beginning the serious play of the day. At the craps table I have a method of play, I wouldn't call it a system, because a system implies that you can beat the house odds, and there is no way to beat the house odds on the craps table. You can avoid it, stretch it out, know what the best and worst bets are, so I play the best bets, the Don't Come line, which incorporates both statistics and superstition. Statistics in that it's the best odds bet on the table, and superstition in that I wait for the roller to establish a point before I establish my point, then there are actually rolls where we can both win. I drop a couple hundred while Karen has disappeared to her slot corner. At noon, I head to the poker room, present my ticket, and am assigned a seat. The announcer comes on and tells us that there are over three hundred players today, and that we'll play into the evening as needed, but probably won't be able to complete the tournament until the following evening. And that's the way it goes, starting with thirty-plus tables. By 5:00 we are narrowed down to ten, and I'm still there, with a small stack, just enough to nose around and hope for something to help me survive the night. Just before 9:00, the assigned ending time, I hit an A-high flush on the river with no possibility of a boat on the board, and I go all in, am called by someone with the king-high flush, and my stack grows at the perfect time, not a good way to climb into bed hoping for some rest, given that my adrenaline is sky high, but I'm thrilled, and Karen has hit another jackpot, so we stay awake and watch *The Late Show*.

We sleep in, which is rare, because we usually want to be back at it as soon as possible. But today, we're looking forward to what's coming, have breakfast delivered to our room, bowls of fruit and oatmeal, a pitcher of water to make sure we hydrate early. By noon we're out the door. My tourney doesn't restart until 4:00, so I've got four hours to dedicate to blackjack, which I haven't played yet. Blackjack is really my game. I'm a card counter and have been doing so since I was eighteen. Of all the possible addictions in this place, if I were forced to rank them, yesterday it would have looked like this: 1) blackjack, 2) poker, 3) craps, and 4) poker slots with Karen. But as of yesterday, the list now adds Evan's restaurant at #1. I hit the $25-minimum-bet blackjack table because generally the steep limit helps to control the quality of the partner gamblers at your table. I start slow, lose a few hundred but work my way back up, hitting a couple of blackjacks, nailing a couple of double-downs, getting some friendly dealers who are easy to train, meaning I bet for them when I know the odds are in my favor and rather than shuffle up as they're supposed to do, they finish out the deck and increase both our odds of winning. I so love this game! So love that it's the only game in the whole building where you can find your odds better than the house in certain situations where you increase your bet size to maximize your overall chance of winning.

I walk away ten minutes before the tourney begins $600 ahead, having won $300 for the dealer on matching bets. I'm happy. He's happy.

Daily Fresh

I take my seat. There are four tables left, thirty-six players. They have added bleachers for the crowds to have tiered viewing options. Karen is sitting in the top row. She has her cell phone, and if I make it to the final table, she'll call my mom and dad so they can be part of it.

I do make it to the final table. They take a half-hour break, and we come back tensions high, blood pressure pounding. After another three hours, there are three of us left. I hit a straight and knock one guy out. That leaves two of us. He reaches his hand across the table says, "Eric Cloutier. I'm a professional hockey player in the Canadian League." I'm impressed, but not sure if he meant for me to be intimidated. I want to say something like "Jory Post, professional teacher of fifth and sixth graders from Happy Valley, CA," but instead say, "Jory. Pleasure to meet you." He backs up a bit, seemingly surprised that I don't know him, but I don't, so maybe he's a little intimidated now.

We play for another two hours, me gaining a bit of a stack advantage, when he calls for a bathroom break. He nods, suggesting I follow him to the bathroom. We get there, standing in front of our urinals, and he says, "How do you want to play this?" I have no idea what he means and tell him so. "What I mean is winner gets $44,540, second place gets $24,000. I'm willing to make a deal right now. We both know anything can happen from this point. But I'm willing to say we split first and second place. Not officially. They won't let us. But, once it's over, if I've won, I'll give you $8,000 to bump you up to $32,000, and if you win, vice versa. And because the winner gets one of those World Series of Poker diamond rings, I'm willing to give that to you directly whether you win or lose." I'm not experienced with this kind of finagling, but it sounds pretty good to me. We figure out how we will make the exchange following the conclusion. I win. With a pair of tens. I never discover what he has, as he tosses his cards in face down.

It's not until later, when I have the diamond ring on my finger, a rack of $44,540 in chips, find him in the bathroom and hand him his $8,000, and walk up to our room, ecstatic, that I understand what he did. I have no idea if he could have beat a pair of tens. But that's not what he was after. He wanted to lose, didn't care about the ring. Wanted his $32,000, only having to pay taxes on the $24,400 he officially won, me having to pay taxes on the full $44,540, although I walked out with only $36,540.

It didn't matter much to me. I was thrilled. Thrilled that Karen was there with me, thrilled that my parents were able to follow along, thrilled to think back to when I learned how to play poker by leaning over my dad's shoulder and watching how he played. Taxes and banks and a drive home with all that money buried in our trunk would come later.

The Art of Deflection

S O MANY WAYS TO DEFLECT, to keep the other person or people off guard. I watch the majority of NBA basketball players and am constantly awed by their physical acuity, that they feign one move and at the last second slip into another, leaving opponents grabbing for the floor as they fall. We see similar moves in professional football players, running backs and receivers carrying a ball, planting a foot into the Astroturf so the defendant will move one direction while they turn back, avoiding contact and heading for the end zone.

The majority of modern-day references to deflection are shared by sportscasters behind their microphones, describing a replay, or commenting live on a spectacular move by a player. While I am not a professional sportscaster by any stretch, I am a caster of sorts by tossing out words and sentences that I'm hoping will ensnare readers, make them move in one direction while they should be moving in another. The intention of this whole piece is deflection. I didn't wake up this morning wanting to write about athletes and their bodies. The movements of athletes are simply a metaphorical tool used to compare or suggest an idea to a reader. In this case, I want the reader to be aware that the words are here only to create that deflective shield that hides or puts the truth into the distance, a truth that may eventually land by the last sentence, but possibly not. I want the reader to be trying to discover what it is I'm thinking about, what it is I'm wanting them to be thinking about, possibly a topic that I overwork too often in direct address of my words that I'd like to keep a little more hidden, less transparent and obvious to the world. If folks have read these essays in order, they already have a pretty good idea of who I am, what topics are on my mind, guide my activities, and it's exactly that habitual response I'm hoping to avoid in this piece.

I'm in the most comfortable chair in my house, at the foot-of-the-bed writing studio where I have written the majority of my work over the years. Even though it's supposed to reach the high eighties again today, I am wrapped from toes to chest in a warm alpaca blanket, more for the habit and the weight than for heat. I've already taken a hot shower so the steamy water could run over the left side of my head, my neck, my shoulders, and back. I've already finished my large cup of Sillycow Farms hot chocolate accompanied by two Tylenol. The plucking of a topic or prompt for the morning write is different than usual. Quite often during the night I'll have a circuitous snakelike protagonist or antagonist who accompanies me on the journey, straps itself to my back as I walk to the bathroom to empty my bladder every two hours. But this snake did not wrap itself around my shoulder, loop around my back, flit its tongue softly at me with guidance. No, it slipped between my lips, finding an opening where the missing tooth leaves a gap in the top row of teeth, made its way down my esophagus and managed to slither its way into every vein throughout my body, displacing or swallowing whatever blood it could find, then nested itself there, spread out, filling itself with me, filling me with it, pushing consistently into my skeletal system.

It wasn't a dream. It was an interpretation. An elusive search for what the metaphor was seeking as a companion. And it continues, as I search for the deflective handle on this topic. I'll call on Ron Carlson and Jess Walter, constant companions, to pull me through, carry me to the ends. Carlson who at once tells me to stay in the chair to get it down but get out of the chair and take it sideways, so let me try. I turn right, stand on the second-story deck outside our slider, look down at the green cast-iron blue heron, perched in our backyard, lording over the manor. Nothing stirs her, not the flapping fluttering antics of the ring-necked pigeons or the selfish demands of blue jays and woodpeckers. She stands stoically amid the smoke, watching the two canines new to the property trying to get her to show some emotion, move an eyelid, join in their games. A few feet away the dogs sniff the bushes under the deck, where once again the whine and whistles of potential pumas have been heard all night long by our studio residents who worry about their young daughters. Carlson draws a circle on my paper, his symbol for expansion, tells me to dive into that world, tell that story, are the girls chasing the dogs on the deck too late at night, too close to the canyon, within sniffing range of the cats? Are the adults too engulfed in the excellent smoked ribs and salmon to notice the cats peering hungrily through the railing? Carlson probably never called it deflection, but that's clearly what it is. Going sideways into adjacent worlds and lives and allowing the imagination to fill out the page. And while we're at it, Jess Walter would say, "Now that you've gone sideways and are way off course, jump down one of the many rabbit holes you'll find along the pathway."

And you do. You fling yourself in like you did when you first jumped off Evelyn Dalke's diving board and belly-flopped your way to eventual success. Of course you find rabbits in the hole, extensive families of rabbits who each have their dramatic stories to share with you, along with a carrot. They talk about family outings, racing events with tortoises, and they avoid the same topics you're trying to avoid, better at deflection than you, looking forward to the next day, having no understanding that the year is 2020 and all that it has brought forth to the world above their subterranean lives.

After hours of sideways movements and rabbit-hole diving, the snake around your neck gives up and wriggles away into its own new adventures. You climb back to your world, take another quick shower, more hot water pounding into that same old spot on your neck, return to your chair, hunt for the correct words to define or showcase the elusive deflection of the morning. The words transport themselves into the piece riding puffs of clouds, the wings of wind, a siren whining up the canyon, a fleet of helicopters. That's the key to success. Stay outside yourself, put yourself on the backs of cultural universals, pay attention to what others think about and look forward to rather than your own selfish narrow-minded viewpoint of what you can't change anyway.

This is the true deflection. Get folks to view the world through their own mirrors rather than having to always look through yours. It doesn't matter that the bronco you were trying to ride for eight seconds threw you off its back, stomped on you a few times, smashed a few ribs, dragged you by a rope across the arena a half-dozen times before you let loose, and that you're now sitting in the chair wishing the bull had finished the job. You smile, laugh a little, know you can't wait to get strapped back onto that bronco and try it again, bandaged and bruised. The bull and the fans in the stands will never know, the perfect deflection.

Carryover

And when the deflection fails, you give in, know the failure has altered your mood, your output. It's after dinner, you haven't eaten, haven't written. Your oncologist has decided to eliminate one of your two chemo drugs, give you a better entrance into next week's biopsy process. He talks about the pain in your back, how the chemo could be depleting your electrolytes, recommends stopping by the Running Store to pick up some powders and gels to help you hydrate. They don't help. Yet. He also suggests you take some Norco, a combination of oxycodone and acetaminophen, stay away from the blood thinners they want you to avoid.

You have avoided dipping into these opioids for twenty-three months. You dislike the idea, the physical and mental effects. But it's 5:00 and the pain reverberates with every breath. You slip a pill under your tongue. At 9:00 you take another. At 2:00 a.m. just one more. This is how the addiction begins, you imagine. Not that you've received the expected relief. The pain still throbs across your back, with every intake of breath, settles in a spot in the middle of the high back, moves to your left shoulder, your right shoulder, little sense to its movement. You are not happy that you've given in to this drug, especially given that it hasn't seemed to help. You rotate in bed from one shoulder to the other. You force yourself out of bed to sit up in the chair, keep your head and neck vertical, twist it to the left and back to the right. Finally you get up and turn the hot water on in the shower, stand with your hands planted against the wall as the heat burns into your skin, your remaining muscle structure, creating a temporary numbing effect that doesn't last long, just long enough to dry off, put some clothes on, make a decision about whether to remain vertical or slip back under warm covers in your horizontal cocoon.

There is nothing deflective about the carryover. That you have chosen to carry it over, or that it has chosen you, removes all desire or intention to keep it hidden from others, except that you are mostly holed up in your room to avoid the various noises and activities of others that don't help as distractors, instead act as catalysts for ongoing stress. When you make a public appearance, it is obvious in the careful placement of your feet and legs that you are weak, that you place an open palm against a wall or bookshelf to give you a tripod of support, that your eyes abandon all sense of deflection and bare your worn soul to your soulmates.

Once you've made a decision to throw yourself into the fray, you can't complain about the barking of the dogs, the giggling of the children, the incessant hounding and informing of the news channels about Covid and fires and evacuation schedules and plans to let people move home, or the continual remembrances of possessions lost in the fire, room by room, waves of remembrance, the lists of replacement costs, the never-ending calculator that accrues daily projections. All you can do is wait and hope that the Norco kicks in, as your body gives over to its role as an experimental station. It's a long ride that lasts well into a second day, drains your spirits, your hope, makes you think more about death than you ever have so far. It's one thing to pragmatically know that it's coming and you will have to deal with it, and another for it to feel like it could crawl into your spine and bloodstream and snap you closed whenever it chooses.

You tell a few close friends and loved ones how you feel, that the end could be near. They don't like hearing you say these things, but you have been honest and direct throughout about every phase of the process, so no sense in changing that now. You're supposed to go in for another round of chemo tomorrow. How will that work? Will the Gemzar exacerbate the pain? Will the oncologist need to prescribe something stronger than Norco? Will you wither away even further into your shell?

No. It's chemo day, so you can smear your port access with Emla to numb your skin. And you have to watch your computer for the arrival of the blood-test results that were taken late yesterday afternoon, because of the Monday holiday. A continual oversight on the part of the scheduling "team." The appointment is at 8:30 and the tests finally arrive at 8:22, and the platelet count is 74, lower than it's ever been, possibly too low to sit in the infusion chair and take another jolt of Gemzar. Possibly too low to follow through with the scheduled liver biopsy on Wednesday. All these questions and inconsistencies and seeming oversights taxing a brain that is already feeling the weight of more than one world.

And this carryover that grew out of a deflection now becomes a head-on battle between the professionals and the novices, the professionals without enough time on their hands to make sure all the cracks are spackled closed and secured in the patient's welfare, and the novices with way too much time on their hands, enough time to locate and point out even the tiniest cracks and blow them up and show the professionals. It's about platelet count. Whether it's safe to sit in the chair today. Whether the chemo will reduce them even more. Whether it is your choice as the patient or his choice as the oncologist to determine whether or not it's safe to sit.

The discussion goes on way too long between the nurse, the oncologist, the patient—the nurse playing the key role of advocacy for the patient, the patient asking the oncologist to make the decision, the patient walking out without any more Gemzar loaded into his system this week. It's time to terminate this one, two days long enough for carryover.

Onward to a brand-new topic.

The Sleep of Goddesses

WE FEEL IT IS BEST if our goddesses get a full and unadulterated night of rest that allows them to sleep as if in the palms of peacock feathers. We want them fresh and smooth as their eyes close, with a head free of nightmares as the moon arcs by, with a clear beam of light ready to shine its way through the next day. We want this for them every day.

If they want us to peel grapes and place them on extended tongues as they drop heads to pillows, we're happy to do so. We will also gather the materials needed to make you a five-gallon supply of mead, which will fill fifty-three 12-ounce bottles. We will locate enough honeycombs to squeeze out eighteen pounds of grade A honey, will secure 4.5 gallons of tap water, and will prepare eight grams of dedicated mead yeast. We will sanitize a six-gallon steel vat, boil the water, remove it from the heat, stir in the honey, being careful not to boil the honey. As the water cools, we will put a cup of lukewarm water into a bowl, sprinkle in the yeast, and cover it with a wrap. When the honey water has cooled to 80 degrees, we will stir in the yeast mixture, transfer to a fermentation bucket, and allow to ferment for two weeks. Finally we will siphon the finished mead into sterilized bottles and attach caps.

We are thrilled to be giving our goddesses the attention they deserve, to be pouring them a treasured potion to help them into and through the night.

This is why we were born, spawned from the eggs of giants, from women destined to rule the world. This is our lineage, first to serve, then be served. While our goddesses rest, we slip into the celestial garden and harvest lavender and spray roses, statice and pussy willow, pink peppercorn and larkspur. We sit at the foot of their beds, weave their flower crowns for the next morning as their eyes dance behind lids, reminding them of what's passed, predicting what lies ahead. We protect and treasure their sleep, where all thoughts and models of the perfect world are formulated, where they can practice actions and ideas in the safety of their nests. And we are in training, watch every move, every intake of breath, prepare them for the coming day, prepare ourselves for a coming life.

We are young, prefer to keep our eyes wide and watch it all. To take brief mental notes and write out detailed descriptions in handmade journals that we will carry with us and treasure as bibles as we move from server to servee. Bibles and manuals of style that will pass on to our daughters and granddaughters and all daughters throughout the passage of time.

We craft the hand-embroidered gowns and frocks our goddesses need to address their charges, to present themselves as models of greatness that others should attempt to emulate.

We resist the weariness in our own eyes and lives as we attend to the sleep of our goddesses, because it would be the worst sin ever for our eyes to be closed at the same moments as them, so if one of us sees another drifting off, we rush over to bring them back to full attention, rub their shoulders, massage tired feet, dig thumbs into necks and tell stories of the past and future which often blend into the same story. We revive each other, keep our weariness alive for the time when our goddesses rise and we help them to shine, dress them, brush their long hair, ready them to present to the larger world, see them out to balconies, to carriages, to parades and duties intended to share their magic with the world.

This is the time, when we let them go, comfortable that they are comfortable in themselves, that we slip back inside, lay ourselves down in the impressions of their feathered beds, nestle ourselves into our futures, their presents, the pasts of our great-grandparents long since gone, the upcoming births of daughters, and we allow our own eyes to dance under our lids, to perceive what lies ahead, to see ourselves stepping into our own goddess shoes, to wear them as if they would never fit another, as if they were forged from the light of miracles that wrapped themselves around our feet.

We are practicing our ascent, watch our goddesses carefully to see how it's done, but we're patient, don't allow our dreams to surpass our daily practice, allow our goddesses to come to fruition, reach their apex before transferring the magic and mystery that surrounds their core and hearts.

We know we've arrived when we awake from a meal of peeled grapes, a mug of mead, and at the foot of our beds lie the carefully designed crowns that our own goddesses in training have crafted for us, they as excited as we were to escort us to the balcony, to watch us wave to the crowds, nod to our futures, accept our destinies and act them out as if we've always known how to do it, riding high on the shoulders of ancestors.

Widow's Lament

IT BEGINS WELL BEFORE THE FINAL GURGLE, well before her own birth and scramble for breath on this planet. She is a sentient being long before she knows what it means, thousands of years before the umbilical cord is snipped and she's on her way. Her unborn self makes its way through the first urban civilization of ancient Sumer. She runs her fingers across the Lament for Ur, housed at the Louvre in Paris, hears the guardian goddess sing her words of sorrow for a lost city, attaches each word to a cell and feels it circulate through her body well before she understands the concept of blood, the red flow that permeates the living side.

She has never read Homer's *Iliad* and *Odyssey*, but they exist in her audio data bank, ride the backs of those same blood cells, as she understands the laments and losses of Achilles and Priam, the lament and joy of the recognitions of Odysseus, is able to empathize with every grieving soul who has ever existed.

Even though she considers herself a lapsed Catholic, she hears her own wailing as a friend of Christ who mourns over his body.

She joins in thousands of death wails for people she has never known personally, for the children of friends, the friends of children, for anyone in need of a good wail after passing. She travels to Australia to lament the battles between sides, she occupies houses and helps to smoke them out following the wail. She travels to China, learns the techniques of planned wailings, whether in temples, private lodgings, or in the countryside.

She is in training, her whole life, but doesn't know it. She is in Hawai'i, finds herself in an impromptu wailing and repetition of the syllable *a-a-a*. She imagines herself whining the death wail in the Santa Lucia Mountains as described by John Steinbeck in the short story "Flight." There are others that have squeezed their way into her internal library, like the wail of the Ginginbarra folks of Wide Bay. Places and people where she knows no names, has no maps of routes that have taken her there, but there she is, there she keens, there she falls to her knees and muddies herself with the tears of others.

She believes she has lent her voice to the operatic stage, accompanied often by strings alone, stars in Mozart's *Marriage of Figaro* and Rossini's *Barber of Seville*.

When she finally inhabits her earthly body, lets out a wail for her own arrival, she remembers nothing of her travels, her previous adventures, but feels that something is different about her, that she has been prepared, for something she has no clue about now but is certain will be revealed to her eventually.

As a young child in Sunnyvale, she laments the loss of pets, and when the family moves to Santa Cruz she grieves the loss of friends, a new school, a new life. The wailing continues, for a grandmother, a dog, a parakeet. She begins to understand how the grief is cleansed through the wails, that she can blast them out to be shared and comforted by the larger world.

She gets her hands on a Ouija board early on, plays with its powers, experiments, delves. She marries young, divorces, has two wonderful daughters from the union, doesn't feel the need to grieve or wail, moves on, buys a house, one occupied by a ghost, a friendly one, not to be feared.

She reunites with a high school friend at a twenty-year reunion. They fall in love, live together, marry, and the need for lamentation decreases. There are other reasons to wail throughout her life: the loss of President John F. Kennedy, another grandmother dies, more pets, then her mother goes, followed by her father, her father-in-law. Then the Towers go down on her birthday on September 11, 2001, taking 2,977 lives. The wailing is longer, louder, deeper, but is shared around the earth with others. Every year on her birthday she lives through the joy and sorrow of September 11, remembers to laugh and smile at the miracle of her existence, to wail and grieve the juxtaposition of death. Her hidden training continues, the flexing of blood cells that continue to carry the remnants of sorrow out of her system.

In 2018, she discovers what she has been waiting for. A diagnosis. Her beloved husband, partner, best friend, lover: cancer. The worst flavor. She wails inside every day. Sometimes she hides in the closet and screams at the walls. The cleansing helps, but needs to be refreshed every morning, every night as she turns and tosses in the bed. Even though it's a death knell, they get two more years of glorious time together, and she knows that using words like glorious might feel like overkill to some, but it's exactly what it is, a glory and miracle that they have known each other for over fifty years, spent so much of it together in each other's arms.

Daily Fresh

She prepares daily for the final lamentation, readies herself for the deep wailing that will blast through walls and centuries and ancient lands, that will gather empathizers from every place she's been, family members and friends who will lock arms and cleanse themselves, ready to move on, stronger than ever before, ready for the next joy, the next sorrow.

The Students

I THINK IN THE FIRST SIXTY-SEVEN ESSAYS written I have forgotten to give due respect to my twenty-six years as an educator at Happy Valley School from 1974 to 2000, which is crazy, because they were some of the best years of my life. It's sprinkled throughout, but I haven't mentioned the students yet.

The only reason I became and remained a teacher for twenty-six years was the students. I taught fifth-sixth graders, just the perfect age, with minds ready to think about and explore every topic they could find. It certainly wasn't about the income, nor really even about the status which is so often associated with monetary output. I could engage them in discussions about ancient civilizations and cultural universals and palindromes and Strat-o-Matic Baseball, with its percentages and averages, and creative writing, all topics that I loved and that they would soon come to love.

Daily Fresh

We took field trips to the planetarium in Golden Gate Park, stopped at Tommy's Joint for hamburgers and milkshakes, visited the Monterey Bay Salmon Hatchery on Big Creek, went to Giants and A's games, took cars to Salinas, and hopped on a train to Anaheim, loaded down with days' worth of chocolate chip cookies made by Mrs. Coonerty, stayed at the Disneyland Hotel, and spent all day on rides. We created cultures and poured Rosetta stones made of plaster of paris and built artifacts and buried them behind the school to have our friends from George Merilatt's Gateway School class come dig them up, which they did for us as well.

We turned our classroom into a small city, using Blue Bucks that were donated by County Bank. The students elected a mayor, a sheriff, created jobs, learned how to write resumes, conduct interviews and apply for positions. They established small businesses, washed desks, designed and sold individualized letterhead. They baked goods at home and brought them every morning to stock their bakeries, Toll House cookies and double fudge brownies and chocolate fudge and red velvet cake. And bottles of water, to wash it all down. The real estate agents rented and sold space in the classroom by the square foot. Further away from the teacher's desk was usually more expensive! We held city council meetings, contests, parades, and eventually some financially savvy students created a casino, which caused us to get the principal involved to determine if such businesses were allowable within school boundaries.

We had fun. It was all about the love of learning, and the way I was able to keep myself interested in remaining a teacher was to dig in and have fun with them. I coached their city league softball team, they won citywide spelling bees, math contests. I taught them how to disco dance after coming to work with a new move I learned at Rapid Transit the night before.

We were one of the first classes in the county to have a bank of five Apple computers in the classroom. They learned how to use Bank Street Writer to word process, print, and make handmade books on dot matrix printers, and we loaded into cars and vans with parents and computers and took the whole operation to other classrooms throughout the county and taught their peers how to do the same.

We had so much fun!

We cooked a thirty-pound Diestel turkey on Thanksgivings, my dad and Karen in the kitchen, the kids all bringing a potluck item from home that would feed our class and every aide and teacher and bus driver and life-lab coordinator on campus. They wrote weekly issue essays on every imaginable topic that they would share with the class during writers' workshop on Fridays, topics such as why PBJ sandwiches should be named a national food, why Flubber should be named a national sport, why recesses should last an hour and a half, who should be the next president, why parents should raise allowances, why school lunches should include french fries and Oreos. Every week a new batch of wild and crazy and interesting titles with writing that matched their wit, blueprints for making their lives better and changing the world.

Hundreds of students over the years, some now in their fifties. How extremely lucky I have been to spend a good portion of my life in their company.

They have taught me so much.

Great Scott!
50 Reasons Why Scott Is My Friend

MY GOOD FRIEND SCOTT IS TURNING FIFTY. I've been struggling with the appropriate gift for a guy who seemingly has everything he needs. Material possessions are not what drive him forward, don't motivate him to make more money in his life. I believe his needs have more to do with his thoughts, with his ability to organize and plan, with those things that make him break out in a big smile and laugh. At the world. At himself. At everything.

Short of locating the perfect gift, I'm writing this essay about him, with the subtitle "50 Reasons Why Scott Is My Friend."

1. *Excel*

    Scott is a whiz at Excel. He's been using it as a trusted tool for nearly thirty years. In pool, they have a trick-shot contest where the players do wild and crazy tricks with the cue sticks, balls, and table. If they were to have an International Excel

Spreadsheet "Trick Shot" Contest, Scott would most likely rank in the top two finalists.

2. *PowerPoint*

    Scott's expertise in presentations rivals his abilities with Excel. He pushes the borders of the presentation program to use it to create charts and graphs that help folks to prioritize and analyze their projects.

3. *Piano*

    While many of the items on this list of fifty could be classified as admiration, there are some that fit better under the umbrella of envy. Piano is one of them. I tried to learn piano when I was younger, as my mom played. But it didn't stick. While I succeeded beyond my expectations at dancing, music resisted my grasp. Among other things, Scott plays the piano. He learned quickly, has the mind that allows him to understand and succeed at projects in ridiculously fast time frames.

4. *Guitar*

    More envy. I tried the guitar when I was younger. My mom also played guitar. I blamed my failure on small hands, short fingers, but that's bunk. I didn't have the brain or desire to succeed. Scott is good, takes lessons. He came with me to a jam session at Rick Kleffel's house and fit right in immediately, playing improv riffs to spoken poetry.

5. *Ellis Family Fund*

    Scott and Sabrina have established a fund designed to help people who are helping others. Scott would have to be considered the development officer of the fund, as well as the chief strategist. He donated $5,000 to my Postscript

Publications venture that basically supports all my writing ventures. This extremely generous infusion allowed me to submit more work to more literary magazines and publishers over the past year.

6. *Mr. Organzo*

    Because of Scott's multiple tech skills and his strategist's brain, he is one of the more organized folks I know. He knows how to make a To Do list, how to check things off, how to reach a sense of completion and move on. I mimic his strengths, attempt to be as organized as he is, and even if I fall a little short, I'm much further ahead than I would have been without his influence.

7. *His Shaved Head*

    My baldness occurred late in life, not because the hair fell out naturally due to aging, but rather due to chemotherapy drugs. It was not a conscious choice for me. The hair fell out on its own. Scott, however, made a conscious decision to remove his hair, to shave his head and live with it forever. Not only do I admire his decision, but I also admire the shape of his head.

8. *Ankylosing Spondylitis*

    Scott suffers from this chronic inflammatory disease that occurs when the immune system attacks healthy joints in the spine. There is no known cure. He doesn't complain, has learned to live with it, to adapt as in every other aspect of his life.

9. *Sabrina*

    He had the good sense to fall in love with and marry Sabrina!

10. *Vivian and Ryan*

    They had the good sense to have children and produce Vivian and Ryan.

11. *New Teacher Center*

    Where we met, when he volunteered his skills to help the center enter a new phase as its own entity, using his organizational and management skills to break away from the University of California, Santa Cruz's administrative stranglehold.

12. *NaNoWriMo*

    We agreed to participate in the National Novel Writing Month, November, for thirty straight days, with the goal of writing 50,000 words toward a novel. We tracked our daily work on a Google Drive spreadsheet, inspired each other daily, and both succeeded in exceeding our intended output.

13. *USA 2020*

    Through our NaNoWriMo venture, Scott succeeded by completing *USA 2020*, and having it published within a year.

14. *Copyediting Skills*

    He has one of the quickest eyes when it comes to finding errors in grammar and spelling, and I have been the recipient of his expertise on many of my pieces.

15. *Amazingly Deep and Rich Critique*

    Scott has an extraordinary sensibility for offering suggestions to fix redundancies and inconsistencies, having read a paragraph on page 13 of a novel and 251 pages later, on page 264, noticing a discrepancy in the color of the neighbor's Mini Cooper.

16. *That He Speaks French*

    Yes. You'll notice that I compare myself to him often. I barely completed second-year Spanish in high school, my abilities bordering on *muy poquito* at best. Scott speaks fluent French, and lived in France for part of his life. It fascinates me, motivates me.

17. *McKinsey*

    That he worked for the world's premier consultancy firm.

18. *SPaM at HP*

    That he managed this organizational unit for Hewlett-Packard.

19. *Harvard*

    That he had a best friend at Harvard named Francine, and that this is also when and where he got his first electric guitar, a gift from his mom.

20. *Stanford*

    Scott's conscious decision on entering Stanford that he didn't want to worry about getting good grades, that it was more about playing golf and having fun in California. Yes!

21. *Live Visits*

    Scott was a regular visitor as I went through chemo over the past two years. He helped me through, helped me, us, focus on topics that didn't need to address pancreatic cancer or ankylosing spondylitis, instead focusing on solving the problems of the world outside our own skin.

22. *Zoom Visits*

    When Covid hit in March 2020, we continued our regular visits through Zoom.

23. *Golf*

    Scott golfs. That should make us blood brothers for life, just that he plays. But it's the way he plays that gets me. A long, lean body that throws his ball high and allows it to land softly. When he practices, he gets better. Some of my favorite times, riding around the course with him.

24. *Tennis*

    Just one more sport that he has taken on and mastered.

25. *Diplomacy*

    This is another game he is addicted to that involves strategy, cooperation, and occasionally deceit. We've never played, but one of these days.

26. *Spelling Bee*

    I might be making this one up. I think we may have this exceptional game in common, but I can't remember. If not, it should be.

27. *Letter Boxed*

    And if I made up the Spelling Bee connection, then Letter Boxed is probably close behind, but should definitely be one more connector.

28. *Dinner and Theater*

    We had the pleasure of attending *Spamalot* in San Francisco with Scott and Sabrina after an Asian-fusion meal on Market Street.

29. *Thinking Way Outside the Box*

    Scott and I worked together on his website Thinking Way Outside the Box. It was such fun, digging into his diverse mind, figuring out which of his ideas to present and how to lay them out.

30. *How to Reduce Wealth Inequality*

    This is how you do it: a 90% marginal tax on all annual household income over $250,000, a 90% inheritance tax. Yes!

31. *A More Interesting Way to Spend $1 Billion*

    A bit of training for billionaires on how to spend their money if certain things were available, like buying one year of living at your current age for $1 million, or reducing your current age by one year for $10 million, or buying immunity from death from disease or accident for $100 million.

32. *A Better Keyboard Layout—Dvorak*

    Always looking to bring efficiency to the forefront of his life, when he first learned of the Dvorak keyboard, Scott bought a plastic overlay for his keyboard and proceeded to switch over from the age-old QWERTY style. It slowed him at first, but not for long, as I'm guessing he's probably in the neighborhood of 100 words per minute now.

33. *Using Reverse Auctions to Select CEOs*

    How about this Scott brainstorm? Corporations create a list of eligible CEOs, then offer the job to the one willing to do the job for the least amount of compensation.

34. *A New Structure for College Football*

    How about a tiered system where teams move up or down based on performance? A more consistent and entertaining season.

35. *A New Scoring System for Golf*

In his spare time, Scott created a new scoring system for golf based on scoring points for only the good shots. That's my kind of game.

36. *New Rules to Make Soccer More Entertaining*

Increase the size of goals, change the offside rules to match hockey, conduct penalty kicks at the beginning of games.

37. *Simplifying Coinage*

Let's eliminate the penny, nickel, and dime, says Scott, and round all prices to the nearest 25 cents, so we can shop better, faster, and easier.

38. *Proxy Voting for Children*

To ensure that we are thinking about the future, not just today, parents receive proxy votes for up to two children.

39. *The Veil of Ignorance*

I didn't know about John Rawls and the veil of ignorance until Scott. Now I do.

40. *Firewalk*

That he drove to South Fort Collins to participate in a firewalk with his mother, being the first one to break loose and expose his bare feet to the fire.

41. *The Learning Accelerator*

That he knew after working with the New Teacher Center his strengths would be best utilized as the CEO of an educational nonprofit and proceeded to create his own.

42. *Mastery Track*

That his ability to quickly understand the needs of students and teachers to progress led to his creation of the Mastery Track system that enables mastery-based progression.

43. *Kung Fu*

That he has the physical and mental drive and perspicuity to achieve belts in his chosen martial art, all the way up to black belt.

44. *The Northern Lights*

That he made time in his life to travel with his mother and father to view the Northern Lights.

45. *Yosemite School Trips*

My main vacations as a youngster were to Yosemite, which I loved. When I learned of Scott's parent-chaperone trips with both kids, that further sealed the deal for me.

46. *Travel*

More of my envy—I, who have taken one trip out of the country, very few trips out of the state, am enamored by Scott's sense of adventure, his trips and experiences all over the world.

47. *National Merit Scholarship*

Just another of Scott's accomplishments, the landing of this prestigious national honor.

48. *Love of Vanilla Milkshakes*

Scott is an epicure when it comes to vanilla milkshakes. He has studied and compared their qualities from Japan to Paris to London to our living room. He enjoyed the one from

Carpo's Restaurant in Soquel, but I think the homemade one I created using our VitaMix came closer to his ideal.

49. *Zoom*

Three years ago, Scott introduced me to Zoom. Who knew at that point how instrumental Zoom would become in my future, my present, a tool I use every day to communicate and share in the time of Covid.

50. *ADD Genius*

I started referring to Scott as the ADD Genius a number of years ago, because of his tendency to explore and experiment with anything and everything and his ability to master it all so quickly.

If I spent another week or two at this, I'm certain I could come up with another fifty items, but I'll wait until his hundredth birthday for that.

When the Music's Over

THE DEATH OF A LOVED ONE or close personal friend always reminds me of my impermanence, of the fleeting miracle that has allowed me to breathe, walk, love, bleed, and laugh on this planet. Expected deaths like those of Lane Sharp and Debbie Analauren were more of a crockpot slow brew, left the odor of mortality on plates and spoons, in my hair follicles, and in my clothes. Unexpected deaths like my father and Joe Allen and Don Rothman came like spikes of lightning that tattooed my brain with quick, hot reminders.

I've attended the memorials for these and other friends and family members, and each time I'm overwhelmed by the sorrow felt by others and myself. And while the logical me understands the importance of the grieving process to allow us to heal, there's the other me that wants a bash that heartily celebrates the lives of those who have gone. It was at the colorless Lutheran ceremony for my friend Lane Sharp, who left at the age of thirty-nine, that I began writing the playlist for my memorial, a bash designed to only allow tears when mixed together with deep laughter.

When my own diagnosis became imminent and threw a shortened time frame in my face, I decided it was time to finish the playlist, finalize it and hand it off to others who would be in charge of implementing it. Thus it seemed fitting to include it as the final essay in this book, ten songs intended to promote belly laughs and maybe a few tears. In backward order, here are the ten songs that comprise my memorial playlist:

10. "This Moment" by Katy Perry.
    She talks to us about living in the moment, the time when you get to the "finish line" and realize "that you just can't push rewind."

9. "Once in a Lifetime" by the Talking Heads.
    David Byrne tells us that life is the "same as it ever was," and reminds us to let the "days go by."

8. "Like You'll Never See Me Again" by Alicia Keys.
    Her honey voice pulling us in, as she wonders if, with "no more time," we'd "cherish what we had."

7. "If Today Was Your Last Day" by Nickelback.
    They tap into your heart, asking if at the last we'd be able to "say goodbye to yesterday" and give away our last dime.

6. "Living in the Moment" by Jason Mraz.
    Who brings us along with him as he finds peace in his heart and soul and realizes he's "already home," "living in the moment."

5. "Another One Bites the Dust" by Queen.
   This one could just as easily be the finale, but I think it's a better starting point, a signal about the relativity of our existence, pointing to the need to celebrate our lives, to treat each other well while we can.

4. "Please Don't Bury Me" by John Prine.
   After requesting that his arms be given to the Venus de Milo and his feet to the footloose, Prine stays forever Prine, telling us to "kiss my ass goodbye." Amen.

3. "I'm Going Home" from *The Rocky Horror Picture Show*.
   Just before singing this eighteenth song of the movie version of *The Rocky Horror Picture Show*, Tim Curry, as Frank, says he can explain, then goes on to explain nothing—which is why I feel it's perfect for any memorial playlist, especially mine.

2. "Keg on My Coffin" by the Push Stars.
   Charlie telling his friend to stop praying and "throw a party" where the guests can smile and "know I loved you 'til the end."

1. "When the Music's Over" by the Doors.
   Although I haven't smoked pot in almost thirty years, I was stoned when I first heard this song wailed out by Jim Morrison, which is probably why the eleven-minute song felt more like it was two hours long. Usually sung as an encore at the Doors' live shows, it serves as the encore to my memorial playlist. As the song approaches the final seconds in the final minute, Morrison shares the secret we all know: that music is our "only friend/ Until the end."

I expect at least one of my friends to make sure this playlist finds a home, is looped during the duration of any memorial that might arise, be it in the time of Covid on my website, or live in a field or on a beach or a hilltop or in the backyard overlooking Rodeo Gulch Road and canyon.

About the Author

Jory Post was an educator, writer, and artist who lived in Santa Cruz, California. He and his wife, Karen Wallace, created handmade books and art together as JoKa Press. Jory was the co-founder and publisher of *phren-z*, an online literary quarterly, and founder of the *Zoom Forward!* reading series.

His first book of prose poetry, *The Extra Year*, was published in 2019, and was followed by a second, *Of Two Minds*, in 2020. His novel, *Pious Rebel*, also appeared in 2020. *Smith: An Unauthorized Fictography*, a collection of fictional interviews, was published in 2021.

His work has been published in *Catamaran Literary Reader, Chicago Quarterly Review, Rumble Fish Quarterly, The Sun*, and elsewhere. His short stories "Sweet Jesus" and "Hunt and Gather" were nominated for the Pushcart Prize.

Also by Jory Post

PIOUS REBEL

After her partner dies suddenly, Lisa Hardrock realizes how little she knows about the life she's been living—and starts exploring her questions in a blog that unexpectedly goes viral.

SMITH: An Unauthorized Fictography

In this kaleidoscopic, episodic joy ride, Jory Post treats us to thirty interviews that may or may not be real, with an array of "ordinary" people who turn out to be anything but.

Available from Paper Angel Press in
hardcover, trade paperback, and digital editions
paperangelpress.com

www.ingramcontent.com/pod-product-compliance
Lightning Source LLC
Chambersburg PA
CBHW021438070526
44577CB00002B/213